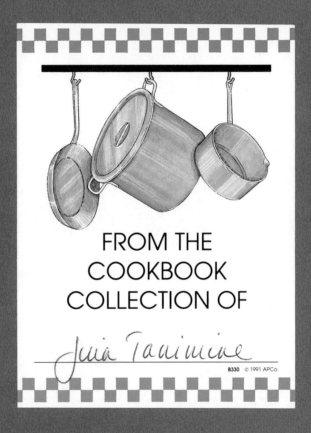

FROM THE
COOKBOOK
COLLECTION OF

Julia Tanimine

B330 © 1991 APCo.

LORENZA'S PASTA

LORENZA DE'MEDICI

LORENZA'S PASTA

200 RECIPES FOR FAMILY AND FRIENDS

CLARKSON POTTER/PUBLISHERS
NEW YORK

Published by Clarkson N. Potter, Inc., 201 East 50th Street, New York,
New York 10022. Member of the Crown Publishing Group.

Random House, Inc. New York, Toronto, London, Sydney, Auckland

CLARKSON N. POTTER, POTTER, and colophon are trademarks of
Clarkson N. Potter, Inc.

Originally published in Great Britain by Pavilion Books in 1996.

Printed and bound in Great Britain

Library of Congress Cataloging-in-Publication Data is available on request.

ISBN 0-517-70440-4

10 9 8 7 6 5 4 3 2 1

First American Edition

CONTENTS

FOREWORD

ALMOST THIRTY YEARS HAVE PASSED SINCE I WROTE MY FIRST PASTA RECIPE BOOK. It was fairly fundamental, meant for young Italian wives and mothers who had not had the chance to learn the basics of making their national dish at the apron-strings of their mothers or grandmothers. No longer did two or three generations of the same family live in the same house, or even in the same city. At the time, that was a new social situation in Italy.

Since then a lot of boiled pasta water has passed under the proverbial bridge. I have raised four children for whom I must have cooked thousands of kilos of pasta over the years, and now I frequently serve this nourishing dish to a table full of hungry grandchildren. At Badia a Coltibuono, our family wine estate in Tuscany, I include it on the menu for simple meals with friends, as well as for elegant luncheons when we entertain important guests from all over the world. It is the first food I think of when I eat on my own, as well as one of the dishes I prepare for the buffet that follows our annual summer chamber concert, when I have the challenging task of serving supper to several hundred guests. During this past decade I have also written half a dozen cookery books in which I have included recipes for pasta. Most decisively, for the past twelve years I have taught the art of making pasta to hundreds of students who have attended my cooking classes at Coltibuono.

All of which brought me to the point where I wanted to write a comprehensive book dedicated exclusively to what is personally, when all is said and done, my preferred food both to cook and to eat.

And there is something very personal about pasta. I know of no other dish with which the cook can so easily express his or her taste and appetite at the moment, whether it be for the light, rich, sweet, savoury, for meat, fish, or greens and vegetables. The repertory of recipes covers such an amazingly wide range. Pasta is truly a food for all seasons. It is also a food naturally suited to improvisation, which is not to say that anything goes. As with any craft, successful improvising comes only when you have mastered the basic discipline of the art.

In the recipe chapters I include both classic pasta dishes as well as more innovative creations. In the introductory chapters I give information and guidelines that provide background to the uniquely Italian culture of pasta, which will help you successfully adapt it to your own kitchens and tables.

And the place pasta holds in Italian culture is unique. There is a marvellous scene in the film, *A Taxi Driver in America*, in which the great Italian comedian, Alberto Sordi, is passing through customs in an American airport. When the officer discovers that he has a suitcase full of pasta, Sordi explains in his inimitable English, "For the Italian people, where there is pasta there is hope." If I remember the ending correctly, the customs officer lets him through with his pasta. Well, we all need to be nourished by hope, and through this book I hope to share some of the richness both traditional and personal of my Italian culinary heritage as expressed in pasta, certainly one of the world's greatest foods.

The Story of Pasta

IT IS EVEN MORE DIFFICULT TO UNRAVEL THE HISTORICAL ORIGINS OF PASTA THAN IT IS TO UNTANGLE A MANAGEABLE MOUTHFUL OF SPAGHETTI AROUND YOUR FORK. PASTA IS ONE OF THOSE PRIMEVAL FOODS, LIKE BREAD, WHOSE CREATION SEEMS TO HAVE OCCURRED SPONTANEOUSLY WITH THE CULTIVATION OF WHEAT AND THE PRODUCTION OF FLOUR AND SEMOLINA. CULTURAL ANTHROPOLOGISTS REASON THAT A PASTA-TYPE FOOD PROBABLY PRECEDED BREAD. AS NO FERMENTATION OR BAKING ARE INVOLVED, PASTA WOULD HAVE BEEN MUCH SIMPLER FOR A PRIMITIVE PEOPLE TO PRODUCE. CERTAINLY NOODLES IN ONE SHAPE OR ANOTHER ARE, AND ALWAYS HAVE BEEN, A UNIVERSAL DIETARY STAPLE.

What concerns me here, however, are not the Oriental or Northern and Eastern European versions of this food, but what Italians—and now the world, using the Italian word—call pasta. One sure way around the often tedious arguments about who invented pasta is simply to state that Italians may not have been the first people to produce noodles but they were certainly the first to make pasta, to say nothing of maccheroni, spaghetti, lasagne and ravioli!

While there is no written evidence that the ancient peoples who inhabited the Italian peninsula ate pasta as we know it, they did leave behind several indications that they made a kind of food which can correctly be considered the historical antecedent of pasta. The first of these comes from the Etruscans, the people whose civilization emerged in central Italy during the early centuries of the first millennium BC. North of Rome, outside of Cerveteri, an ancient Etruscan city with numerous underground burial chambers, there is a tomb with painted stucco reliefs depicting scenes of everyday life. One series shows several cooking utensils, including a jug of water, a board with a raised edge for mixing flour and water, a rolling pin and a fluted pastry wheel that resembles the one still used to cut ravioli today. These illustrations do not convince some historians, who point out that you can do other things with those implements besides making pasta. However, as any Italian knows, what they are most used for *is* making pasta. Personally, the idea appeals to me that the Etruscans, who are credited with creating the first civilization on the Italian peninsula, were also the first to cook our most civilizing domestic dish.

Written testimony exists that the Greeks, who began to immigrate to southern Italy around the eighth century BC, and then the Romans, who conquered the Greeks and assimilated not only Etruscan culture but the Etruscans themselves, ate thin strips of stiff, unleavened dough made from flour and water, called *laganum* in Latin, that resembled our modern-day lasagne. The Latin poet, Horace, in a letter to a friend, claimed he would much prefer to eat a simple dish of *laganum* with leeks and chick peas in the comfort of his own home, rather than be forced to attend the lavish banquets of the Emperor Augustus. About this same time, the Roman gastronome, Marcus Gabinus Apicius, the reputed author of history's first cookery book, *De Re Coquinaria* (*Concerning Culinary Matters*), was creating dishes served at the imperial banquets that used these same distant cousins of our lasagne to enclose elaborate baked moulded dishes and meat pies.

The problem with calling these foods "pasta" is that they were cooked by baking them in ovens or by grilling them on hot stones, more like pizza. What distinguishes pasta is that it is the first cooking of unleavened dough by boiling it in liquid.

For the genuine beginnings of pasta in Italy we have to jump ahead almost a thousand years and on to the island of Sicily, where so much of what is most delicious in Italian gastronomy—ice cream, for example—had its origins. By the first half of the ninth century, Sicily, the largest and strategically the most important island in the Mediterranean Sea, had been conquered by the Saracens, as the later Greeks and Romans called the nomadic peoples of the Syro-Arabian desert. The Arabs brought with them not only a refined gastronomic tradition, but also their highly developed agricultural technology, especially their efficient methods of irrigation. On the arid plains of Sicily, grain began to be cultivated on a scale impossible before.

In the early-twelfth century, knights from Normandy descended upon Sicily to drive out the Saracen "infidels" and then, of course, decided to occupy the island for themselves. It is from this period that we have the first documentation of the production of pasta, and it is dried pasta, as we know it today.

In a book written in 1154, commissioned by Roger II de Hauteville, a Norman king, Arab geographer Abu Abdullah Muhemmed ibn Idris recounts that the people of Trabia, a town near Palermo, produced a kind of spaghetti called *itrijah*, the Persian word for string, "in great quantities". *Itrijah* are still a favourite pasta today in Sicily where they are called trii or tria.

Idris goes on to say "large shipments were exported, especially to Calabria as well as to other Muslim and Christian territories". The obvious advantages of this dried pasta are precisely that it could be conserved for long periods of time in a hot climate and could also be transported.

During this period the Mediterranean grain market was controlled by the great maritime republic of Genoa. Several manuscripts from the thirteenth century kept in the state archives of Genoa document the fact that along with grain from Sicily, Genoese merchants also imported dried pasta and distributed it in the northern regions of the peninsula.

In a notarized document dated 1244, a doctor from Bergamo, Ruggero Brusa, insists that his patient, a certain Signor Bosso, a wool merchant suffering from an infection, promise to refrain from eating "fruit, beef, dried foods, spaghetti (literally "string pasta") and cabbage". So much for the Mediterranean diet! On the other hand, about this same time in a manuscript from

Bologna, *tria genovese* cooked in salted almond milk are recommended as a food for the infirm.

The first recipe we have for making dried pasta was written around the middle of the fifteenth century by Maestro Martino da Como, the celebrated personal cook to the Patriarch of Aquileia. In his recipe booklet, called *Libro de Arte Coquinaria* (*Book of Culinary Art*), and composed in the work-a-day language of a professional cook and vernacular Italian, not the Latin of scribes and scholars, Maestro Martino prescribes several ways to make pasta. For vermicelli you begin with a dough made from "the finest flour (*farina bellissima*), egg whites and rose water or plain water". From this dough you then cut "little strips (*bastoncelli*) as thin as straws...roll them with your fingers... and dry them in the sun". He says they will last for "two or three years".

To make what Maestro Martino calls *Siciliani*, acknowledging the Sicilian origins of dried pasta, the procedure is much the same, except that this type of pasta is shaped by "rolling the dough around a little metal rod" (*bacchettina metallica*), so the pieces remain hollow on the inside. Further on, when he is giving instructions on how to cook pasta, he mentioned *le tritte*, a corruption of the words *tria* and *trii*, a common term, as I have already mentioned, for dried pasta in the Middle Ages.

When it comes to cooking pasta, all similarity to contemporary tastes ends. Maestro Martino recommends boiling the pasta in a fatty broth of meat or chicken and dressing it with "sweet spices and sugar".

About a quarter of a century later, in 1475, Bartolomeo Sacchi, the great Renaissance humanist,

known as Platina, in his exhaustive and learned culinary treatise, *De Honesta Voluptate ac Valetudine* (*Concerning Honest Pleasure and Well-Being*), edited and translated Maestro Martino's recipes for dried as well as fresh pasta into Latin, the literary language of the time. In this form they became the standard for cooks in the following centuries until the industrialization of pasta in modern times.

Johann Wolfgang von Goethe, in the diary he kept during his journey through Italy in 1786–88, describes how maccheroni was made in a home where he stayed in Sicily:

The dough is first moulded into the shape of a pencil as long as a finger; the girls then twist this once with their fingertips into a spiral shape like a snail's. We sat down beside the pretty children and got them to explain the whole process to us. The flour is made from the best and hardest wheat, known as **grano forte***. The work calls for much greater manual dexterity than macaroni made by machinery or in forms.*

The story of fresh pasta follows a separate, if sometimes parallel, history to that of dried pasta, as befits a food with a distinct culinary identity. The *laganum* from Roman times seems not only to have survived the Dark Ages, but to have evolved during those obscure centures, for lasagne emerges in the literature of the High Middle Ages as an accepted part of medieval Italian life.

In a mid-thirteenth-century chronical Fra Salimbene de Adam, from Parma, describes, not without a certain admiration, a corpulent friar from Ravenna, who excelled at stuffing himself full of "lasagne with cheese" (Parmesan, one would suppose). Salimbene goes on to

OPERA DI
BARTOLOMEO
S C A P P I
MASTRO DELL'ARTE DEL CVCINARE,
con laquale si può ammaestrare qual si voglia Cuoco,
Scalco, Trinciante, o Mastro di Casa.
DIVISA IN SEI LIBRI.

NEL
{ Primo si intende il ragionamento che fa l'Autore con Giouanni suo discepolo.
{ Secondo si tratta di diuerse viuande di carne, si di quadrupedi come di volatil.
{ Terzo si parla della statura, e stagione di ogni sorte di pesci.
{ Quarto si mostra le liste del presentar le viuande in tauola di grasso, & magro.
{ Quinto si contiene l'ordine di far diuerse sorti di paste, & altri lauori.
{ Sesto si ragiona de' conualescenti, e molte altre sorte di viuande per gli infermi.

Con le Figure che fanno dibisogno nella Cucina.

Aggiontoui nuouamente il Trinciante, & il Mastro di Casa.

DEDICATE AL MAG. M. MATTEO BARBINI
Cuoco, e Scalco celeberrimo della Città di Venetia.

IN VENETIA, Per Alessandro de' Vecchi. MDCXXII.

note that "in the same year, on the feast of Santa Chiara (he ate) for the first time ravioli made without being wrapped in pasta". These would have been a type of gnocchi similar to today's *malfatti*.

Towards the end of the Middle Ages, Giovanni Boccaccio, the famous Bolognese writer, of the *Decameron*, published in 1348, gives the most telling description of just how much his fellow Italians had come to enjoy their pasta. Boccaccio depicts a mythical earthly paradise of delights where "there was a mountain made entirely of grated Parmesan cheese, on top of which people did nothing else but cook ravioli and maccheroni in capon broth and roll them down to the bottom where whoever caught the most got to eat the most".

As in the case of dried pasta, the first real recipes for fresh pasta began to appear during the Renaissance. Platina, in the work cited above, describes how noodles should be made:

To make the dough sift the flour well and mix with water and extend on a table. Then roll with an oblong piece of polished wood such as bakers use. Draw it out and cut into the length of a little finger or ribbon. Boil in a fatty broth.... Serve with cheese, butter, sugar and sweet spices.

Documentation from this period presents pasta, not as a food of the common folk, but as luxury item for the privileged few. Price control lists from this time show that pasta cost three times as much as bread. In the case of dried pasta, at least, this was due in part to the fact that it was usually imported from the kingdoms in the south of the Italian peninsula and therefore subject to various duties and taxes that would make it marketable at a price only the aristocracy and the wealthier middle classes could afford. As we have seen, it was also prepared as a rich man's dish, dressed with sugar and spices, other imported and expensive items.

By the seventeenth century, however, pasta had crossed all class barriers. Its wide popularity is attested to by the guilds that were formed by pasta makers to protect their product. They banded together to limit the number of pasta shops in a given town and to prevent bakers of bread from also making and selling pasta.

It was not, however, until the late-nineteenth and early-twentieth centuries that pasta attained the status of having become the national food of Italy. During the intervening years several historical events crucial to this evolution took place: the tomato was "discovered"; the kingdoms and republics of the Italian peninsula were united, more or less, into one nation; the industrial revolution produced mach-ines that could crank out high-quality pasta for the masses on an industrial level; it also caused masses of southern Italians to immigrate to the industrial north and to the New World, bringing their taste for pasta with them.

The centre of what has been called the "national people's pasta movement" was Naples. In the late-eighteenth century, Naples was still capital of a kingdom that included the vast countryside of the peninsula's southern provinces where *grano duro*, durum wheat, was cultivated in abundance and made into semolina for pasta. Also, the city's climate, a combination of sea breezes, hot winds from Mount Vesuvius and sun, was found to be ideal for drying pasta. It allowed the dough to dry at a perfect pace, slow enough so that it would not break but not so slow that it could become mouldy.

During this period literally hundreds of shops where pasta was made, sold, cooked and even eaten on the spot, lined the streets and narrow alley-ways of the capital. The picturesque scene has been documented in the diaries of dozens of travellers making the Grand Tour; as well as depicted in numerous contemporary sketches, drawings, engravings, paintings and even a few turn-of-the-century photographs.

The semolina was ground by hand in granite mills and the dough was kneaded by foot in troughs by bare-footed men and children stomping to the musical accompaniment of mandolins. The pasta was cut by primitive machinery and hung outside to dry, draped over wooden rods.

Long strands of spaghetti tied together like sheaves of wheat were stored in large wooden barrels and sold at street stalls, where you could also buy it cooked over charcoal fires to eat on the street with your fingers. In the pictures you also see heaping bowls of grated sheep's milk cheese on the counters ready for use.

Exactly when and where the marriage of the tomato and pasta took place is not known. There is good reason

in their books. In his *Cuoco Galante* (*Gallant Cook*), Corrado has a recipe for tomato sauce, and Leonardi, in his *L'Apicio Moderno* (*The Modern Apicius*) includes one for a tomato and meat *ragú*. Amazingly, neither of them mentions dressing pasta with these, perhaps because they were both concerned with an aristocratic cuisine and considered it too proletarian. The agriculture-based industry of cultivating, processing and canning tomatoes started about one hundred years later and ever since then, at least, tomatoes have provided a delicious, widely available, cheap and easily prepared way to dress pasta dishes.

In the mid-nineteenth century, Giuseppe Garibaldi, the great Italian patriot and military leader, initiated

(49)-2013-Macaroni drying in the dirty streets of Naples, Italy.
Copyright Underwood & Underwood.

to think it happened in Naples. One thing is for sure, it was made in heaven. The tomato originally came from Peru and was brought to Europe by the Spanish explorers in the sixteenth century. For several centuries it was thought to be poisonous and was valued only as an exotic, ornamental plant—the "golden apple" (the first variety was yellow), as it was nicknamed, *pomodoro*, in Italian.

From Spain it made its way to the Spanish kingdom of Naples and it was there that its culinary attributes were recognized. Two Neapolitan chefs and cookery writers, Vincenzo Corrado and Francesco Leonardi, active in the latter half of the eighteenth century, were the first to include numerous recipes for using tomatoes

the revolution that would free the Italian peninsula from foreign domination and unify the country in one nation. While in the midst of liberating Naples from Spanish rule, he is credited with having come up with an unusual battle cry, "It will be maccheroni, I swear to you, that will unite Italy!" His prediction did not really come true for almost another hundred years, when there was mass immigration from the poor rural regions of the south to the industrial north. The immigrants brought with them their culinary traditions, and from then on Italians have been united, at least in their taste for pasta.

At about this same time the taste for pasta began to spread beyond its national boundaries and across the seas, where it underwent some curious mutations. Since the eighteenth century English travellers to Italy had been bringing back home maccheroni (the generic term for dried pasta) and baking it with lots of cheese and cream and in sweet custards. British Italophiles who aff-ected Italian manners in dress and comportment were even called "macaronis" by their fellow coun-trymen. And, of course, when "Yankee Doodle" came to town, he struck a feather in his cap and called it macaroni. The "macaroni" was the name of a dandified hairstyle, and doodle/noodle was a term for a foolish person.

Thomas Jefferson obvi-ously developed an appetite for pasta after his visit to Naples in 1789. He had two cases shipped back home, together with a "maccarony machine". Ten years later, the first successful pasta factory in the New World was opened in Philadelphia.

It was not until the end of the following century and the beginning of the twentieth, however, that pasta became firmly established on the American table. During that period close to six million Italians, mostly from the south, immigrated to the United States. They soon began to manufacture pasta in their adopted country, although studies show that those who could afford it still preferred to import it from its native land.

In their restaurants, which by the Twenties had become the most popular "foreign food" restaurants in America, Italian-Americans served a new dish, spaghetti and meatballs, unheard of here in Italy. It combined the two national dishes, spaghetti with tomato sauce and hamburger. Which brings this history up to the time of my first trip to the United States in the Fifties, when I saw, but thankfully never had to taste, canned "spaghetti" and grated "Parmesan" cheese in card-board containers.

In this second half of the twentieth century the evo-lution of pasta as an inter-national dish has taken a new and more promising direction, a return to its roots, which it continues to follow. Three main fac-tors are responsible for this positive development: the possibility of easy and rea-sonable inter-continental travel with a migration back to Italy in this case; inter-est in the health benefits of the Mediterranean diet, of which pasta is a staple; and intelligent dedication to the art of authentic Italian cooking, both in home and in restaurant kitchens as well as in cookery books. All of which promises well for the future of one of the world's greatest foods.

Opposite page: Dried Spaghetti

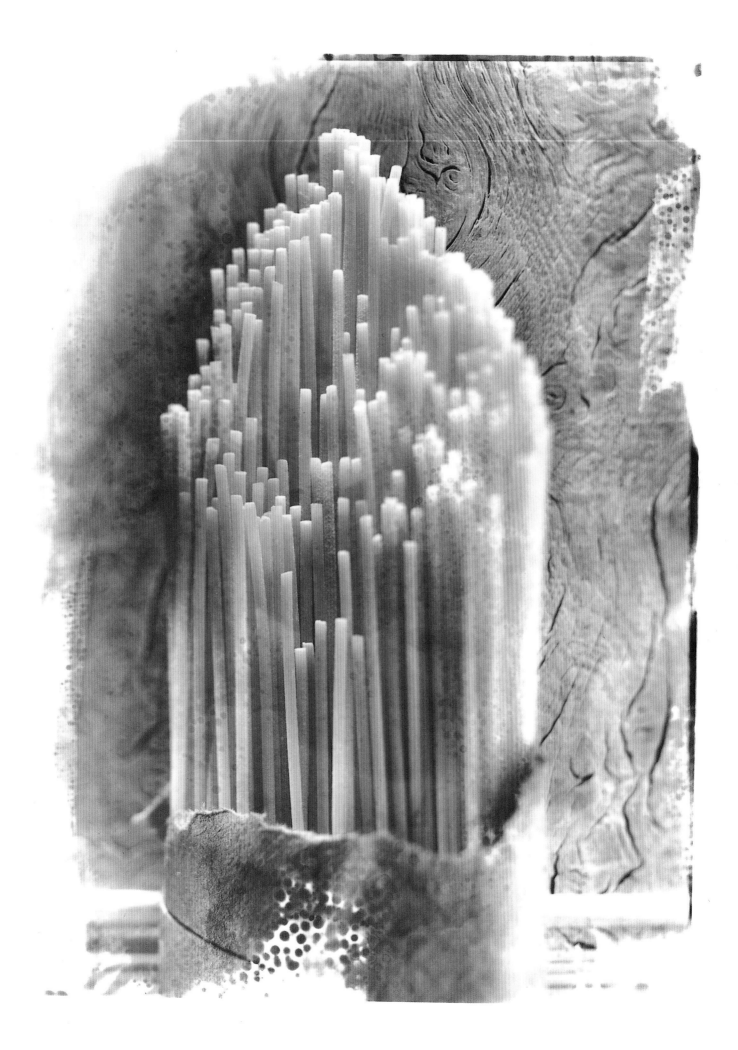

PART I

A Delineation of Pasta Types

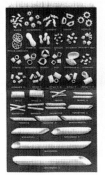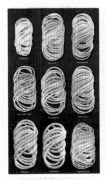

It is often said that there are at least three hundred names for a hundred different types of pasta. The opposite, however, is also true. The same name frequently refers to several different types of pasta. Fusilli, for example, can refer to long spirals or to short springs of dried pasta, and in the Silena area of southern Italy, to fresh pasta made by wrapping dough around a piece of metal the size of a knitting needle.

Even if it were possible, I do not think it would be desirable to sort out this sometimes perplexing babel of nomenclature. Here, as in other matters of gastronomy, the trend to standardization should be vigourously resisted. Pasta, like the rest of Italian cuisine, has evolved in local, regional kitchens, and the Italian peninsula is divided into twenty regions, each with its own distinct and diverse character. Down through the centuries every region has given its own particular twist to the shape of pasta.

Today commercial producers of dried and fresh pasta, in an effort to promote their product, have added to this happy confusion by resurrecting long-forgotten names for familiar forms, as well as inventing new shapes. And why not? As with life itself, variety is the spice of pasta. Just remember that one woman's ravioli could be another's tortelli.

Some types of pasta are little known outside their place of origin; others have reached the national and international marketplace. Is there any place under the sun where Neapolitan spaghetti is not known? On the other hand, even most Italians have never heard of *piccagge*, the Genoese version of tagliatelle.

In this section I have included the varieties and shapes of pasta that will be of most practical interest to you in the kitchen, as well as ones that will be helpful to recognize when you travel and eat in Italian restaurants. I have also included a few eccentric forms because they illustrate the whimsical element in the evolution of pasta.

FRESH AND DRIED PASTAS

Fresh and dried is the fundamental division of all pasta types.

Traditionally fresh pasta is home-made, usually with eggs and soft wheat flour, and sometimes in southern Italy with semolina (*semola* or *semolino* in Italian), flour ground from hard durum wheat, mixed with water. The dough is rolled out by hand or by machine and cooked while it is fresh. Today, thanks to modern methods of food production, good-quality commercially produced fresh egg pasta is often dried before packaging.

Dried pasta is factory made from semolina flour and water and dried before being packaged. The quality of dried pasta is determined not only by the quality of the flour and water, but also by the means used for shaping it and the length of time that it is allowed to dry, which should be gradual and slow. (See Preparing Dried Pasta, pages 26-9.)

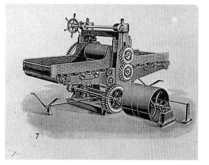

I cannot emphasize enough that dried pasta is in no way inferior to fresh pasta. Among many non-Italians a widespread prejudice against dried pasta in favour of fresh pasta seems to exist, as if the difference were the same as that between canned vegetables and fresh ones. Participants in my cooking classes have often expressed surprise that I even deign to use dried pasta. Frankly, I could not imagine life without it.

I suspect this popular misconception dates back to the Seventies when Americans, in particular, were introduced to the art of making fresh pasta. For cooks and eaters alike it was a new and delicious experience. Understandably they must have felt that since they could now enjoy fresh pasta, why bother with the packaged variety? As a result many have deprived themselves of one of the world's tastiest, easiest and most versatile dishes.

Fresh and dried pasta are simply two different types of the same food. Each satisfies diverse culinary and gastronomic intentions. Fresh egg pasta, whose origins are in the northern regions of Italy, combines well with sauces based on butter and cream. Dried pasta, traditional in central and southern Italy, is most suitable for sauces cooked with olive oil. I think of fresh pasta, especially the filled varieties such as ravioli, more as a dish that stands on its own, whereas I like to use dried pasta as a base for eating a variety of greens and vegetables. In the South, for example, it is not unusual to hear a dish described as "such and such a vegetable with a certain type of dried pasta", rather than the other way around. In other words, with dried pasta dishes the sauce gets first billing. With fresh pasta the pasta itself is primary.

FRESH PASTAS

Sheets of *lasagne* are the prototype of fresh pasta. They are made in various parts of Italy but their realm is the northern region of Emilia-Romagna, where they have achieved perfection and reign supreme.

Classic lasagne are home-made. The traditional dough is made of flour and eggs only. It is rolled out thin and cut into squares of about 10 x 10cm/4 x 4 inches. Sometimes cooked, finely chopped spinach is added to the eggs before the flour is mixed in to colour the dough green, making *lasagne verdi*. Italian brands of dried egg lasagne are now commercially produced.

Sheets of lasagne are used for baked pasta dishes. They have, in fact, become practically synonymous with a dish that originated in Emilia-Romagna called *lasagne al forno*, baked lasagne, usually prepared with alternate layers of green lasagne, coated with a rich meat *ragú* mixed with a white sauce and topped with grated Parmesan cheese that forms a light golden crust after baking. So popular is this dish that travellers going by train to northern Italy can jump out at the station in Bologna, the capital of Emilia-Romagna, and buy a single portion of hot *lasagne al forno* from vendors who push their carts along the track.

Tagliatelle is another shape of classic fresh egg pasta from Bologna. The dough must be rolled paper-thin and then cut into ribbons about 1cm/½ inch wide. Tagliatelle are usually wrapped into little nests and once they are dried in the open air and covered with a cloth, they can be kept for at least three months. You can also buy good commercially produced dried egg tagliatelle. Meat sauce is the classic dressing for tagliatelle.

In Italian, *tagliare*, the word from which tagliatelle is derived, is the verb "to cut" and there are several cuts of the tagliatelle form of pasta. *Tagliolini* or *taglierini*, for example, are thinner, about 0.25cm/⅛ inch wide, and particularly suitable for soups.

Fettuccine is the name of tagliatelle made in Rome. They are narrower and a little thicker than tagliatelle and delicious with butter and cream, as made famous by the Roman restaurant, Alfredo. In Liguria the same type of pasta is called *trenette*, and goes perfectly with that region's creamy pesto sauce.

Pizzoccheri are short, wide noodles made of buckwheat flour, a speciality of the cool Alpine valley, Valtellina, where buckwheat is grown.

Pappardelle are another ribbon shaped, fresh egg noodle pasta, wider and shorter than tagliatelle, measuring about 3cm/1¼ inches wide and 10cm/4 inches long. They are one of only two pasta shapes traditional to Tuscany. *Pici* (see page 54) is the other. *Pappardelle con la lepre*, a mound of these large noodles dressed with a rich gamy sauce made with pieces of wild hare, is a classic autumnal dish in the Chianti region of Tuscany. If you order it in a restaurant and ask for some grated Parmesan cheese, your concerned waiter will probably advise you that the two do not go together, at least for local taste-buds.

FRESH FILLED PASTA

Ravioli are the best-known filled pasta and are made in most regions, shaped in little squares and stuffed with a variety of seafood, meat and vegetables. They can also be oval, round or shaped in the form of a half-moon.

Tortelli are like ravioli, when bigger called *tortelloni*. They are traditionally stuffed with spinach and ricotta cheese and often simply sautéed with butter and sage and served with lots of grated Parmesan cheese.

Agnolotti, square, round or half-moon, with ruffled edges, are a popular stuffed pasta made in Piedmont. They are usually filled with meat and in autumn often have the honour of being topped with a shaving of white truffles.

Cannelloni are shaped completely differently from any other filled pasta. They are sheets of pasta spread with a variety of fillings and rolled up into tubes. They are then baked. Cannelloni are mostly associated with the South, although similar stuffed pasta tubes are also made in some central and northern regions of the peninsula.

Cappelletti are shaped like little paper hats. They vary in shape—in Emilia-Romagna they have turned-up peaks, in some central regions they are round—but their meat stuffing is invariably rich. These are a festive pasta and the smaller forms are usually served in a hot capon broth.

Pansoti, meaning little bellies, are triangular packets of pasta from Liguria, filled with a local herb mixture called *preboggion* and traditionally served with a walnut sauce.

COOKING FRESH PASTA

To cook really fresh pasta, within a couple of hours of making, bring the water to a high boil, then add the salt and pasta. Flat pasta, such as fettuccine, lasagne, pizzoccheri and taglierini will be *al dente* when the water returns to the boil and they float to the surface. Filled pastas, such as ravioli, will be *al dente* after they have cooked for 2 minutes after the water returns to a high boil. Thicker pasta, such as orecchiette and pici, have to cook a bit longer, depending on how fine or thick you have made them. They will take about 5 minutes after the water returns to the boil.

If the pasta is a day or two older, it will take longer to cook. In which case, you will have to taste a piece to test when it is done.

DRIED PASTA

Dried pasta forms can be divided into four main groups: long pasta, spaghetti, for example; short pasta (*pasta corta*) of the tubular maccheroni type; traditional fantasy forms, in the shape of snails, shells, etc.; and tiny bits of pasta for soups. I have added a fifth contemporary category, recent innovations in shapes and colour.

Spaghetti are certainly the best-known form of long dried pasta. The Italian word means "little strings". Spaghetti are associated with Naples and with the sauces of southern Italy based on olive oil and tomato, ingredients which keep these little strings slippery and separate. No Neapolitan, at least, would add cheese. Spaghetti was originally a generic term for string-like dried pasta and they have always been commercially

produced in several thicknesses, each with its own specific name or even names.

Spaghettini are thinner than the standard spaghetti size and perhaps the most versatile of all pastas. Today this shape is sometimes called *vermicelli*, or little worms, whereas originally vermicelli was the name for the long pasta size that is now simply called spaghetti. Spaghettini are especially suitable for sauces made with shellfish.

Chitarra, named after the Italian word for guitar, are square-shaped spaghetti, about 2mm/^{1}/$_{12}$ inch thick.

Bucatini are a fatter form of spaghetti with a *buco*, a little hole. That is, they are hollow and not unlike drinking straws. This is a shape popular in Rome and central Italy, where they are served with the local hefty *carbonara* and spicy *amatriciana* sauces.

Angel hair, *capelli d'angelo*, are the thinnest and most delicate form of spaghetti. They are usually added to broth or used for sweet or savoury pasta pies.

Linguine, or tongues, are a long spaghetti-type pasta whose borders have been flattened while the centre remains round. This is the pasta you need at hand for those times when you fancy a quick dish of *aglio, olio e*

peperoncino, spaghetti dressed with a simple and savoury sauce of garlic, oil and hot pepper flakes. This form can also be called *bavette*.

Tubular pastas can be divided into two groups. *Penne*, meaning pens, which refers to the shape of their ends, which are cut at an angle and resemble the end of a quill, are short and of various widths. They come either with a smooth surface and are called *penne lisce*, or with a ribbed surface and are called *penne rigate*. Penne are suitable for rich and hearty sauces and are probably the most popular pasta for a working man's mid-day meal. The smooth type is often used with vegetable sauces, while chunky meat sauces cling best to ribbed penne.

Maccheroni are the other tube shaped pasta. They come in various lengths and widths. Their ends are cut straight, while their body can be slightly bent or shaped at an angle. Like spaghetti, the word "maccheroni" was often used to refer to pasta in general. *Rigatoni* are the most popular form of the maccheroni-type pasta. Large and chewy, their wide cavity is ideal for catching chunks of meat in heavier sauces of sausage or game.

Manicotti are large tubes, similar to cannelloni, for stuffing.

Pipe, another popular tubular pasta, are shaped more like little crescents than pipes, their ends bent back so that they practically touch each other. Like *conchiglie*, they are especially good for catching sauce.

Ziti are long maccheroni, about 25cm/10 inches, which can sometimes be quite fat and are then called *zitoni*. They are broken in half by hand before being cooked. Because of their length and, therefore, the extra time required for drying, the pasta assumes a fuller flavour, which is what makes this form special. *Zita* is the word in Neapolitan dialect for an "old maid" (rather than a maiden), who is about to be married, and ziti were the traditional pasta for the wedding dinner. They are still used on festive occasions in the south of Italy.

Most fantasy shapes of dried pasta were originally made fresh and sometimes still are for special festivals, especially in southern Italian villages. Today few cooks have the time or the talent to shape them and so they live on thanks to manufacturers of packaged pasta.

Conchiglie, or shells, are a natural shape for pasta since the hollow is an ideal receptacle for the sauce.

Eliche are small twists or spirals.

Farfalle means butterflies and is also the Italian word for a bow tie, which is what this form of dried pasta most resembles. Their attractive and delicate shape make them one of the few dried pasta forms suitable for creamy sauces.

Fusilli look like tight little springs. The fresh version is longer and has a hollow centre formed by wrapping the dough around a thin rod the size of a knitting needle.

Lumache, or snails, are the Neapolitan version of French *escargots*, with the advantage that you can even eat the shell.

Orecchiette are "little ears" and are a traditional shape much favoured by commercial producers of dried pasta. The women of Puglia, the region that forms the heel of the boot-shaped Italian peninsula, still make fresh orecchiette with flour and water by pressing their thumb on a tiny circle of dough (page 55).

Ruote, or *ruote di carro*, are miniature cartwheels. Their spokes can hold a substancial sauce.

Besides these traditional fantasy forms commercial pasta producers are inventing new forms in the shape of bunches of grapes, mushrooms, and who knows what else is still to come. In general, I have never found these novelties, decorative though they may be, to be a significant advance in the art of pasta making.

Personally I would place coloured and flavoured pasta in the same category as the above innovations. Green, spinach-flavoured pasta is, of course, an exception. As mentioned above, it is a traditional form of lasagne and more recently of ravioli and of *paglia e fieno*, or hay and straw, a yellow and green mix of tagliolini. Less successful are the newer colours and flavours—tomato and beetroot-red, black-squid ink, brown-mushroom—as well as the many varieties speckled with herbs and seasonings. It would be difficult to improve upon the warm yellow to rich gold hues of natural wheat pasta. The infinite variety of sauces with which they can be matched provide all the gastronomic and artistic inspiration for flavour and colour imaginable. (Yet, for anyone who wants to master these coloured pastas, the instructions are on page 56.)

A final category of dried pasta is *pastina*, tiny bits of pasta in the shape of small tubes, rings, squares, stars and even letters of the alphabet. *Pastina* are put in minestrone, a broth made with a light meat stock, a popular dish in Italy for children as well as adults who are recovering from an illness or are on a diet. For a delightful and quick first course for evening meals I often serve *quadrucci in brodo*, tiny squares of dried or fresh pasta, cooked in stock, often with a few strips of julienned fillet of beef. Usually one spoonful of pastina is sufficient for a bowl of soup as they should float in the stock.

GRANDE DEPOSITO di PASTE
NAPOLI
OLII FINISSIMI D'OLIVA - VINI - FABBRICA DI LISCIVA
GIUSEPPE BRAJA
TORINO
BARRIERA di NIZZA · 122
CATALOGO delle FORME
Pasta lunga forme rotonde
1. Zitoni
2. Ziti
3. Mezzani
4. Mezzanelli
5. Maccheroncelli
6. Perciatelli
7. Bucatini
8. Vermicelloni
9. Vermicelli
10. Vermicellini
11. Capellini
Pasta a mano
64. Orecchi
63. Orecchietti
Pasta lunga forme piatte
12. Lasagne
13. Mezze lasagne
14. Fettucce
15. Fettuccette
16. Fresini.
17. Tagliatelli
18. Tagliatellini
19. Linguine
62. Tortellini speciali (aumento 10 %)
Pasta corta forme grosse
20. Rigatoni
21. Mezzi rigatoni
22. Cannelloni
23. Fascette
24. Anelloni lisci
25. Canneroni
26. Mezze fascette
27. Anelloni ricci
28. Occhi di lupo
29. Conchigliette
30. Conchiglie
31. Canneroncini
32. Mezzi canneroni
33. Ditali
Pasta corta forme mezzane
34 Mezzi canneroni ricci
35. Riccetti
36. Fagiolini
37. Ditalini
38. Premiere
39. Orzo
40. Anelli
41. Rosamarina
42. Stelle
43. Stortini
Pasta corta forme piccole
44. Peperini
45. Tubettini
46. Stelline
47. Stellettine
48. Pepe
49. Anellini ricci
50. Pernicette
51. Rosamarina
52. Anellini lisci
53. Semi peperoni
54. Orzo
55. Crocette
56. Semi cicorie
57. Triglie
58. Fiori di sambuco
59. Semi melloni
60. Alfabeto
61. Croci di Malta
Il presente Catalogo annulla i precedenti
SPECIALITÀ SAPONE POLVERE PER BUCATO
Vero tesoro delle Famiglie per Igiene e Pulizia
Fate il vostro Bucato colla semplice immersione di poche ore
GARANZIA ASSOLUTA
Cent. 30 al pacco di grammi 500 coll' Istruzione
In vendita presso tutte le Drogherie e Magazzini Alimentari
LIT. MAURER, TORTA & C. TORINO

PREPARING DRIED PASTA

I CANNOT IMAGINE ANY DISH MORE SIMPLE TO COOK THAN DRIED PASTA. BOIL A POT OF WATER, ADD SALT, TOSS IN THE PASTA AND WITHIN MINUTES IT IS READY TO DRESS. ON THE OTHER HAND, SIMPLICITY IS AN ART. A LITTLE KNOWLEDGE ABOUT THE NATURE OF PASTA, HOW AND WHY IT COOKS SO SIMPLY, CAN BE A HELP NOT ONLY TO PREPARE IT PERFECTLY BUT ALSO WHEN IT COMES TO PURCHASING A QUALITY PRODUCT.

Four basic components constitute dried pasta: two ingredients, semolina and water for making the dough, and two technical processes, shaping and drying the pasta. The excellence of the final product depends on the quality of all four factors.

By Italian law dried pasta "made in Italy" must be produced from semolina. On the packet you will read: *Pasta di semola di grano duro. Semola*, or semolina, is made by grinding durum wheat (*grano duro*) into relatively coarse granules. Durum of the species, *triticum durum*, is *hard* wheat, in fact, the hardest wheat grown, as distinct from the soft wheat, *triticum vulgare*, used to make flour for bread and fresh pasta.

The hardness of wheat is the measure of protein contained in its kernels. Superior semolina is obtained by grinding the endosperm, or heart, of the kernel which contains the highest concentration of proteins. It will contain an average of twelve to fourteen per cent protein, whereas standard soft flour has about nine per cent protein. The highest-grade semolina can even have a protein content of around seventeen per cent.

Because semolina is so rich in proteins and low in starches, relatively little water needs to be added to make dough, about thirty per cent less than for bread or flour-based pasta. It is starch that absorbs water. This is an advantage since the dough will have to be dried. When mixed with water the proteins in semolina form a semi-solid structure called gluten, which stretches under pressure and at the same time resists that pressure. In other words this gluten-rich dough is stiff and sturdy, not brittle like flour dough, and can stand up to being put through the machines that mould it into its various shapes, as well as not turning crunchy or gummy when it is cooked.

Pasta produced in other countries can be made from soft wheat flours or from blends with semolina. These are less expensive than Italian brands made from one hundred percent pure *semola*, but they are vastly inferior in texture and taste and do not hold up while being cooked in boiling water.

PASTE
ALIMENTARI

MARCA
REGISTRATA

PASTIFICIO
TRIESTINO
SOCIETÀ ANONIMA
TRIESTE

Creazione: S. POLLIONE

Durum wheat is grown in North and South America, Russia, the Middle East and, of course, in the Mediterranean. Although quality durum wheat is grown in many Italian regions, particularly in the south, the national pasta industry relies heavily on imports. Mediterranean durum wheats have a higher degree of yellow pigments than other types, which account for the warm amber colour of some Italian dried pasta, while other brands add artificial colouring to achieve this effect.

The quality of water that is added to semolina to make the dough might be regarded as the "mystical element" in the manufacture of dried pasta, just as it seems to be in the brewing of beer and the making of a superior cup of espresso coffee. In the nineteenth century Neapolitans proudly proclaimed that their water made the local pasta the very best. Today most artisan producers note on their packets that pure spring water has been used to make their pasta.

With increasing frequency another important qualification now appears on the packets of some artisan pasta. It states that the pasta is a *prodotto biologico*, the Italian way of saying that it is organically produced. This means that the farmer who raised the wheat used no chemical fertilizers, pesticides or other noxious compounds at any stage of cultivation, nor were any of these added during the processes of production and conservation before the pasta was put into its packet. Both European Community regulations and the Italian Ministry of Agriculture govern this sector. Implementation of their norms is entrusted to several government-approved private agencies who supervise production and confer a mark of guarantee on products that qualify.

Once the semolina is mixed with water and the dough is ready it is forced under pressure through pierced metal plates or dies that stamp, cut or mould the pasta into its particular shape. Nowadays industrial manufacturers use Teflon-lined plates. Some artisan producers still use the traditional *trafile di bronzo*, unlined bronze drawplates. In contrast to Teflon, these have a rough surface, which confer a porous texture to the pasta, enabling it to cook more homogeneously, and an irregular surface, making it better suited for holding and absorbing sauce. By all accounts, the technical step in the manufacture of dried pasta that most influences flavour and texture and the overall quality of the final product is the drying process. The trick is to reduce the moisture in the dough from about twenty-five per cent to about twelve per cent, at a rate that will allow it to dry uniformly. If the dough dries too quickly the

outside will crack. If it dries too slowly, bacteria and mould will form and the dough will acidify. For industrial manufacturers this is also an economic problem. Time is money.

In bygone days pasta was dried in the open air, draped over cane poles. Neapolitans boasted about the benefits of local sea breezes for beneficially flavouring their pasta. Today basically two drying methods are used by commercial producers.

In industrial plants pasta is dried in large chambers for several hours by means of alternating rapid sequences of dry air and steam at extremely hot temperatures. Artisan producers employ a much more time-consuming, but ultimately satisfactory, method that begins with a fast first phase lasting about thirty minutes, during which the pasta is set into its shape, and then a second phase during which the moisture is slowly and gently reduced and redistributed at low temperatures around 40°–45°C/106°–116°F. For most shapes of pasta this takes up to fifty hours, whereas pasta dried industrially can be ready to package in five.

About 170 companies in Italy produce packaged pasta. Happily, all recent and objective consumer reports unanimously grade the standard of mass-produced pasta as good. This evaluation includes the product of producers now owned by multinational corporations and nationally owned companies, as well as lesser-known "discount" labels.

Beyond "good", however, are *buonissimo* and excellent. These are honours usually reserved for the products of the dozen or more of Italy's artisan pasta producers. They obtain their superior results first of all by a careful selection of semolina from choice durum grains. Carlo Latini, owner of Pastificio Latini, for example, even raises the grain for his pasta to ensure its quality. Next comes the careful mixing and "soft" pressing of the dough, its shaping through traditional bronze plates, and finally the slow, low-temperature drying process.

Obviously, the costs and prices of these products are also superior. Fortunately for the state of the art, many consumers are prepared to pay more than double the price of standard brands for a superior artisan pasta.

The ultimate test of quality is in the pot and on the palate. Good pasta must hold its shape and texture while cooking. If the boiling water becomes cloudy, that is a sign that the pasta contained too much starch which was released while cooking and conversely was low in protein.

Most people think of the sauce as that which gives

flavour to a bowl of pasta. Superior pasta, however, when tasted on its own, cooked but not dressed, will have a definite flavour and even a subtle aroma, like any other product made from high-quality grain. With a firm and flavourful base, all you really need to add for a tasty bowl of pasta is an equally superior extra virgin olive oil. In any case, I recommend you try tasting different brands in this way before you choose the family staple.

COOKING DRIED PASTA

Cooking pasta is so simple that the only problem is to keep it that way—the art of simplicity. All it takes to achieve this is a little trial and error.

The first and most important thing to remember is that pasta must be served just as soon as it is cooked. In Italy, when pasta is the first course of a meal, a way of asking family and friends if they are ready to come to table is, *si butta?*, meaning "should I toss the pasta in the water?" In the short time it takes everyone to be seated the pasta will be ready to serve. On the other hand, if you were to cook it before calling them to table, in the short time it would take to gather the group the pasta might easily have become a sticky mass.

Begin with a deep, light-weight, easy-to-handle saucepan for boiling water. The pan has to be big even if you are cooking only a small portion. Pasta needs ample space to swell and move around and enough water so that it can absorb some and there still be plenty in which to cook. Otherwise it will stick together in the starch that is released while it cooks. Remember to leave room in the pan so the water does not boil over and extinguish the flame.

Normally it is advisable to use about 4.8 litres/8½ pints/5 quarts water for cooking up to 450g/1 lb pasta. I know Neapolitans, born to the art of preparing pasta, who use 950ml/1½ pints/1 quart water to 450g/1 lb pasta. In this way, they claim, the flavour of the pasta remains more concentrated since it is not diluted in a lot of cooking liquid. If you adopt this procedure, it is essential to use a high-quality brand of pasta and to watch it carefully while it is cooking, giving it an occasional stir with a wooden spoon, so it does not stick together. In any case, I would not recommend cooking more than 900g/2 lb pasta in the same pan. It gets too cumbersome. In Italy the usual portion per person of pasta when it is a first course is about 90g/3oz.

When the water begins to boil, add a little sea salt to flavour the pasta. Two tablespoons is sufficient. After the water returns to a brisk, rolling boil, add the pasta. If it is short pasta, give it a stir with a wooden spoon to ensure that it doesn't stick to the bottom of the pan. If it is spaghetti, ease the strands under the boiling water with the spoon as they begin to bend. Never break the strings in half. All the pasta must be added at the same time so that it will cook uniformly. During cooking, continue to give the pasta a few stirs.

Actual cooking time will depend on the kind of pasta. Ignore the time instructions that are often printed on the packet. The only sure method is to test it from time to time until it has arrived at the point called *al dente*. Just when that point has been reached will require a judgment on your part, and like all judgments it will be based on objective and subjective criteria.

Objectively, *al dente* simply indicates that perfectly cooked pasta should be chewy while still remaining firm to the bite. The Italian phrase literally means "to the tooth". Over-cooked pasta will be completely limp on the fork and mushy in the mouth. Undercooked pasta is rigid on the fork and raw to the bite. *Al dente* is the perfect mean between these two extremes.

While Italians and connoisseurs of pasta of all nationalities would agree that pasta should be cooked *al dente*, some prefer it more *al dente* than others. Neapolitans say that pasta should be taken out of the boiling water *all'impiedi*, or still standing, in other words, it is ready just as soon as it begins to yield to your fork. I find that tubular pasta like penne are best on the far side of *al dente*, while long pasta such as spaghetti are tastier with a little more bite. This subtlety is totally subjective. There is, however, nothing subtle or subjective about what constitutes *al dente* itself and with a little experience it becomes readily palpable. Remember, too, that the more pasta is cooked, the more difficult it is to digest.

To test the point your pasta has reached, extract a noodle from the boiling water. If you have not yet developed asbestos fingers, there exists a special long wooden spoon with prongs that facilitates this operation. Even before the piece of pasta reaches your mouth, both its flexibility and colour will give you clues to its state. If it is rather dark and stiff, it still has a couple of minutes to go. If it is soft and almost white, well, better luck the next time.

Sometimes it is not the fault of the chef when pasta overcooks. It can be the brand of pasta that is faulty. Perhaps the flour was made from inferior types of grain or the drying process was defective. In these cases the pasta does not properly "seal" the first couple of minutes after it has been placed in boiling water and will not be able to stand up to the cooking process.

When the pasta has reached the right degree of *al dente* (and remember to allow for the fact that it still cooks during the first few seconds after you have taken it out of the water), pour the contents of the pan, pasta and water, into a large metal colander in the sink.

Help the water to drain completely away by giving the colander a few shakes. Then transfer the pasta immediately to a warmed serving bowl or platter. Pour over the sauce, toss and serve immediately. Pasta cooked perfectly *al dente* will sustain its sauce, while over-cooked pasta will be overcome by it.

One last suggestion. So essential is it that pasta be enjoyed as soon as it is cooked that the usual table etiquette of not starting to eat until everyone has been served is abrogated. Invite your guests to begin immediately.

DRESSING PASTA

ACHIEVING A SUCCESSFUL MATCH BETWEEN A PARTICULAR TYPE OF PASTA AND A SUITABLE SAUCE IS FUNDAMENTAL FOR THE FAVOURABLE OUTCOME OF THE DISH. FOR THOSE WHO HAVE GROWN UP ON PASTA THE MATTER IS MOSTLY INSTINCTIVE. FOR THOSE WHO HAVE NOT, A FEW GUIDELINES CAN BE HELPFUL FOR MAKING THE PERFECT MATCH. THESE ARE NOT RULES THAT MUST BE RIGOROUSLY APPLIED. RATHER THEY ARE TRADITIONAL STANDARDS BASED ON TASTE AND COMMON SENSE. IT TAKES ONLY A LITTLE EXPERIENCE AT THE TABLE TO DISCOVER THAT EACH TYPE OF PASTA HAS ITS OWN PERSONALITY WHICH MUST BE RESPECTED WHEN IT COMES TO CHOOSING HOW YOU ARE GOING TO DRESS IT. THE FOLLOWING ARE A FEW GENERAL GUIDELINES FOR PAIRING PASTA WITH SAUCE. I HAVE GIVEN MORE SPECIFIC SUGGESTIONS IN THE RECIPE CHAPTERS.

Perhaps the most important consideration to keep in mind when combining sauce and pasta is that the two should form something which transcends the sum of their parts. You sometimes read a description of a pasta dish in which all the ingredients sound interesting and delicious, yet when it arrives on the table you find yourself confronted with a pasta and a sauce that for some reason turn out to be incompatible. The two even seem to go their separate ways on the plate. On the other hand, when the marriage has been successful, their union is one of the most satisfying taste experiences in Italian cooking.

The principle with the broadest application for pairing pasta and sauce is that dried pasta has an affinity with sauces made with olive oil and fresh pasta with sauces based on butter. A corollary is that seafood sauces, since they are almost always made with olive oil, go especially well with spaghetti-type pasta. Spaghettini, in particular, is the classic mate for seafood. In general, tomato sauces, because they are usually made with olive oil, are most successfully combined with the whole range of dried pasta, long and short. Sauces thickened with butter and cream are absorbed best by fresh egg and flour pasta.

Common sense dictates that pasta of light consistency should be paired with light sauces. In structure slim pasta is slippery and subtle. It would go against its nature to weigh it down with a heavy sauce. *Aglio, olio e peperoncino*, garlic, olive oil and chilli pepper, perhaps the most simple and minimal, as well as tastiest, of all sauces, is only imaginable with thin strands of spaghetti. Even grated cheese should only be added to thin and medium pastas with discretion, if at all. Neapolitans would not grate it over their native spaghetti.

As the diameter of the pasta increases, so does its capacity for coping with weightier ingredients. Chunky meat sauces, a hearty *ragú*, for example, and those made with game such as hare and wild boar, need thick noodles like pappardelle and tagliatelle. And you can grate cheese over maccheroni to your heart's content.

Very rich sauces with cream and cheese are ideal for baked pasta dishes. On the other hand, filled pastas can be stuffed with either light and subtle or rich and complex ingredients because by their very nature the quantity that goes into them is circumscribed and can be savoured in single bites.

There are occasions when I feel like featuring the quality of the pasta itself and times when I want to emphasize the sauce. I often use dried pasta as a base for eating my favourite vegetables as they come into season. In these cases, the larger the pieces of vegetable, the larger the form of pasta.

Some forms of pasta are natural for catching the

MDXXXV.

E. B. 488.

Allium oleraceum, var. genuinum.   Field Garlic, var. a.

goal here is to coat every strand or noodle with the olive oil or butter, as the case may be, and to spread around the other ingredients as uniformly as possible. You can also toss the pasta for a couple of minutes in the saucepan itself. This sometimes helps to dress the pasta more evenly, especially with heavier and thicker sauces.

When the serving bowl is brought to the table, everyone should be able to lift out a portion in which the pasta and sauce have been evenly combined. It seems that inevitably some of the best bits remain for the last to be served, which in a family is usually the youngest child and therefore a reward for having waited patiently until served.

Whether it is a family meal or a dinner with guests, pasta should be served in a large bowl and each participant allowed to help himself. Only in restaurants is pasta presented at the table already in individual dishes.

Ideally pasta should be neither dry nor soaked in sauce. If a puddle of sauce remains on the plate after the pasta has

ingredients of a sauce. Other shapes are more suited to be wrapped around the ingredients. A bite of penne with a bit of diced meat or vegetable inside or an orecchiette that has caught some tomato sauce is a delight, as is a fork full of tagliatelle wrapped around some sliced fresh porcini mushrooms.

Since the moment to dress the pasta is immediately after it has been taken off the heat and drained, it is important that the sauce be ready and waiting. Just as soon as the pasta is in its serving bowl, pour over the sauce and begin to toss the pasta to mix in the sauce. I find that two large serving forks do the job best. The

been eaten, you will know to use less the next time. If, after you have tossed the pasta and sauce, you sense the dish is a little dry, add a touch of fresh olive oil or butter, depending on the sauce.

One last remark, and this *is* a rule to be rigorously applied. Pasta should be eaten from a proper dinner plate, never from a soup bowl, and only with a fork. No knives or spoons allowed! There is really no mystery in mastering the skill of twirling a mouthful of spaghetti around your fork. As every Italian child has been reminded at least a dozen times, the secret to success is managing a small mouthful only.

GRATING CHEESE OVER PASTA

Sometime, somewhere, after the taste for pasta had passed beyond the boundaries of its native land, the practice of grating cheese over any and every dish of Italian noodles took hold. I would imagine many people thought, "this is how they do it in Italy". Cooks and eaters alike seem to have simply taken it for granted that a little, and usually a lot, of grated cheese enhanced the flavour of all pasta dishes, without first stopping to consider the tastes and textures of the other ingredients involved.

Undoubtedly this foreign malpractice was also encouraged by the industrial cheese companies that packaged pulverized products suggestive of sawdust for that purpose. And who knows, maybe the taste of some of those pasta dishes was improved by smothering them with grated cheese.

Notwithstanding the recent advances made in preparing pasta outside of Italy, the unfortunate practice of indiscriminately adding grated cheese still lives on. Your taste-buds, however, as well as Italian culinary tradition, will tell you that only particular pasta dishes are complemented by the addition of grated cheese, and only if the cheese is of a certain type and quality.

"Parmesan" is the word pasta recipes often employ to indicate the use of any cheese whose grainy texture makes it suitable for grating. This usage derives from the name of the Italian grating cheese *par excellence*, *Parmigiano Reggiano*, for which there is absolutely no substitute. Happily, the genuine product is now widely available.

Parmigiano Reggiano is a denomination strictly protected by law and only cheese with this name branded all over the rind is the authentic article. Production is subject to strict standards and exacting quality control. It is made exclusively from the partially skimmed milk of cows whose pasture is located in several provinces of the region of Emilia-Romagna, including areas around Parma and Reggio, where this cheese originated. Only rennet which causes milk to coagulate is added. The milk is heated for about 30 minutes to separate the curd, which is pressed, moulded into huge solid drums, salted and slowly aged for a minimum of one year.

Ripe *Parmigiano* is of a pale straw colour which becomes golden with age. It is a hard cheese, yet has minute, pinpoint holes on its firm surface that allow it to break apart easily. *Parmigiano* in good condition has a mellow, nutty flavour and practically melts in the mouth. It is these qualities that make it perform so perfectly in cooking. It melts easily, binds with other ingredients and does not become stringy.

Because it is a cow's milk product, it combines best with pasta sauces based on butter and cream rather than olive oil. It is indispensable with the many fresh egg pastas of its native region, lasagne, ravioli and tagliatelle. With very few exceptions, it is not grated over pasta with seafood sauces, since these are almost always made with olive oil. To the taste of many Italians it does not complement porcini mushrooms, perhaps because these are usually sautéed in olive oil, and Tuscans, in particular, do not sprinkle it over sauces made with game. It also tends to suppress the tang of spicy sauces, so Romans would never put it on *spaghetti alla amatriciana*, for example.

When you wish to add *Parmigiano* to a pasta dish, wait until you are ready to eat before grating it. That way it will remain moist and aromatic. *Parmigiano* is often described as *formaggio di rifinitura*, a cheese for adding the "finishing touch" to a dish. Almost like salt, it should be used sparingly so the taste of the pasta itself, cooked perfectly *al dente*, and the flavours of the sauce are heightened, not submerged.

When you buy a piece of *Parmigiano*, ask for a wedge still attached to the rind. It will stay fresh longer. It should be stored tightly wrapped first in cheese paper and then in foil, and kept on the bottom shelf of the refrigerator.

Parmigiano Reggiano is the most prestigious of a family of other cow's milk cheeses known as *grana* due to their hard, grainy texture. The other three, all produced in the northern regions of Emilia-Romagna and Lombardia, are *Grana Piacentino*, *Grana Lodigiano* and *Grana Padano*, the most famous after *Parmigiano Reggiano*. These are all excellent grating cheeses and are less expensive than *Parmigiano*.

From southern Italy comes another classic grating cheese that belongs to the pecorino, sheep's milk cheese, family. *Pecorino (Romano)* develops a hard consistency and slightly oily texture after months of aging. It has a sharp, salty taste which is well suited to many of the piquant sauces of the South cooked in olive oil.

THE PASTA PANTRY

BECAUSE PASTA IS SUCH A SIMPLE, VERSATILE, EASILY PREPARED DISH, YOU CAN KEEP ON HAND ALL THE ESSENTIALS FOR DOZENS OF RECIPES, BOTH IN THE LINE OF PROVISIONS AND EQUIPMENT, IN EVEN THE SMALLEST AND MOST MODEST OF KITCHENS. THESE ARE THE BASIC NECESSITIES.

PROVISIONS

The secret of a successful pasta dish is the quality of its ingredients. Never use an inferior product. There are so many ways of dressing pasta that you will almost always be able to use seasonal produce. Keeping in store a variety of dried herbs, spices and preserves will enable you to prepare tasty dishes in the leaner months of winter, as well as for a last-minute midnight supper.

ANCHOVIES

Try to find Italian anchovy fillets in olive oil that are packed in jars, as you can use a few at a time and keep the rest in the refrigerator for several weeks. On their own anchovies have a very strong flavour, but when cooked they disintegrate and bring out the other flavours in a sauce. Never substitute anchovy paste. Do not use the oil as it is almost always low grade.

BREADCRUMBS

Use a blender or food processor to make dry breadcrumbs and store the crumbs in a sealed glass jar, not in the refrigerator. Avoid packaged "seasoned" breadcrumbs. In some of my recipes fried breadcrumbs are sprinkled over pasta dishes instead of grated cheese. (You'll find the recipe for these on page 67.)

CAPERS

Italian capers, especially from the Aeolian islands off the coast of Sicily, are the best in the world. They are preserved in salt or vinegar. The ones in salt are preferable. Be sure to wash away the salt before adding them to a sauce.

CHEESES

Parmigiano Reggiano is the finest of all Italian grating cheeses. Like extra virgin olive oil it is expensive but well worth the investment. Never buy pregrated Parmesan in packets. A chunk of *Parmigiano* tightly wrapped first in cheese paper then in foil will keep for months in a refrigerator. Grate finely just before serving.

Pecorino (Romano) is a well-matured sheep's milk cheese traditionally used for grating over some southern Italian pasta dishes. It has a stronger flavour than *Parmigiano* and can be stored in the same way.

DRIED PASTA

If you always keep a couple of packets each of spaghetti- and maccheroni-type pasta in the cupboard, your family will never go hungry. With a little garlic and extra virgin olive oil you have the makings of a quick and tasty last-minute supper. Buy pasta made from *semola di grano duro* only, produced in Italy.

FLOUR

For making fresh pasta in Italy we use grade 00 flour. Unbleached plain (all-purpose) flour is a good substitute.

GARLIC

Buy firm heads of garlic and store in a dry place. They will keep for several weeks. Never substitute with dried or powdered garlic.

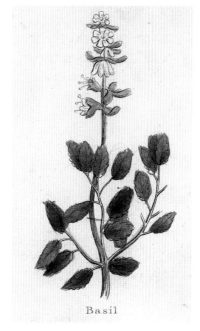

Basil

HERBS

These are essential for pasta sauces. They are always better when fresh but some may be substituted with the dried, but not the powdered, variety.

Basil does not dry well but it is easy to grow on a sunny windowsill. If that is impossible, store some leaves in pure olive oil in the refrigerator. They will keep for about one week. Or chop and freeze with a little salt to preserve the green colour.

Bay leaves Italian bay leaves, or *alloro*, are less pugent than the Pacific variety and have a very distinctive flavour. They are available dry from Italian grocery stores.

Marjoram The wild Mediterranean variety has a stronger flavour than cultivated sweet marjoram. Dries well.

Oregano is similar but stronger than marjoram and also dries well.

Parsley Use the fat-leaf Italian variety which has a definite flavour of its own. It loses all of it's flavour when dried but may be frozen.

Rosemary is a very popular Italian herb that retains its flavour when dried but not for more than a few months.

Saffron is expensive because it is the tiny stamen of the crocus flower. Only use the best because inferior products are either flavourless or are mixed with turmeric and will make your pasta taste like curry.

Sage has a strong, musty flavour and is sometimes sautéed in butter and poured over pasta as a dressing. It dries fairly well.

MUSHROOMS

Porcini are full of flavour even when dried. Choose packets containing large slices. They keep indefinitely in a jar stored in a dry place.

OIL

Use only cold pressed extra virgin olive oil. Nothing else gives the authentic flavour to pasta sauces, and anything less will spoil the taste of your dish.

OLIVES

Always buy olives loose. A lot of their flavour disappears when they are stoned and canned.

ONIONS

Keep at least a couple of red onions on hand, stored in a dry place.

PANCETTA

This is Italian unsmoked bacon, cured with salt and spices. Smoked bacon can be used as an alternative. You can hang a small slab of pancetta in a cool, well ventilated place or keep it wrapped in the refrigerator. If you only have smoked bacon, blanch it in boiling water for 5 minutes before using it.

PINE NUTS

Pinoli, in Italian, are the seeds of the Stone pine. Keep a small amount of these in store for when you want to make pesto sauce.

SPICES

Cloves should be used whole. Buy nutmeg whole and grate straight into the pan or dish. Black and white peppercorns should be ground as they are required. Use crushed dry *peperoncini*, or hot pepper flakes.

TOMATOES

Pasta sauces require perfectly ripe plum tomatoes. If these are not available use only Italian peeled tomatoes in cans, as tomatoes are often picked too soon in other countries.

If you are fortunate enough to have a surplus of ripe plum tomatoes, they are very easy to freeze whole and then use as required. Of course, every pasta pantry should have several jars of good tomato sauce.

Tomato purée (paste) in tubes is easier to keep than the canned variety.

Sun-dried tomatoes Buy the ones preserved in olive oil, otherwise you will have to go through a tedious process of reconstituting them and storing them in olive oil yourself.

TUNA

Canned in oil or brine, it is handy to have tuna in your pasta pantry. It is even worth investing in a couple of cans of imported Italian tuna, which comes from the belly of the fish, and is superior in taste and texture to that you get from other countries.

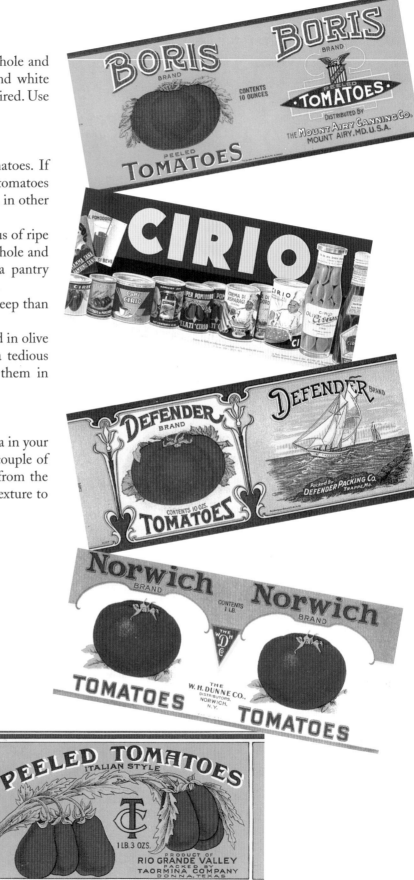

39

EQUIPMENT

Happily Italian kitchens are generally gadget-free. There are, however, a few pieces of equipment that will help you to produce superior pasta.

BISCUIT (COOKIE) CUTTERS

Straight or fluted 5cm/2 inch and 7.5cm/3 inch diameter cutters are perfect for cutting circles for stuffed pasta.

CHEESE GRATER

Choose a rotary or half-cylindrical shredder to grate Parmesan and pecorino (Romano) very finely.

COLANDER

Invest in a good metal colander with sturdy handles and feet. The holes should be large and well distributed so the pasta drains quickly.

DOUGH SCRAPER

Use a flexible metal scraper to clean the work surface before rolling out pasta or pastry dough.

FOOD MILL

You will need a food mill with three assorted discs, as a food processor is not suitable for puréeing tomatoes.

HAND-CRANKED PASTA MACHINE

Optional for thinning and cutting pasta.

MEZZALUNA

This is a crescent-shaped blade with a wooden knob at each end. It is rocked back and forth on a board to chop herbs and vegetables quickly and efficiently without "bruising" them. Once you have acquired the knack, you will find it much easier and more satisfactory to use than an ordinary knife.

MOULDS

You should have a springform mould, as well as a ring mould, for making pasta pies and timbals.

OVENPROOF DISHES

For baked pasta, use heavy ovenproof porcelain, glazed earthenware or glass dishes that can be taken directly to the table.

PASTA PAN

Use a deep, light pan so that the water boils quickly and it is not too heavy and awkward to handle when full of boiling water and pasta.

PASTRY WHEELS

A rolling cutter can be used for slicing flat pasta with fluted edges or cutting and sealing stuffed pasta.

PESTLE AND MORTAR

Although you can make satisfactory pesto sauce in a blender or food processor, the process and end-result are far more satisfying using a marble mortar and a wooden pestle.

ROLLING PIN

Not too thick and at least 60cm/24 inches long.

SLOTTED SPOON or SKIMMER

Perfect for removing and draining cooked stuffed pasta from the pot. If stuffed pasta is poured into a colander it is likely to break. Also essential for removing gnocchi from boiling water.

WOODEN FORK

It is preferable to own one with prongs, for stirring pasta and lifting from water to test.

WORK SURFACE

You will need a large wooden or plastic surface for rolling out pasta dough. Marble is too cold.

PART II

BASIC RECIPES

MAKING FRESH PASTA

I heartily recommend to anyone who delights in the pleasure of pasta that they make the effort to learn the gentle craft of making pasta at home. I guarantee it will be an investment of your time that will reap benefits a hundredfold.

Home-made pasta is so much lighter than the fresh pasta available in shops that the latter is only a poor substitute. In fact, unless you have savoured egg pasta made in an Italian household, it is highly unlikely that you have ever tasted genuine home-made pasta. The fresh pasta made in shops and served in restaurants is nearly always made in elaborate commercial pasta machines which work by extrusion and alter the structure of the gluten in the flour and the end-results of texture and taste.

I know of few culinary skills that give the satisfaction of transforming a heap of flour and a few eggs into yards of golden pasta. And, as most Italian women and not a few men know, nothing is quite as soothing as kneading and rolling pasta following a stressful day.

Preparing pasta has none of the pitfalls of making bread or pastry. There is no yeast to prove or temperamental shortening to worry about. It would be misleading, however, if I said that all you need do to successfully make pasta completely by hand is carefully follow instructions. Practice and patience are required. It is a very tactile craft and your hands have to learn to recognize instinctively well-kneaded dough. You will find, however, that you have mastered the craft much sooner than you expected. Then you can begin to relax and take satisfaction in this process that provides so much enjoyment in the kitchen and pleasure at the table.

WORK SURFACE

Choose the largest area available to work on. A depth of 60–84cm/2–3 feet is sufficient but the bigger it is, the easier it will be to work. Space gives you a freedom of movement that is especially important when you are learning. Ideally the surface should be of hardwood but Formica or other hard materials will do. Special pasta boards can be purchased. Always keep the work surface clean and free from pots and jars.

Cucina principale

reduto da pani

lucerna

Camino per arzan

ordegno

murello per piguatte

banche

Colonna col mortaro

Tauola per imbandire

fa | uola
da | pasta

PASTA ALL' UOVO
Fresh Egg Pasta

Pasta making is not an exact science. The amount of flour you actually use will vary slightly, depending on how large the eggs are, how absorbent the flour is and especially whether you are working in a dry or humid atmosphere. So do not be alarmed if you find that you require a little less or a little more flour to achieve a smooth, elastic dough.

There are two ways of mixing flour and eggs for pasta dough. The method I call Method One is the one explained in all cookery books. It uses a bowl. The other way, which I call Method Two, or The Italian Way, is the method really used by every Italian housewife when she wants to make dough for fresh pasta. It is much more flexible and adaptable to variables, not only in the weather but especially in the human condition!

Both these methods make about 360g/12oz, enough for four first courses.

METHOD ONE

210g/7oz/1⅓ cups plain (all-purpose) flour
2 eggs, size 3 (U.S. large)

In this method, a bowl rather than a board should be used to mix the flour and eggs. Otherwise you will find that it is virtually impossible to keep the eggs from running out of the well. Remove a couple of spoonfuls of the measured flour and put them on the side of the board. You might need them later. Heap the rest of the flour in a mound in the middle of a large mixing bowl. Make a deep well in the centre and break the eggs into it.

Beat the eggs lightly with a fork until the yolks and whites are well blended. Then gradually draw in the flour from the lower inside of the well, using a circular movement. When the egg and flour are well amalgamated, transfer the dough on to the work surface and start kneading (see below).

METHOD TWO
The Italian Way

Heap a generous amount of flour on to a large work surface without regard to exact measurement, but use at least 900g/2 lb of flour for 2 eggs. Make a well in the centre, break the eggs into it and then begin to mix the eggs and the flour with a fork into the well with a circular motion.

When the eggs and part of the flour are well mixed and have become too resistant to be worked with a fork, scrape the dough formed and transfer it on to a clean board before kneading it. (Sift the leftover flour which can be used again.)

KNEADING

The work surface should be perfectly clean before you start kneading or the dough will gather tiny lumps which will cause the pasta to split when it is rolled out.

Lightly sprinkle the work surface with a veil of flour. Place the ball of dough in the centre of the surface and knock it down with the flat of your hand. When the dough is flat, knead it from the middle outwards using the heel of your hand.

Fold the dough in half and, giving it a half-turn, press down hard with the heel of your hand. Repeat this operation for at least 10 minutes, always turning the dough in the same direction. By this time the dough should be elastic and as smooth as the proverbial baby's bottom.

When the dough seems ready, wash and dry your hands. Poke a finger into the middle of the dough and, if it comes out clean, you require no more flour. If your finger is sticky, work in a little of the flour you have set aside. If the dough seems hard and too dry, add a little moisture by working it a little with wet hands.

When the dough is neither too dry nor too sticky, cover it with a bowl. Carefully scrape the work surface to get rid of any loose flour or scraps of dough and immediately roll out the dough. The more thoughly you knead the dough, the easier it will be to roll out, stretch and cut.

ROLLING

ROLLING PASTA BY HAND

There is a knack to rolling out pasta by hand. At first it might appear to be complicated but once you have acquired it, you will find it quicker than setting up a machine.

It is essential that you have a really long rolling pin. If you have one with ball-bearings, do not hold it by the handles but to have firmer control, place your hands at each end of the actual roller.

Choose a clean work surface large enough to comfortably accommodate a big circle of dough. Sprinkle it with a little flour. Lightly flour the rolling pin as well as your hands. The dough should never be allowed to stick, but at the same time it should not be over-floured or it will get too stiff to handle.

Flatten the dough with the palm of your hand, then start rolling out a circle, much as you would if you were preparing pastry (dough) for a tart. Always roll away from you and roll evenly, turning the disc of dough by a quarter after each movement. Work quickly and lightly and avoid pushing the rolling pin into the pasta.

It is essential that the disc is uniformly thick. To achieve this, constantly rotate the dough in the same direction and remember to roll all the way to the edge. You can tell how evenly you are rolling by how round your disc is.

STRETCHING

When the dough is about 2mm/$\frac{1}{16}$ inch thick, it will be too thin to turn easily, so you will need to change your method. Place the rolling pin on the far side of the disc. Curl the pasta around the pin, making sure that it is centred. Starting with your hands together in the centre, make quick rolling movements. While you roll the pin towards you, keep the pasta round it by sliding your hands towards the edges and then back towards the centre again.

Try to work lightly and evenly and as quickly as possible so the pasta does not have time to dry out.

Once the entire disc of pasta is wrapped around the rolling pin, unfurl it back on to the work surface on its reverse side. Repeat this operation until the pasta is paper thin, about 1mm/$\frac{1}{32}$ inch for ribbon noodles, such as tagliatelle, and 0·5mm/$\frac{1}{64}$ inch for filled pasta.

At this point, the pasta can be cut out or left to dry before cutting.

ROLLING PASTA BY MACHINE

Attach the machine to your work table and cover the rest of the surface with cloth kitchen towels.

Divide the dough into equal parts. Remove one piece of dough and wrap and cover the others.

Lightly dust your portion of dough with flour and flatten it with your hand. Adjust the rollers to the widest setting and, using your right hand, crank the machine. Your left hand should be under the machine where the pasta emerges, with your fingers palm up and the thumb well out of the way so it cannot tear the pasta, ready to guide the strip of pasta as it comes out of the machine.

Place the rolled strip flat on the table and fold it into three, as you would a sheet of paper before putting it into an envelope. Flatten the dough with your hands to push out any air between the layers. If sticky, lightly sprinkle one side with flour and run it through the widest setting again. Repeat this folding and rolling operation three or four times, as it is an essential part of the final kneading process and also results in even strips of the same width.

Reset the rollers to the next setting and pass the pasta through all the settings once until you have reached the desired thinness. Machines vary, but unless otherwise specified, pasta is thin enough when it has been rolled through the last setting. If the pasta becomes too sticky during this thinning process, just dust it lightly with a little flour.

As you finish rolling the strips of pasta, place them on the cloths and, if your surface is narrow, allow the strips to hang over the sides.

Opposite page: Fresh Lasagne

USING A MACHINE TO MAKE FRESH PASTA

Less experienced or adventurous cooks will find that making pasta dough with a machine is a very simple and straight-forward operation. If you follow the instructions carefully, you can make "perfect" pasta on the first try. The results are superior to any bought pasta but not as soft and subtle as that made and rolled by hand.

The only machinery I recommend is a food processor fitted with plastic blades or a dough hook. Add the eggs and pulse for a few seconds. Pour the flour into the bowl and pulse the machine briefly a few times to combine the ingredients. Stop and then run the machine for longer periods, for about 2 minutes in total, until the dough forms a ball around the blade.

Turn out the dough on to a lightly floured work surface and knead it following the instructions for the hand method (page 47), but only for a few minutes.

Then follow the instructions for rolling pasta by machine (page 51).

CUTTING FRESH PASTA

Cutting noodles of various widths is very simple. The rolled out pasta should be left to dry but sliced while it is still soft and flexible, after 10–30 minutes, depending on the relative humidity of the ambience. The pasta can then be cooked immediately or stored (page 56).

CUTTING BY HAND

On a clean work surface, using both hands, carefully roll the pasta into a cylinder, as you would a parchment, about 7.5cm/3 inches wide. If the dough seems sticky, sprinkle it very lightly with flour to prevent the layers from sticking together. The thickness for ribbon noodles and lasagne should be about 1mm/$\frac{1}{32}$ inch. For filled pasta it should be 0.5mm/$\frac{1}{64}$ inch.

Using a long, very sharp knife, cut across the roll at very regular intervals. For example, 3cm/1$\frac{1}{4}$ inches for pappardelle; 1cm/$\frac{1}{2}$ inch for tagliatelle and fettuccine; and just 0.25cm/$\frac{1}{8}$ inch for tagliolini and taglierini.

Pasta for lasagne should not be rolled up. Instead, the rolled-out dough should be cut into 10cm/4 inch squares.

To make quadrucci, cut 1mm/$\frac{1}{32}$ inch thick pasta into strips 1cm/$\frac{1}{2}$ inch wide. Cut into 1cm/$\frac{1}{2}$ inch squares.

Lift a few strips of pasta at a time, roll them into little nests about 7.5cm/3 inches wide and leave them to dry on a lightly floured cloth.

CUTTING BY MACHINE

All pasta rolling machines have attachments which slice pasta to at least two widths, one of tagliatelle and the other for taglierini. Before you start, the pasta dough should be rolled out to 1mm/$\frac{1}{32}$ inch thick. Run the rolled pasta through the blades with the desired width and leave the pasta to dry on a floured cloth.

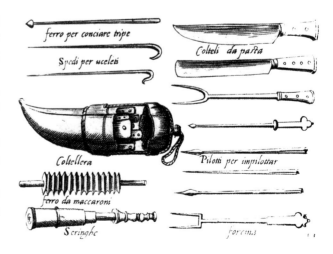

SHAPING FRESH PASTA

AGNOLOTTI, RAVIOLI, TORTELLI

These are different names for stuffed pasta, depending on the regions. Their shapes will also vary from region to region, and they can be square, round or even half-moon shaped.

The pasta dough should be 0.5mm/$\frac{1}{64}$ inch thick. Cut the pasta into strips about 5cm/2 inches wide. Place small spoonfuls of filling along the strips at regular intervals about 5cm/2 inches apart and moisten the edges of the pasta and between the fillings with a damp pastry brush. Place another strip on top and press with the tip of your fingers round each mound of filling to seal well. Cut into squares with a fluted wheel, or rounds with a pastry cutter.

CAPPELLACCI, TORTELLONI

These are made using the same procedure, only the size is bigger. The rolled out pasta should be cut into strips of about 7.5cm/3 inches wide and filling should be placed at regular intervals about 7.5cm/3 inches apart. When the pasta strips are filled and sealed, cut out 7.5cm/3 inch squares for tortelloni or 7.5cm/3 inch rounds for cappellacci.

PIZZOCCHERI

Fresh Pizzoccheri

A speciality of the Valtellina, north of Milan, these are made with a mixture of buckwheat and plain (all-purpose) flours.

120g/4oz/1 cup plain (all-purpose) flour
120g/4oz/1 cup buckwheat flour
1 egg, size 3 (U.S. large)
60ml/2fl oz/$\frac{1}{4}$ cup milk

Mix the flours in a bowl and make a well in the centre. Add the eggs and milk and combine to form a smooth dough, following the instructions for making Fresh Egg Pasta (page 47).
Roll out thin layers of pasta and cut into noodles about 1cm/$\frac{1}{2}$ inch thick.
Serves 4; makes about 360g/12oz.

CANNELLONI

Cylinders of pasta, these are not sealed and are usually baked, topped with bechamel or other sauce. Cut the rolled-out pasta into strips about 9cm/3¾ inches wide and then into 9cm/3¾ inch squares. To use, boil the squares in salted water, drain and place in a bowl filled with cold water to stop further cooking. Drain again and lay on a cloth until dry. Add the filling and roll up to form cylinders. Cook the cylinders in one layer in a greased overproof dish, covered with the chosen sauce. The usual cooking time is about 20 minutes at 180°C/350°F/Gas 4.

ANOLINI, CAPPELLETTI, TORTELLINI

Each of these shapes can be described as a twisted ravioli and they can be made from a round or triangle of pasta. The method of twisting is the same, but if the pasta is round, it will resemble rings, which is why it's called anolini, and if it is a triangle, it will resemble little hats, or cappelletti. To shape anolini, lay the rolled-out strips of pasta on a lightly floured work surface. Cut out 3cm/1¼ inch rounds. Dot the rounds with a little filling, brush the edges with water, fold in half and pinch to seal. Holding the straight edge of the half circle against the tips of your index finger, gently wrap the pasta around the finger and turn the sealed edge up to make an upturned pleat. Pinch the pointed edges together.

For cappelletti use the same method, starting from a 3cm/1¼ inch square of pasta. Close the filling into a triangle, then proceed with the same twisting method.

PICI

Fresh Pici

Very popular in Tuscany and Umbria, are like thick spaghetti.

120g/6oz/1½ cups semolina
120g/6oz/1½ cups plain (all-purpose) flour

Put the semolina and flour in bowl and make a well in the centre. Follow the method for orecchiette, adding about 120ml/6fl oz/¾ cup water.
Once the dough is formed, roll small pieces into cylinders about 30cm/12 inches long and 0.2cm/1⅛ inch thick.
Serves 4; makes about 360g/12oz.

ORECCHIETTE

Fresh Orecchiette

Said to resemble little ears, these are a Pugliese speciality. Look for semolina at gourmet delicatessens or Italian grocery stores.

120g/6oz/1½ cups semolina
120g/6oz/1½ cups plain (all-purpose) flour

Put the semolina and flour into a bowl and make a well in the centre. Add water a little at a time, stirring with a circular movement until you form a dough that is not too wet and not too dry. The exact quantity of water is difficult to give because it depends a lot on the climate and the absorption rate of the flours; it will be about 180ml/6fl oz/¾ cup.

Put the dough on a work surface and work with the palm of your hands following the method for kneading fresh pasta (page 47). When the dough is smooth and elastic, roll into long cylinders about 1cm/½ inch thick. Cut little pieces about 1cm/½ inch long. Press them with your thumb against the board to give them a curved round shape before cooking in boiling salted water.

Serves 4; makes about 360g/12oz.

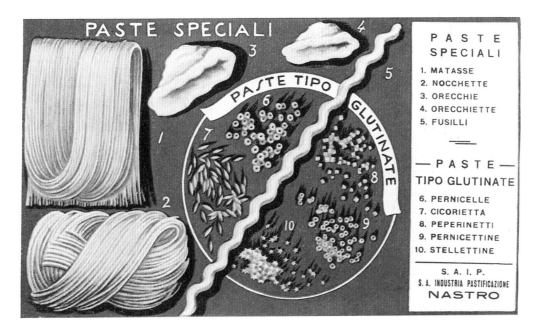

COLOURED PASTA

We hardly ever eat coloured pasta in Italy because we consider it a nonsense. The only coloured pasta that is generally acceptable is the green one, made from fresh spinach because it gives colour and a definite flavour to the pasta. I know that outside Italy smoked salmon and truffle pastas, among others, have become fashionable but I think they are a rip-off because they are expensive and all the flavour just gets lost in the cooking water. You are much better off just adding a little smoked salmon or sliced truffle to freshly cooked pasta.

To make *green pasta*, cook 75g/2½oz fresh spinach in a little salted water. Drain and leave to cool. When the spinach is cool enough to handle, squeeze it hard to get rid of as much water as possible. Purée the spinach and stir it into the eggs before you start drawing in the flour. Green pasta must be very well blended and kneaded to get an evenly coloured dough. The spinach replaces one egg in any recipe.

If you insist on making other coloured pasta, however, here are instructions for the most popular variations.

Use the Fresh Egg Pasta recipe on page 47:

Black pasta Replace one egg with 70ml/2½floz/⅓ cup black squid ink. Mix the squid ink with the remaining egg before you incorporate the flour.

Red pasta Replace one egg with 70g/2½oz/⅓ cup cooked and puréed fresh beetroot (beet). Mix the beetroot purée with the remaining egg before you start to incorporate the flour.

Yellow pasta Soak one pinch of saffron threads in 1 teaspoon water, then mix with the eggs before you start to incorporate the flour.

STORING FRESH PASTA

Although fresh pasta is generally cooked when it is still soft, it may be dried and stored very successfully. To avoid any risk of mould forming, the little nests of noodles should be left to dry on a towel for a whole day. Once the pasta is dry, handle it with the greatest care as it breaks easily. The little nests can be stored in layers, with paper towels between them, on a tray or in a bowl for up to three months with a towel over the top. By the way, the reason for forming ribbon pasta into little nests is that it is less likely to break when dried. When the nests are dropped into boiling water, the ribbons gradually spread out again as they become soft and flexible.

Ribbon pasta cannot be refrigerated because it becomes sticky. When dry it can be frozen.

Stuffed pasta, however, can be refrigerated but only for two or three days. It also keeps well when frozen. To freeze, spread the filled pasta out on a baking tray so that no two pieces touch. Transfer the tray to the freezer and leave it until the pasta is frozen. The pasta can now be put in plastic bags, sealed and stored for at least two months. Neither the texture nor the flavour are spoilt by drying or freezing. If boiled while still frozen, the pasta ribbons will take about 30 seconds longer to cook and the stuffed pasta about 5 more minutes longer.

GENERAL NOTES ON MAKING FRESH PASTA

• *When making fresh pasta time is of the essence. If you work slowly the dough will dry and become very difficult to handle. Roll and stretch the dough as quickly as possible.*

• *Do not make pasta near a hot oven or radiator because it should be kept as moist as possible and any extra sources of heat would dry it out.*

• *Should your sheet of pasta tear, patch it with a small slice of pasta cut from the edge. If it seems not to stick, dampen it slightly with your fingers and roll to smooth it out. If using a machine, fold the pasta over and pass it through the rollers once again.*

• *Never put your wooden rolling pin in water. Anything stuck to the pin should be very lightly scraped off with a knife, then the rolling pin should be brushed and hung up to prevent warping. Should the wood become very dry, treat it by rubbing the wood with a cloth dipped in a little vegetable oil. Remove any excess oil with a paper towel.*

• *Pasta rolling machines should never be allowed to get wet. To get rid of flour or little pieces of dough, set the rollers on the largest opening and clean them with a pastry brush. Wipe the rest of the machine with a slightly damp cloth. Always keep the machine in its box. Before rolling out the pasta, run a small quantity of dough through the rollers and cutters to get rid of any dust it might have gathered.*

BASIC SAUCES

THESE SAUCES ARE BASIC IN TWO DIFFERENT WAYS. SOME, LIKE THE WHITE SAUCE MADE WITH BUTTER, FLOUR AND MILK, AND TOMATO SAUCE, USING EITHER RAW OR COOKED TOMATOES, ARE THE BASIS FOR CONSTRUCTING MORE COMPLEX PASTA DRESSINGS, MADE BY ADDING TO THEM A VARIETY OF OTHER INGREDIENTS—MEAT, FISH, HERBS AND VEGETABLES. OTHERS, SUCH AS THE STEWED MEAT, FISH AND VEGETABLE SAUCES, ARE BASIC IN THE SENSE OF BEING AMONGST THE MOST SIMPLE, FUNDAMENTAL AND CLASSIC OF THEIR CATEGORY. ANY COOK WHO ENJOYS PREPARING PASTA WOULD WANT TO HAVE ALL OF THESE IN HIS OR HER REPERTOIRE.

Basic sauces vary from region to region. In Bologna, for example, they make a rich *ragú* with ground lean veal sautéed in butter and add a spoonful of cream at the end. Tuscans, on the other hand, prepare their meat sauce with beef rump cooked in olive oil and sometimes add a few dried porcini to the other aromatic vegetables. The popular Neapolitan ragú is often based on pork traditionally browned in lard.

A word about tomato sauce, perhaps the most classic pasta dressing of all. For a long while there was a popular misconception that all you had to do to render almost any dish alla Italiana was to add some tomato sauce. More recently there seems to have been a reaction against tomato sauce, as if it were somehow vulgar to serve any dish that had been even slightly reddened by a tomato.

While it is true that there are hundreds of different and delicious ways to prepare pasta, dressing it with a sauce made from good tomatoes seasoned with aromatic herbs and vegetables has always been and remains one of the most satisfactory. When you have mastered the two basic tomato sauces I have given here, variations on seasonings will come easily.

Travelling outside of Italy I have more than once come across a pasta dish dressed with tomato sauce listed on menus as alla marinara, or sailor's style, which is incorrect. In Italy, a marinara sauce is made with garlic and olive oil and sometimes chilli pepper but no tomatoes are added. In the days when that sauce was invented, sailors did not have tomatoes aboard ship, not even canned ones, which did not become widely available until early this century.

Most Italian sauces are based on olive oil. Always use a good-quality extra virgin olive oil. As anyone knows who has developed a taste for fine extra virgin oil, bad oil cannot be disguised by any amount of cooking or seasoning. It is immediately detectable and will ruin the taste of your sauce.

RAGÚ DI CARNE
Meat Sauce

In Italy there are about as many different meat sauces as the people cooking them. Everyone makes his or her own variation, changing the meats, the herbs, the spices and the condiments, and then there are all the regional variations as well. This is a basic recipe, inspired by recipes from Bologna.

Generally speaking, meat sauces are traditionally served with fresh pasta, rather than the dried varieties, but currently this is changing and many sauces are used on dry pasta. The important thing to remember when you are making a meat sauce is that the meat should never be minced (ground) before cooking, which would cause it to cook in lumps. The second rule is that the longer the sauce cooks, the better it will taste.

This sauce can be kept in the refrigerator for about 24 hours, or frozen for up to 3 months.

Handful of dry porcini mushrooms
60g/2oz/4 tbsp unsalted butter
2 tbsp finely chopped onion
60g/2oz pancetta, chopped
2 tbsp finely chopped flat-leaf Italian parsley
2 tbsp finely chopped carrot
2 tbsp finely chopped celery
1 bay leaf

300g/10oz stewing beef, cut into 2.5cm/1 inch cubes
300g/10oz stewing veal, cut into 2.5cm/1 inch cubes
300g/10oz stewing pork, cut into 2.5cm/1 inch cubes
120ml/4fl oz/½ cup good-quality red wine
300g/10oz/2 cups very ripe tomatoes, peeled and chopped, or canned with the juice
Salt and pepper

Soak the mushrooms in water to cover for about 30 minutes, then drain and squeeze dry; finely chop and set aside. Filter and reserve the soaking water.
Melt the butter in a heavy saucepan over low heat.
Add the onion and pancetta and cook, stirring occasionally, for about 3 minutes until the onion is translucent. Add the parsley, carrot, celery and bay leaf and continue cooking for 2 minutes.
Add the meats, raise the heat to medium and continue cooking, stirring occasionally, until the meats start to brown. Remove the meat from the pan and chop it finely.
Return to the pan, add the wine and simmer until it evaporates. Add the tomatoes and reserved mushrooms, then season with salt and pepper to taste and stir. Cover the pan, lower the heat to minimum and simmer gently for about 3 hours until all the excess liquid is absorbed. If necessary, add a little water from time to time.
Makes about 900g/2 lb/4 cups.

SALSA DI POMODORO A CRUDO
Raw Tomato Sauce

This should only be prepared in full summer, when tomatoes are very ripe and tasty. The best way to appreciate its great flavour, is to mix with well-drained, freshly cooked spaghetti, and let cool to room temperature. The flavours will be enhanced by the heat of the pasta. For extra flavour, fresh herbs are added to the finished sauce, the most traditional of which is basil. But flat-leaf Italian parsley, fresh oregano, fresh thyme and marjoram can also be added. Even fresh coriander (cilantro) is delicious.

900g/2 lb very ripe plum tomatoes
4 tbsp extra virgin olive oil
2 tbsp chopped fresh herb (see above)
Salt and pepper

Bring a pan of water to the boil, then add the tomatoes and cook for 1 minute. Drain and pass under cold water, then pull off the skins. Cut the tomatoes in half, discard the seeds and dice.
Put the tomatoes in a bowl with the olive oil, the herb, salt and pepper to taste, and stir together. Serve immediately with well-drained, freshly cooked pasta. If you want to keep the sauce in the refrigerator for a few hours, do not add the herb until you are ready to serve. Let the sauce return to room temperature before serving.
Makes about 720ml/24fl oz/3 cups.

Opposite page: Meat Sauce

SALSA DI PESCE
Fish Sauce

I like to serve this light sauce with any type of long pasta, such as spaghetti, bucatini or linguine. You can use most type of fish provided it is not too fatty, and I think cod has a good texture and flavour. You can also use porgy or porrpano.

120ml/4fl oz/½ cup extra virgin olive oil
1 small onion, chopped
2 bay leaves
900g/2 lb fish, such as cod,
skinned and chopped into large pieces
1 tbsp chopped flat-leaf Italian parsley
Salt

Heat the oil in a frying pan. Add the onion and cook for about 3 minutes, stirring often, until translucent. Add the bay leaves and the fish. Continue cooking for about 10 minutes, stirring a couple of times, until the fish is golden. Discard the bay leaves and the parsley.
Add salt and about 480ml/16fl oz/2 cups water. Simmer over low heat, covered, for about 30 minutes, adding more water if necessary to keep it quite moist. Remove the pan from the heat and let the fish cool a bit, then remove any bones.
Pass the fish and onions through a food mill into a saucepan. Add enough of the cooking liquid to dilute the sauce which should not be too thick.
When you are ready to serve, reheat the sauce and toss it with well-drained, freshly cooked pasta.
Makes about 480ml/16fl oz/2 cups.

SALSA DI VERDURA
Vegetable Sauce

This type of lightly cooked and puréed sauce is becoming very popular because of its fresh taste. It can be made all year round, providing you use seasonal vegetables that are tasty. In summer, for example, use courgettes (zucchini), tomatoes, sweet (bell) peppers and green beans; in autumn and winter, use fennel bulbs, artichokes, broccoli and turnip leaves; in spring, try broad (fava) beans or peas. Be sure to peel vegetables such as sweet peppers, fennel bulbs and broad beans.

240g/8oz of your chosen vegetable (doubling the quantity if using artichokes, because there is a lot to discard)
120ml/4fl oz/½ cup extra virgin olive oil
Salt and pepper

Clean and slice thinly the chosen vegetables, or wash the turnip leaves. Discard the outer pod of the broad (fava) beans if they are very small and tender, otherwise peel them also.
Heat half the oil in a large frying pan over medium heat. Add the vegetables and sauté them for about 5 minutes until they are barely tender. Sprinkle with salt and pepper and put in a blender or food processor and purée until creamy, adding the rest of the oil and about 120ml/4fl oz/½ cup of the pasta cooking water. Reheat the sauce when pasta is ready. Do not keep this in the refrigerator more than a couple of hours.
Makes about 480ml/16fl oz/2 cups.

PESTO ALLA GENOVESE
Pesto Sauce

You will find that pesto only keeps its fresh green colour on pasta when it is freshly made, otherwise it becomes dark and less appetizing looking. And as it is so quick to make, I suggest you always serve it fresh and never try to freeze it. In Liguria cooks make pesto with young basil plants not more than about 10cm/4 inches tall. The quality of the leaves is important for the freshest flavour. They should not be too large or too small, and, of course, they should be very fresh.

60g/2oz/1 cup fresh basil leaves
Salt
45g/1½ oz/3 tbsp freshly grated Parmesan cheese

30g/2oz/2 tbsp freshly grated pecorino (Romano) cheese
3 tbsp pine nuts
2 garlic cloves
120ml/4fl oz/½ cup extra virgin olive oil

Combine the basil with a little salt to taste in a blender or food processor and process a few seconds until chopped. Add the cheeses, pine nuts, garlic and olive oil. Process until a smooth sauce is formed. Add 280ml/10fl oz/1¼ cups of the pasta cooking water and process again briefly. Pour over well-drained, freshly cooked pasta and serve.
Makes about 180ml/6fl oz/¾ cup.

Opposite page: Pesto Sauce

BATTUTO DI VERDURE
Primavera Sauce

This sauce descends from what is called *soffritto* in Italy, a mixture of finely chopped vegetables, such as carrots, onions and celery, with parsley, which are fried in olive oil or butter, or a mixture of the two, depending on the region. *Soffritto* is actually the base for many Italian sauces, and in this version for pasta the vegetables can be varied. The result is known outside of Italy as primavera sauce. This goes very well on short pasta, such as farfalle, conchiglie, penne or rigatoni, and is also perfect on noodles. In authentic versions, such as this one, no cheese is added.

30g/1oz/2 tbsp unsalted butter
120ml/4fl oz/¹/₂ cup extra virgin olive oil
1 small courgette (zucchini), diced
1 carrot, diced
4 asparagus tips, diced
1 handful green beans, diced
75g/3oz/¹/₂ cup shelled very small peas
1 large very ripe tomato, peeled, seeded and diced
1 tbsp chopped flat-leaf Italian parsley
Salt

Melt the butter with half the oil in a large frying pan over low heat. Add all the vegetables, except the tomato, and cook for about 5 minutes, stirring frequently. Add the well-drained, freshly cooked pasta, tomatoes and parsley and cook for 2 more minutes. Add the rest of the oil and mix together, then serve immediately while still very hot. Adjust the salt if necessary.
Makes about 450g/1 lb/2 cups.

SALSA BESCIAMELLA
White Sauce

In the old cookery books this was called *balsamella*, and by old I mean thirteenth-century books, such as *Anonimo Toscano* or *Anonimo Veneziano* (*Anonymous from Tuscany* or *Anonymous from Venice*). And to think French chefs declare béchamel to be a French sauce—in the thirteenth-century there were not even any French cookery books! You can add some grated Parmesan cheese to the finished sauce for extra flavour. You can also use semi-skimmed (low-fat) milk.

30g/1oz/2 tbsp unsalted butter
4 tbsp plain (all-purpose) flour
480ml/16fl oz/2 cups milk
Salt

Melt the butter in a heavy saucepan over medium heat. Add the flour and cook, stirring constantly with a wooden spoon, until the flour is well blended to form a soft paste. Add the milk a little at a time, stirring constantly, and let it absorb before adding more. When you have finished adding the milk, sprinkle the sauce with salt to taste and cover the top with cling film (plastic wrap) to prevent a skin forming if you are not using it right away. You can keep the sauce a few hours in the refrigerator before reheating and using. If it sits in the refrigerator, however, it may become a little too thick, so dilute it with more milk when you reheat it.
Makes about 480ml/16fl oz/2 cups.

Opposite page: Primavera Sauce, pictured here with Farfalle

SALSA DI POMODORO COTTA
Cooked Tomato Sauce

There are many variations on this sauce, but this is the version I use most of the time. In Italy we use canned tomatoes for this recipe more often than fresh ones, but it is very important that the quality is good and the tomatoes are very ripe with a thick juice. Only at the height of summer, when the tomatoes are at their peak of ripeness do we use the fresh ones.

1 tbsp chopped onion
2 garlic cloves, chopped
1 tbsp chopped flat-leaf Italian parsley
4 tbsp extra virgin olive oil
900g/2 lb/6 cups canned chopped tomatoes with the juice, or fresh peeled and chopped tomatoes
Salt and pepper

Combine the onion, garlic and parsley in a heavy-based saucepan over low heat. Add the oil and fry gently for about 3 minutes until the onion and garlic are translucent.
Stir in the tomatoes and half cover the pan so the steam can escape. Cook until all the liquid evaporates and the sauce is thick. Season with salt and pepper. This keeps for a couple of days in the refrigerator.
Makes about 480ml/16fl oz/2 cups.

SALSA ALL'ALFREDO
Alfredo Sauce

This sauce gets its name from when it was first served in a popular Roman restaurant called Alfredo alla Scrofa, where a golden fork and spoon were used to mix the sauce and fettuccine. This sauce is also excellent in filled lasagne or ravioli, or simply tossed with traditional hollow pasta such as penne or rigatoni.

240ml/8fl oz/1 cup double (heavy) cream
30g/1oz/2 tbsp unsalted butter
120g/4oz/1 cup freshly grated Parmesan cheese
Salt and pepper

Put the cream and butter in a saucepan over low heat and let it boil for a couple of minutes.
Take the pan off the heat and stir in half the Parmesan cheese and salt and pepper to taste. Mix with well-drained, freshly cooked pasta and sprinkle the rest of the Parmesan on top.
Makes about 240ml/8fl oz/1 cup.

SALSA AGLIO E OLIO
Garlic and Olive Oil Sauce

Here's one of the most typical sauces for spaghetti, which originated in Naples. The only secret is not to let the garlic burn because it will become bitter. The colour should be barely golden. Variations include a couple of anchovy fillets or anchovies and fennel seeds. But I always think the simpler the better. Make this sauce during the last three minutes of the pasta's boiling time.

240ml/8fl oz/1 cup extra virgin olive oil
8 garlic cloves, finely chopped
1/2 tsp hot pepper flakes

Heat the oil, garlic and hot pepper flakes in a large frying pan over medium heat and cook for about 3 minutes, or until the garlic becomes slightly golden. Immediately add well-drained, freshly cooked pasta with a ladleful of the pasta cooking water. Cook for 2 more minutes, then serve.
Makes about 240ml/8fl oz/1 cup.

Opposite page: Cooked Tomato Sauce

OTHER USEFUL RECIPES

BRODO DI CARNE O POLLO
Meat or Chicken Stock

Sometimes I like to make a meat stock or a chicken stock, with separate distinctive flavours, but often I make a stock with a mixture of meat and chicken which I think is perfect for almost every soup. To make a veal stock, replace the beef with stewing veal.

900g/2 lb beef chuck or brisket, or 1 chicken, or 450g/1 lb beef and 1/2 chicken
1 onion, cut in large pieces
1 leek, cut in large pieces
1 carrot, cut in large pieces
1 celery stalk, cut in large pieces
Handful of flat-leaf Italian parsley
1 bay leaf
Salt

Combine all the ingredients in a large saucepan. Add 2.4 litres/4 pints/2½ quarts water and slowly bring to the boil, skimming the surface as necessary. Lower the heat, partially cover the pan and simmer for about 2 hours, skimming a couple of times. Remove the meat from the stock and set aside, to use for another dish. Strain the stock into a large bowl through a fine sieve (strainer). Add salt to taste and leave to cool. Transfer the stock to the refrigerator. When the fat has congealed on top, remove it and discard. Keep the stock refrigerated until required, up to 24 hours. Otherwise freeze.
Makes about 1.8 litres/3 pints/1³/4 quarts.

BRODO VEGETALE
Vegetable Stock

Sometimes I use a chicken or meat stock to enhance the flavour of soup, but often I prefer a vegetable stock. You can use almost any vegetables, but I suggest you omit strongly flavoured ones such as cabbage because they cause the stock to overwhelm any other flavours in your soup.

2 carrots, scraped
1 large onion
2 small courgettes (zucchini)
2 celery stalks, halved lengthwise and well rinsed
1 leek, halved lengthwise and well rinsed
1 fennel bulb, halved lengthwise and well rinsed
Handful of flat-leaf Italian parsley
2 bay leaves
Salt

Put the vegetables, parsley, bay leaves and 1.5 litres/2½ pints/6 cups water into a large saucepan and bring to a slow boil, skimming the surface as necessary. Leave to cook over low heat, partially covered, for about 1 hour.
Add salt to taste and strain. Leave to cool, then cover and refrigerate until required, up to one day. Otherwise freeze.
Makes about 1.2 litres/2 pints/5 cups.

PANGRATTATO FRITTO
Fried Breadcrumbs

Fried breadcrumbs are often used in the south of Italy instead of Parmesan cheese on pasta dishes, as until quite recently Parmesan cheese was a speciality from northern Italy. They are also used instead of cheese on dishes that contain fish. These store very well for up to one week, at room temperature. Do not put in the refrigerator or they will become mushy. You can buy the breadcrumbs in Italian food stores or make them yourself, grating dry bread.

1 tbsp extra virgin olive oil
150g/5oz/1¼ cups dry fine breadcrumbs
1 anchovy fillet in oil or brine, drained and chopped
1 garlic clove, very finely chopped

Heat the oil in a saucepan over medium heat. Add the breadcrumbs, anchovy fillet and garlic, and fry, stirring constantly, for about 5 minutes until golden. Watch closely that they do not become too dark, or they will become bitter.
Makes about 180g/6oz/1 cup.

PASTA FROLLA NEUTRA
Shortcrust (Piecrust) Pastry

210g/7oz/1⅓ cups plain (all-purpose) flour
90g/3oz/6 tbsp unsalted butter, diced
Salt

Put the flour in a food processor fitted with a metal blade. Add the butter and a pinch of salt. Process until the mixture becomes crumbly. Add 45ml/1½fl oz/3 tbsp chilled water and continue processing until the mixture forms into a ball around the blade. Shape the pastry (dough) into a ball, wrap in cling film (plastic wrap) and chill for at least 1 hour before using.
Makes enough to line a 20cm/8inch tart pan, about 360g/12oz.

PASTA SFOGLIA
Puff Pastry

It is very important that the pastry (dough) and the butter are the same consistency and at the same temperature, or the butter will tear the pastry (dough) when it is rolled out. The water quantity is only approximate because it depends on how much the flour absorbs, due to the climate.

180g/6oz/1½ cups plain (all-purpose) flour
180g/6oz/½ tbsp unsalted butter
Salt

Set aside one fifth of the flour and heap the rest on a work surface in a mound. Make a well in the centre and add 45ml/1½fl oz/3 tbsp chilled water and a pinch of salt. Using the tips of your fingers work until the mixture resembles coarse crumbs. Add an additional 45ml/1½fl oz/3 tbsp chilled water and knead the pastry (dough) until it is smooth and elastic. Roll into a ball, wrap in cling film (plastic wrap) and refrigerate for at least 1 hour.
Soften the butter and, using your fingers, work into the reserved flour until the mixture has the same consistency as the pastry (dough). Shape this mixture into a 9cm/3½ inch square.
Using a rolling pin, roll out the pastry (dough) on a lightly floured surface into an 18 cm/7½ inch square about 1cm/½ inch thick. Place the square of the butter mixture in the centre and fold the corners of the pastry (dough) over the butter, enclosing it but without allowing the edges to overlap. Wrap and refrigerate for at least 20 minutes.
Unwrap the pastry (dough) and place it on a lightly floured surface. Roll out into a rectangle about 30 x 20cm/12 x 8 inches. Fold the rectangle into thirds, folding the bottom third up and the top third down, like folding a letter. Flatten lightly with a rolling pin. Wrap and refrigerate again for 20 minutes. This completes the first turn.
Repeat this step five times more for a total of six times, always turning and rolling the pastry (dough) in the same direction. After you have folded the rectangle for the sixth time, it is ready for rolling out to the required size. Use at once, or cover and chill until required.
Makes about 360g/12oz.

PART III

PASTA IN SOUPS

To someone who is not Italian, pasta in soup may be totally unfamiliar and probably seems like a very minor culinary category. Not so in Italy where we make the fundamental distinction between *PASTASCIUTTA*, which literally means "dry pasta" (not *dried* pasta as the word is often erroneously translated), that is, fresh egg or dried pasta dressed with a sauce, and *PASTA IN BRODO*, pasta cooked in stock (and therefore not dry but "wet"). Dishes in this category include all the regional variations of hearty pasta and bean soups, as well as minestrone, a thin meat broth enriched with pasta.

A popular type of soup pasta is *pastina*, small shapes of pasta, many even quite tiny, in the form of *tubetti* (little tubes), *anellini* (rings), *quadrucci* (squares), *stelline* (stars), *maccheroncini* (tiny maccheroni), *gramigna* (tiny ovals), *tempestina* (another type of tiny ovals) and *alfabetini* (letters of the alphabet), to encourage a child's appetite and education all at the same meal. *Pastina* is floated in stock to thicken it for added nourishment, as well as for its decorative effect. Particularly fine strands of pasta, such as *capelli d'angelo*, or angel hair pasta, and *taglierini* are also cooked in soup, as are stuffed forms of pasta, such as *cappelletti* and *tortellini*. *Ditalini* (little fingers) are frequently added to thicken minestrone.

These soups with pasta can be refined and elegant, as well as delicious. Since *pastasciutta*, apart from special moulded dishes, is not normally served for supper in Italian homes, I often serve a seasonal choice of these soups with pasta at evening meals both to my family and when I entertain friends. These soups also make a perfect first course for a light luncheon.

Dried soup pasta can be purchased in packages but the flavour and consistency of home-made egg pasta (page 47) can raise a humble soup to a new height. And remember when you are making fresh egg pasta that a good use for the leftover scraps of dough is to turn them into pastina for soup.

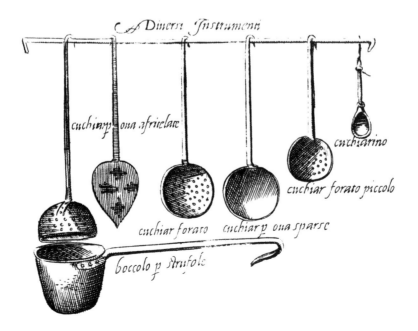

MINESTRA DI DITALINI E FAVE

Ditalini and Broad (Fava) Bean Soup

When broad (fava) beans are young and fresh you
need only discard the outer, inedible pods; the inner
skins will be so tender that you don't need to remove
them. If they are older and quite big, however, remove
the inner shell as well. When they aren't in season,
you can use dry ones if you soak them overnight in
cold water. The next day, drain them and put them in
a pan with enough water to cover and boil for 1½
hours until tender. Drain the beans and follow the
recipe below.

60g/2oz pancetta, sliced
1 large onion, sliced
210g/7oz/1 heaped cup fresh broad (fava) beans,
shelled, or 90g/3oz/½ cup dry
2 large plum tomatoes, peeled and puréed
Salt and pepper
210g/7oz/1 heaped cup ditalini
60g/2oz/4 tbsp freshly grated pecorino (Romano) cheese
6 tbsp extra virgin olive oil

Put the pancetta and onion in a large saucepan. Cook
over low heat, stirring occasionally, for about 5
minutes until translucent and the pancetta fat melts.
Raise the heat to medium and add the beans, tomato
purée, salt and pepper to taste and a glass of water.
Simmer for 5 minutes over low heat, then add 1.2
litres/2 pints/5 cups water and bring to the boil.
Add the ditalini and continue boiling until *al dente*.
Sprinkle with the cheese and extra pepper. Pour in a
warmed soup tureen, drizzle with olive oil and serve
immediately.
Serves 4.

MINESTRA DI CAPELLI D'ANGELO E FRUTTI DI MARE

*Angel Hair with Mussels
and Clams Soup*

This soup, a speciality from Naples, has all the
perfumes of the sea. The angel hair can be replaced
with home-made taglierini (make half the quantity of
fresh egg pasta on pages 47 and 51 and cut into
taglierini following the instructions on page 52), if
you really feel like working a little more, but dry pasta
is perfectly suitable for this recipe.

1.8kg/4 lb very fresh mussels and clams in equal quantities
4 tbsp extra virgin olive oil
2 garlic cloves
4 ripe plum tomatoes, peeled and puréed
120ml/4fl oz/½ cup dry white wine
Salt and pepper
210g/7oz angel hair pasta
Handful of flat-leaf Italian parsley, finely chopped

Wash and scrub the shellfish carefully and discard any
mussels or clams that remain open when you tap
them. Drain the shellfish, place them in a large
saucepan over a high heat and cover. After about 5
minutes, or when the shells are open, drain and
remove the flesh from the shells; set aside. Discard
any shells that have not opened.
Strain the liquid left in the pan and set aside.
Heat the oil in a large pan over low heat. Add the
garlic cloves and fry, stirring occasionally, for about 5
minutes. Discard the garlic, then add the tomato
purée, reserved cooking liquid, wine and 1.2 litres/2
pints/5 cups warm water. Add salt and pepper to taste
and bring to the boil.
Add the pasta and mussels and clams and boil for
about 3 minutes until the pasta is *al dente*. Sprinkle
with the parsley and extra pepper. Pour into a warmed
soup tureen and serve immediately.
Serves 4.

MINESTRA DI CAPELLI D'ANGELO E CIPOLLINE
Angel Hair and Baby Onion Soup

Taglierini, very thin, flat noodles, make a good alternative for angel hair pasta. If you can't buy any, make half the quantity of Fresh Egg Pasta on pages 47 and 51 and follow the instructions on page 52 for cutting the dough into taglierini.

450g/1 lb baby (pearl) onions
4 tbsp extra virgin olive oil
1.5 litres/2½ pints/6 cups chicken stock (page 66)
salt
½ tsp hot pepper flakes
210g/7oz angel hair pasta
60g/2oz/4 tbsp freshly grated pecorino (Romano) cheese

Place the onions and the oil in a large saucepan over low heat and fry, stirring occasionally, for about 10 minutes until golden.
Add the stock and salt to taste. Sprinkle with the hot pepper flakes and boil for about 1 hour.
Add the pasta and cook until it is just *al dente*.
Sprinkle with the grated cheese. Pour into a warmed soup tureen and serve immediately.
Serves 4.

MINESTRA D'OVOLI
Angel Hair and Ovoli Mushroom Soup

Ovoli mushrooms are very special and becoming more difficult to buy. They have a very subtle flavour and resemble eggs, which is where the name comes from—*ovo* means egg in Italian. Porcini are the most appropriate substitute. Clean the mushrooms by wiping them with a dry cloth; do not wash them or they will become mushy and lose their flavour.

4 tbsp extra virgin olive oil
300g/10oz ovoli mushrooms (see above),
wiped and thinly sliced
1.2 litres/2 pints/5 cups vegetable stock (page 66)
Grated zest of ½ lemon
Salt and pepper
210g/7oz angel hair pasta
Handful of flat-leaf Italian parsley, finely chopped

Heat the oil in a large saucepan over medium heat. Add the mushrooms and sauté for about 3 minutes, stirring occasionally. Add the stock and lemon zest and bring to the boil. Add salt and pepper and the pasta. Continue boiling until the pasta is *al dente*. Sprinkle with the parsley. Pour into a warmed soup tureen and serve immediately.
Serves 4.

MINESTRA DI CAPELLI D'ANGELO E ASPARAGI
Angel Hair and Asparagus Soup

Eggs enrich the taste of this soup, but you will also get a delicious result if you use chicken stock (page 66) instead of water.

900g/2 lb fresh asparagus, washed and the tough ends of the stalks removed
4 tbsp extra virgin olive oil
Salt and pepper
210g/7oz angel hair pasta
2 eggs, size 3 (U.S. large)
Grated zest of 1 lemon
60g/2oz/4 tbsp freshly grated pecorino (Romano) cheese

Steam the asparagus tips for about 5 minutes in very little salted water, then drain them well.
Heat the oil in a large saucepan over low heat. Add the asparagus tips and sauté for about 3 minutes.
Sprinkle with salt and pepper, add 1.2 litres/2 pints/5 cups salted water and bring to the boil. Stir in the pasta and cook until *al dente*.
Meanwhile, crack the eggs into a cup and beat in the lemon zest with a fork.
When the pasta is cooked, remove the pan from heat, add the beaten egg mixture and mix well. Pour into a warmed soup tureen, adjust the seasoning and serve immediately with the cheese in a side dish.
Serves 4.

MINESTRONE DI VERDURA
Ditalini and Vegetable Soup

The lighter version of an infinite series of popular Italian vegetable soups. Instead of starting by frying the vegetables in oil, a small amount of oil is poured into the finished soup with the cheese. I think ditalini or tubetti pasta are the best shapes to use for this.

1 small carrot, diced
1 potato, diced
1 celery stalk, diced
1 courgette (zucchini), diced
Handful of shelled peas
Handful of fresh borlotti beans
Salt and pepper
180g/6oz/1 cup ditalini
2 tbsp extra virgin olive oil
60g/2oz/4 tbsp freshly grated Parmesan cheese

Put all the diced vegetables, peas and beans in a large saucepan and add 1.5 litres/2½ pints/6 cups water. Bring to a slow boil and continue cooking over low heat for a couple of hours, covered.
Add salt and pepper to taste and the ditalini. Continue cooking until *al dente*. Pour into 4 soup bowls, sprinkle with the oil and Parmesan cheese and serve immediately, very hot.
Serves 4.

MINESTRA DI CAVOLO NERO E DITALINI
Ditalini and Black Cabbage Soup

Black cabbage is a speciality in Tuscany. It is very tall with long, fat dark leaves. Savoy cabbage makes a very good substitute.

4 black cabbage leaves, or 8 savoy cabbage leaves
1 onion, chopped
1 carrot, chopped
1 celery stalk, chopped
Handful of flat-leaf Italian parsley, chopped
120ml/4fl oz/½ cup extra virgin olive oil
2 large tomatoes, peeled and puréed
1.5 litres/2½ pints/6 cups meat stock (page 66)
210g/7oz/1 heaped cup ditalini
Salt and pepper

Wash the black cabbage and slice into thin strips, discarding the tough stalks. Put onion, carrot, celery and parsley into a large saucepan. Add half the olive oil and fry over medium heat for about 3 minutes, stirring occasionally, or until the vegetables look translucent. Add the cabbage to the pan with the tomato purée and the stock. Cook over low heat for about 1 hour.
Add the ditalini and continue cooking until it is *al dente*. Pour into a warmed soup tureen, sprinkle with the rest of the oil and salt and pepper to taste. Stir together and serve immediately.
Serves 4.

MINESTRA DI DITALINI E BORRAGINE
Ditalini and Borage Soup

Borage is a sky blue flowering herb often found in the wild, as well as cultivated in gardens. It is used in Genoese cuisine for enhancing vegetables and ravioli fillings. The flavour is quite mild.

120g/4oz/⅔ cup lentils
Salt
450g/1 lb/3 cups ripe plum tomatoes, peeled and chopped, or canned with their juice
2 handfuls borage leaves, finely shredded
4 tbsp extra virgin olive oil
210g/7oz/1 heaped cup ditalini

Leave the lentils to soak overnight in cold water. The next day, discard any which rise to the surface and wash the rest well. Drain.
Place the lentils in a large saucepan and pour in 1.5 litres/2½ pints/6 cups water. Add salt, the tomatoes, borage and olive oil and bring to the boil. Lower the heat and simmer for 1 hour, then add the ditalini. Increase the heat and boil until *al dente*. Pour into a warmed soup tureen and serve immediately, very hot.
Serves 4.

Opposite page: Ditalini and Vegetable Soup

MINESTRONE DI CAVOLO

Ditalini and Cabbage Minestrone

The best pasta to use in this hearty soup is ditalini or tubetti. If you cannot find good-quality prosciutto, pancetta is the best substitute.

150g/5oz/1 cup dry beans, such as borlotti or cannellini
4 tbsp extra virgin olive oil
4 garlic cloves, chopped
60g/2oz prosciutto or pancetta, chopped
450g/1 lb/5 cups savoy cabbage, shredded
1.5 litres/2¹/₂ pints/6 cups meat stock (page 66)
1 tbsp tomato purée (paste)
1 sprig fresh rosemary
Salt and pepper
180g/6oz/1 cup ditalini

Cover the beans with cold water and leave them to stand for about 12 hours. Drain.
Heat the oil in a saucepan over low heat. Add the garlic and the prosciutto and fry, stirring, for about 3 minutes until the ham looks translucent.
Add the cabbage and fry, stirring constantly, for 3 more minutes.
Stir in the stock, tomato purée (paste), beans, rosemary sprig and salt and pepper to taste and simmer for about 2 hours, covered.
Add the pasta and continue cooking a few more minutes until *al dente*. Discard the rosemary. Pour into a warmed soup tureen and serve immediately, very hot.
Serves 4.

MINESTRA DI FAGIOLI E MACCHERONI

Maccheroni and Bean Soup

Borlotti beans, with their characteristic stripy red skin, make especially creamy soups. If you use the dried beans, start with half the weight and soak them for at least 12 hours in cold water. This recipe also works well with maccheroncini.

210g/7oz shelled fresh borlotti beans
6 tbsp extra virgin olive oil
60g/2oz pancetta, chopped
1 onion, thinly sliced
180g/6oz/2 cups savoy cabbage, thinly sliced
1 carrot, thinly sliced
4 ripe plum tomatoes, peeled and chopped
1 garlic clove, sliced
1 celery stalk, thinly sliced
Salt and pepper
Handful of fresh basil, finely chopped
1 sprig rosemary, finely chopped
1 tsp fresh thyme leaves
210g/7oz/1 heaped cup maccheroni

Cook the beans, just covered with salted water, for about 1¹/₂ hours over very low heat. Drain, reserving the cooking water, and pass half the beans through a food mill.
Meanwhile, heat half the oil in a large saucepan over low heat. Add the pancetta and onion and fry, stirring occasionally, for about 3 minutes until the onion is translucent. Add the cabbage, carrots, tomatoes, garlic, celery, whole beans, bean purée, cooking water from the beans and 1.2 litres/2 pints/5 cups water. Sprinkle with salt and pepper to taste and simmer for about 30 minutes.
Add the basil, rosemary and thyme. Add the maccheroni and continue cooking until *al dente*. Pour into a warmed soup tureen and serve immediately, very hot. It is not customary to serve cheese with this soup.
Serves 4.

Opposite page: Maccheroni and Bean Soup

MINESTRA DI MANZO E FARFALLINE
Farfalline and Beef Soup

Beef in Tuscany is renowned for its tenderness and quality. If you would like to subtly alter the flavour of this soup, add a bay leaf and some grated black truffle as a final touch. Farfalline are tiny pasta twists, but you can just as easily use ditalini.

1 carrot, finely sliced
1 leek, finely sliced
1 celery stalk, finely sliced
4 tbsp extra virgin olive oil
210g/7oz minced (ground) beef
1.5 litres/2½ cups/6 cups meat stock (page 66)
Salt and pepper
210g/7oz/1 heaped cup farfalline
Freshly grated Parmesan cheese

Put the carrot, leek and celery in a large saucepan. Add the olive oil and fry over low heat, stirring occasionally, for about 5 minutes until the vegetables look translucent. Add the minced (ground) beef, stock and salt and pepper to taste. Simmer over low heat for about 1 hour.
Stir in the farfalline and continue cooking until *al dente*. Pour into a warmed soup tureen, sprinkle generously with the cheese and serve immediately.
Serves 4.

MINESTRA DI ORTICHE E FETTUCCINE
Fettuccine and Nettle Soup

If you have never experienced the flavour of nettles, don't be afraid to try them. They grow wild in the spring and autumn. Use good thick gloves and harvest just the top, tenderest parts. You can substitute spinach or Swiss chard.

60g/2oz pancetta, diced
1 onion, sliced
4 tbsp extra virgin olive oil
4 ripe plum tomatoes, peeled and chopped
600g/1¼ lb fresh nettle tops, washed and
torn into small pieces
1.2 litres/2 pints/5 cups vegetable stock (page 66)
½ quantity Fresh Egg Pasta (pages 47 and 51),
cut into fettuccine (page 52)
Salt and pepper

Put the pancetta, onion and oil in a frying pan over low heat and fry for about 3 minutes, stirring continuously, until translucent. Add the tomatoes and simmer for about 10 minutes, then stir in the nettles and stock. When the stock comes to the boil, add the fettuccine and salt and pepper to taste. Continue cooking until the water returns to the boil and the fettuccine float to the top. Pour into a warmed soup tureen and serve immediately.
Serves 4.

MINESTRA DI FINOCCHI E DITALINI
Ditalini and Fennel Soup

In Italy, we prepare many dishes with fennel bulbs, both raw in salads and cooked. They are also delicious in *pinzimonio*, where raw chunks are dipped into extra virgin olive oil and sprinkled with a pinch of salt.

4 fennel bulbs, outer leaves removed, halved and thinly sliced
1 garlic clove, finely chopped
1 handful fresh flat-leaf Italian parsley, finely chopped
Salt
210g/7oz/1 heaped cup ditalini
4 tbsp extra virgin olive oil
pepper

Place the fennel, garlic and parsley in a large saucepan with 1.2 litres/2 pints/5 cups lightly salted water and bring to the boil. Reduce the heat and simmer for about 20 minutes until vegetables are tender. Add the ditalini and continue simmering until it is *al dente*. Pour into a warmed soup tureen. Add the oil, sprinkle with pepper to taste and serve immediately. It is not customary to serve cheese with this soup.
Serves 4.

PASTA E CECI

Pappardelle and Chick Pea Soup

When we first opened the restaurant here at Badia a Coltibuono, I enjoyed giving ideas to the chef and trying out new recipes. This was one of the ideas that soon became popular with the customers.

Chick peas have a wonderful flavour that perfectly complements the pasta, but you'll find cannellini beans also have a suitable flavour and texture. As well as using pappardelle, I sometimes make this with ditalini.

120g/4oz/²/₃ cup dried chick peas
1 sprig fresh rosemary, finely chopped
4 garlic cloves, finely chopped
6 tbsp extra virgin olive oil
30g/1oz/2 tbsp tomato purée (paste)
¹/₂ quantity Fresh Egg Pasta (pags 47 and 51),
cut into pappardelle (page 52)
Salt and pepper

Soak the chick peas overnight in plenty of cold water. Drain and place them in a large saucepan. Add 1.5 litres/2¹/₂ pints/6 cups water and bring to a slow boil. Reduce the heat and simmer for about 2 hours. Purée the chick peas and their cooking liquid through a food mill. Return the purée to the rinsed-out pan and bring to the boil.
Meanwhile, fry the rosemary and garlic in a saucepan with half the oil over low heat, stirring occasionally, for about 3 minutes. Stir the tomato purée (paste) and the pappardelle into the puréed chick peas and cook until the pasta is *al dente*. Pour into a warmed soup tureen and pour the sizzling oil with rosemary and garlic on top. Add the rest of the oil, sprinkle with pepper and serve immediately.
Serves 4.

MINESTRA DI PAPPARDELLE E FAGIOLI
Pappardelle and Fresh Bean Soup

In Tuscany we generally use cannellini beans, similar to great northern beans in the United States, but you can try this with your local varieties. Ditalini or ditali make good substitutes for the home-made pappardelle.

300g/10oz fresh cannellini beans, shelled, or 90g/3oz/½ cup dried cannellini beans, soaked in water overnight
60g/2oz prosciutto, chopped
1 onion, chopped
6 tbsp extra virgin olive oil
300g/10oz ripe plum tomatoes, peeled
1 large potato, thinly sliced
1 celery stalk, thinly sliced
Salt and pepper
½ quantity Fresh Egg Pasta (pages 47 and 51), cut into pappardelle (page 52)

Place the beans in a large saucepan with 1.5 litres/2½ pints/6 cups water and slowly bring to the boil over low heat. Simmer for 1 hour, then add salt to taste.
Meanwhile, fry the prosciutto and onion with 2 tablespoons of the oil for 3 minutes, stirring occasionally, over a low heat. Set aside.
Pass the tomatoes through a food mill or use a food processor to purée. Add the potato and celery to the beans with the prosciutto and tomato purée. Add salt and pepper to taste and stir well. Continue cooking for a further 30 minutes.
Drain half of the beans and purée through a food mill or in a food processor. Return the purée to the soup and let it come back to the boil. Add pappardelle and continue boiling until *al dente*. Pour into a warmed soup tureen and serve immediately, very hot.
Serves 4.

MINESTRA DI SPAGHETTI E LENTICCHIE
Spaghetti and Lentil Soup

For this soup, use any lentil, such as brown, green, or red.

120g/4oz/²/₃ cup lentils
2 garlic cloves, chopped
1 small onion, chopped
2 celery stalks, chopped
210g/7oz spaghetti
Salt
4 tbsp extra virgin olive oil
1 tbsp fennel seeds

Soak the lentils overnight in cold water. Wash and drain them, making sure you discard any that have floated to the surface.
Put the lentils in a large saucepan with 1.5 litres/2½ pints/6 cups salted water. Add the garlic, onion and celery and bring to the boil. Lower the heat and simmer, partially covered, for about 1 hour, skimming the surface as necessary; the consistency should be quite thick.
Break the spaghetti into small pieces, add to the soup and cook until *al dente*. Season to taste with salt. Pour into a warmed soup tureen and season with the olive oil and fennel seeds. Mix well and serve immediately.
Serves 4.

QUADRUCCI IN BRODO
Quadrucci Soup

After a few years of marriage, my husband and I were lucky enough to hire a husband and wife team as our butler and cook. The couple came from Marche, a region where pasta is made just with flour and egg yolks. By not including the egg whites, Nunziata, the cook, produced pasta with a firm bite. Often she would make fresh quadrucci floating in a delicious home-made stock for just the two of us, as the children always prefered fettuccine with a meat sauce.

This is a more refined version of the *pastina in brodo*, with very tiny squares of home-made pasta. As fresh pasta can easily be stored for a couple of months, you can make quadrucci in a large quantity so they are always handy.

1/2 quantity Fresh Egg Pasta (pages 47 and 51),
cut into quadrucci (page 52)
1 litre/1³/₄ pints/4¹/₂ cups meat stock (page 66)
5 tbsp freshly grated Parmesan cheese

Put the stock into a large saucepan and bring to the boil. Add the pasta and cook until the squares start rising to the surface. If the quadrucci are dry, cook for about 3 minutes. Season with salt and pepper to taste. Pour into a warmed soup tureen and serve immediately, accompanied by the cheese.
Serves 4.

QUADRUCCI E PISELLI IN BRODO
Quadrucci and Pea Soup

I usually have a good supply of home-made pasta on hand because it keeps easily for such a long time, and once you decide to make the effort to make it, you might as well make extra. If you don't have enough time, however, use stelline or anellini.

60g/2oz pancetta, thinly sliced
1 onion, thinly sliced
1 garlic clove, thinly sliced
60g/2oz prosciutto, thinly sliced
210g/7oz/1¹/₂ cups shelled peas
2 large plum tomatoes, peeled and puréed
1.2 litres/2 pints/5 cups chicken stock (page 66)
Salt and pepper
1/2 quantity Fresh Egg Pasta (pages 47 and 51),
cut into quadrucci (page 52)
1 tbsp finely chopped flat-leaf Italian parsley

Place the pancetta, onion, garlic and prosciutto in a large saucepan and cook over low heat for about 3 minutes, stirring occasionally, until the onion and garlic are translucent. Stir in the peas and tomato purée.
Pour in the stock, add salt and pepper and bring to the boil. Add the quadrucci and continue boiling until *al dente*. Sprinkle with the parsley. Pour into a warmed soup tureen and serve immediately.
Serves 4.

PASTINA IN BRODO
Pastina Soup

Perhaps the most famous of all Italian soups, this is loved by children and adults alike. The very light meat or chicken stock is traditionally home-made, but if you are in a hurry a bouillon cube (*dado*) will do. The best pastas to use are anellini, stelline or gramigna.

1 litre/1³/₄ pints/4¹/₂ cups light chicken or
veal stock (page 66)
90g/3oz/¹/₂ cup pastina of your choice
60g/2oz/4 tbsp freshly grated Parmesan cheese

Put the stock into a large saucepan and bring to the boil. Add the pastina and continue boiling until *al dente*. Pour into a warmed soup tureen and serve immediately, very hot, passing the cheese.
Serves 4.

MINESTRA DI SPAGHETTI E ZUCCA
Spaghetti and Pumpkin Soup

This is a creamy soup. For variety sprinkle a little chopped parsley on top just before serving, or replace the spaghetti with a shorter pasta, such as tubetti.

1.2 litres/2 pints/5 cups milk
450g/1 lb piece of pumpkin, peeled, seeded and chopped
Salt and pepper
120g/4oz/²/₃ cup spaghetti, broken in small pieces
30g/1oz/2 tbsp unsalted butter
60g/2oz/4 tbsp freshly grated Parmesan cheese

Place the milk in a large saucepan and bring to the boil. Add the pumpkin and cook for about 20 minutes until it is soft. Drain well, reserving the milk, and purée the flesh in a food mill or food processor. Return the purée and milk to the saucepan and bring back to the boil. Add salt and pepper to taste and the spaghetti. Continue boiling until *al dente*. Remove the pan from the heat and stir in the butter and Parmesan cheese. Pour into a warmed soup tureen and serve immediately.
Serves 4.

AGLIATA
Tagliatelle and Garlic Soup

Fresh tagliatelle is the traditional pasta for this lovely and tasty soup, but if you do not feel like making any, substitute angel hair pasta.

60g/2oz/1 cup soft breadcrumbs
1.2 litres/2 pints/5 cups milk
210g/7oz unshelled walnuts
8 garlic cloves, peeled
Salt and pepper
¹/₂ quantity Fresh Egg Pasta (pages 47 and 51),
cut into tagliatelle (page 52)

Place the breadcrumbs in a bowl, cover with a little milk and leave to soak for about 20 minutes. Meanwhile, shell the walnuts and place them in a mortar with the garlic cloves. Mash them well (you can also use a food processor).
Squeeze the bread and stir into the walnut-garlic paste to form a creamy mixture. Stir in a pinch of salt and pepper to taste; set aside.
Bring the milk to the boil in a large saucepan and stir in the walnut paste. Add the tagliatelle and heat until the water returns to the boil and the tagliatelle float to the top. Pour into a warmed soup tureen and serve immediately.
Serves 4.

MINESTRA DI TUBETTI E CIPOLLE
Tubetti and Onion Soup

This recipe works well with fresh spring (green) onions, but if you only have the big ones, slice and soak them in the water for a couple of hours before using to make them more digestible.

60g/2oz pancetta
4 tbsp extra virgin olive oil
450g/1 lb spring (green) onions, finely sliced
450g/1 lb/3 cups ripe plum tomatoes, peeled and puréed
210g/7oz/1 heaped cup tubetti
2 eggs, size 3 (U.S. large)
1 tbsp chopped flat-leaf Italian parsley
90g/3oz/6 tbsp freshly grated Parmesan cheese
Salt and pepper

Put the pancetta and oil in a large saucepan over low heat and fry, stirring occasionally, for about 5 minutes until the pancetta's fat melts and the meat is crisp.
Add the onions and salt and pepper to taste and continue cooking, stirring, for about 5 minutes. Stir in 1.5 litres/2¹/₂ pints/6 cups warm water, salt and pepper to taste and the tomato purée. Simmer for about 1¹/₂ hours, covered.
Raise the heat and add tubetti and continue cooking until *al dente*. Beat the eggs in a bowl with the parsley and a little salt. Remove the soup from heat and stir in the eggs and the Parmesan cheese. Pour into a warmed soup tureen and serve immediately.
Serves 4.

Opposite page: Spaghetti and Pumpkin Soup

MINESTRA DI TAGLIERINI E ZUCCHINE

*Taglierini and Courgette
(Zucchini) Soup*

For a less traditional soup, replace the basil with fresh
mint, and if you are in a hurry, use dry angel hair
pasta.

60g/2oz pancetta, chopped
4 tbsp extra virgin olive oil
4 courgettes (zucchini), diced
Salt and pepper
2 eggs, size 3 (U.S. large)
60g/2oz/4 tbsp freshly grated Parmesan cheese
Handful of flat-leaf Italian parsley, finely chopped
Handful of fresh basil leaves, finely chopped
½ quantity Fresh Egg Pasta (pages 47 and 51),
cut into taglierini (page 52)

Place the pancetta and oil into a large saucepan. Cook
over low heat, stirring occasionally, until the pancetta
fat melts and the meat becomes slightly crisp. Add the
cougettes (zucchini) and fry them, stirring constantly,
for about 5 minutes. Add 1.5 litres/2½ pints/6 cups
water and salt and pepper to taste. Cover and bring to
the boil, then reduce the heat to low and simmer for 1
hour.
Break the eggs into a cup and beat with a fork, adding
the Parmesan cheese and chopped herbs.
Add the taglierini to the stock and continue cooking
until the stock returns to the boil and the taglierini
float to the top. Fold in the egg mixture and remove
the pan from the heat immediately. Stir for a few
minutes with a fork to blend all the ingredients. Pour
into a warmed soup tureen and serve immediately,
very hot.
Serves 4.

MINESTRA DI SPINACI E STELLINE

Stelline and Spinach soup

You can substitute Swiss chard or beetroot (beet)
greens for the spinach, or use a different, but always
small, shape of pasta, such as anellini.

600g/1¼ lb fresh spinach leaves, well rinsed
Salt and pepper
60g/2oz/4 tbsp unsalted butter
2 eggs, size 3 (U.S. large)
60g/2oz/4 tbsp freshly grated Parmesan cheese
Pinch of grated nutmeg
1.2 litres/2 pints/5 cups vegetable stock (page 66)
210g/7oz/1 heaped cup stelline

Place the spinach in a large saucepan with very little
boiling water and salt and pepper to taste. Cook for
about 3 minutes until it has just wilted. Drain and
squeeze it dry, then chop very finely.
Melt the butter in a large saucepan. Add the spinach
and cook, covered, stirring a couple of times, for about
3 minutes. Leave to cook completely.
Beat the eggs with the Parmesan cheese and sprinkle
with nutmeg and pepper. Fold into the spinach.
Bring the stock to the boil in a large saucepan. Add
the pasta and cook until it is almost *al dente*. Stir in
the egg and spinach mixture and simmer for 1
minute. Remove the pan from the heat and adjust the
seasoning. Pour into a warmed soup tureen and serve
immediately.
Serves 4.

MINESTRA DI TUBETTI E BROCCOLI

Tubetti and Broccoli Soup

You can substitute cauliflower for the broccoli and add a few finely chopped chives for a stronger flavour. The tubetti can be replaced with any other small pasta, such as ditalini or even broken spaghetti.

1 garlic clove, peeled
60g/2oz/4 tbsp lard
2 large plum tomatoes, peeled and puréed
1.2 litres/2 pints/5 cups vegetable stock (page 66)
450g/1 lb fresh broccoli,
broken into florets with the stalks chopped
Salt and pepper
210g/7oz tubetti
60g/2oz/4 tbsp freshly grated Parmesan cheese

Use a pestle and mortar or a food processor to mash the garlic and lard into a smooth paste.
Place the garlic paste in a large saucepan over low heat and cook, stirring constantly, for about 3 minutes until melted. Add tomato purée, one-quarter of the stock, the broccoli and salt and pepper to taste. Cover and simmer for about 10 minutes.
Add the rest of the stock and bring to the boil. Add the tubetti and continue cooking until *al dente*. Pour into a warmed soup tureen and serve immediately, accompanied by the cheese.
Serves 4.

TAGLIERINI IN BRODO

Taglierini Soup

Taglierini are very fine fettuccine, almost like angel hair, and are perfect for this very famous soup. For a quicker preparation, use dry angel hair pasta.

1 litre/1³/4 pints/4¹/2 cups meat stock (page 66)
¹/2 quantity Fresh Egg Pasta (pages 47 and 51),
cut into taglierini (page 52)
60g/2oz/4 tbsp freshly grated Parmesan cheese

Bring the stock to the boil in a large saucepan. Add the taglierini and cook until the stock returns to the boil and the taglierini float to the top. Pour into a warmed soup tureen and serve immediately, accompanied by the cheese.
Serves 4.

CAPPELLETTI IN BRODO

Cappelletti Soup

Cappelletti or tortellini in stock is a Bolognese speciality. If you don't want to take the time to shape home-made capelletti or tortellini, just make tiny squares of filled pasta like ravioli.

1 litre/1³/4 pints/4¹/2 cups meat stock (page 66)
¹/2 quantity Fresh Egg Pasta (pages 47 and 51),
shaped as cappelletti (page 54)
4 tbsp finely grated Parmesan cheese

Put the stock into a large saucepan and bring to the boil. Add the cappelletti and continue boiling for about 2 minutes after the water returns to the boil. Pour the soup into a warmed soup tureen and serve immediately, accompanied by the grated cheese.
Serves 4.

PASTA GRATTUGIATA IN BRODO

Grated Pasta Soup

To make this soup, you must dry a bit of fresh pasta dough, still in the shape of a ball, and grate it on a cheese grater. Again, this is very typical of Bologna.

210g/7oz Fresh Egg Pasta dough (pages 47 and 51),
still in the shape of a ball
1 litre/1³/4 pints/4¹/2 cups meat stock (page 66)
60g/2oz/4 tbsp freshly grated Parmesan cheese

Leave the ball of dough to dry for about 2 hours, then grate it with a cheese grater on to a cloth. Leave to dry completely, about 1 hour or less in a dry climate. Put the stock into a large saucepan and bring to the boil. Add the grated pasta dough and let it rise to the surface. Pour into a warmed soup tureen and serve immediately, very hot, accompanied by the cheese.
Serves 4.

PASTA WITH VEGETABLE AND CHEESE SAUCES

MANY YEARS AGO WHEN I FIRST VISITED PUGLIA, THE SOUTHERN REGION WHICH FORMS THE HEEL OF THE BOOT OF ITALY, I NOTICED THAT THE LOCALS REFERRED TO THEIR PASTA DISHES, ESPECIALLY ONES DRESSED WITH VEGETABLES, AS *CARCIOFI CON PENNE* (ARTICHOKES WITH PENNE), OR *RAPE CON ORECCHIETTE* (BROCCOLI FLORETS WITH ORECCHIETTE), RATHER THAN THE OTHER WAY ROUND. IN OTHER WORDS, THEY CONSIDERED THE PASTA THE ACCOMPANIMENT FOR THE VEGETABLE, WHICH WAS PRIMARY AND GOT FIRST MENTION. I HAVE ALWAYS FELT THIS SAME WAY ABOUT PASTA DISHES WITH VEGETABLE SAUCES. THE PASTA FORMS A PERFECT SUPPORT FOR MY FAVOURITE, DELICIOUSLY SEASONED VEGETABLES.

I find pasta dressed with herbs, greens, vegetables and pulses (legumes) among the most perfect and satisfying dishes in the world. They are nourishing, simple, seasonal, colourful and usually quick and easy to prepare. What could be simpler than pasta dressed with garlic and olive oil, with a basil sauce, with fresh tomatoes, with chick peas? And think of the lively colours of fresh peas or roasted red and yellow sweet (bell) peppers. Ingredients for many sauces can be grown even in a modest kitchen garden, and that is an added satisfaction. This is also the category of pasta sauce with which it is easiest and most satisfying (and successful) to experiment with different combinations and variations of ingredients and types of noodles.

The combination of vegetables and pasta is typically a southern Italian tradition, so most recipes call for dried types of pasta, but I have also included delicious sauces for dressing fresh egg pasta as well.

Since cheese is not only good grated over pasta but can also be prepared as a tasty sauce in itself, I have also included in this section recipes using the most easily available Italian cheeses—mozzarella, gorgonzola, Fontina, pecorino (sheep's milk cheese), and caprino (goat's cheese), as well as ricotta. Many substitutes are easily imaginable.

CONCHIGLIE CON BROCCOLI E ZAFFERANO
Conchiglie with Broccoli and Saffron

The sauce is so tasty that you want to use large conchiglie that will easily scoop it up. I usually use saffron threads because, although quite expensive, they are very flavourful and the powder is a rip-off. Saffron threads must be dissolved in the hot cooking water to release their flavour, but don't leave them for more than 5 minutes or all the flavour will be lost.

450g/1 lb broccoli, broken into florets with any tough stalks removed and reserved
120ml/4fl oz/¹/₂ cup extra virgin olive oil
4 garlic cloves, chopped
Pinch of hot pepper flakes
Handful of dried blackcurrants, soaked in water to soften for about 30 minutes and drained
Handful of pine nuts
4 anchovy fillets in oil or brine, drained
300g/10oz/2 cups ripe plum tomatoes, peeled and chopped, or canned with the juice
Salt and pepper
1 tsp saffron threads
450g/1 lb conchiglie
90g/3oz/6 tbsp freshly grated pecorino (Romano) cheese

Bring a large saucepan of water to the boil. Add the broccoli stalks and cook for about 10 minutes. Blanch the broccoli florets for the final 3 minutes. Drain the broccoli, reserving the water to cook pasta in. Discard the stalks.
Pour the oil into a large frying pan over medium heat. Add the garlic and pepper flakes and fry, stirring frequently, for about 3 minutes until translucent. Add the currants, pine nuts, anchovy fillets, tomatoes, broccoli florets and salt and pepper to taste. Cover and simmer for about 25 minutes.
Meanwhile, reheat the reserved broccoli cooking water. Put the saffron threads in a small bowl and add a ladleful of the cooking water. Leave for 5 minutes, then stir into the sauce.
Add salt and the conchiglie to the broccoli cooking water and cook until *al dente*. Drain and add to the sauce. Toss gently over medium heat for a couple of minutes and adjust the seasoning if necessary. Sprinkle with half the cheese, stir together and transfer to a warmed serving dish. Cover with the rest of the cheese and serve immediately.
Serves 4.

BUCATINI ALLA CREMA D'UOVO
Bucatini with Eggs and Cream

The sauce in this dish goes very well with any kind of dry, long pasta, such as spaghetti or linguine, but don't try it on fresh pasta because it will stick too much. It is very quick and should be prepared only while pasta is cooking.

Salt
450g/1 lb bucatini
3 egg yolks, size 3 (U.S. large)
240 ml/8fl oz/1 cup double (heavy) cream
¹/₂ tsp grated nutmeg
30g/1oz/2 tbsp unsalted butter
90g/3oz/6 tbsp freshly grated Parmesan cheese
Pepper

Bring a large saucepan of water to the boil. Add salt and the bucatini and cook until *al dente*.
Beat the egg yolks in a bowl with a fork and add 60ml/2fl oz/4 tbsp of the cream, the nutmeg and a little salt. Pour the rest of the cream into a saucepan over low heat and simmer. Add the butter and stir in half of the Parmesan cheese.
Drain the pasta. Transfer it to a warmed serving bowl and stir in the hot cream, the egg mixture and a little pepper. Add the rest of the cheese and serve immediately.
Serves 4.

Opposite page: Conchiglie with Broccoli and Saffron

FARFALLE CON PASSATO DI CECI

Farfalle with Chick Pea Purée

Although farfalle is a nice looking pasta it is a little tricky, because it tends to over-cook on the edges and be under-done in the centre part. So try to find a good balance and remember that under-cooked pasta is more digestible than over-cooked. Conchiglie are also a good choice for this dish because the sauce coats them properly.

120g/4oz dried chick peas
Salt and pepper
6 tbsp extra virgin olive oil
2 garlic cloves, chopped
3 sprigs fresh rosemary, chopped
30g/1oz/2 tbsp tomato purée (paste)
450g/1 lb farfalle

Soak the chick peas in water to cover for 12 hours. Drain and place them in a large saucepan with enough water to cover them completely. Bring slowly to the boil, then reduce the heat and simmer for about 2 hours until tender.
Drain the chick peas and purée them in a blender or food processor, adding salt and pepper and about 1 glass of the cooking water.
Heat the oil in a heavy saucepan over medium heat. Add the garlic and rosemary and fry, stirring occasionally, until the garlic is translucent. Add the chick pea purée and tomato purée (paste) and reheat. Bring a large pan of water to the boil. Add salt and the farfalle and cook until *al dente*. Drain the pasta and transfer it to a warmed serving dish. Add the chick pea purée, discarding the garlic and rosemary, and toss together. If the sauce is too thick, dilute it with a little of the pasta cooking water. Serve immediately, very hot.
Serves 4.

FETTUCCINE VERDI AI PISELLI E ASPARAGI

Green Fettuccine with Peas and Asparagus

The season for both these vegetables is quite short, a good reason not to miss this recipe in late spring. The small piece of prosciutto adds extra flavour, but I'm sure you will enjoy this dish equally well if you keep it vegetarian. I've suggested fresh spinach fettuccine in this recipe but any long, dry pasta is suitable.

4 tbsp extra virgin olive oil
120g/4oz prosciutto, chopped (optional)
2 spring (green) onions, thinly sliced
900g/2 lb asparagus, tough stalks removed and tips sliced
210g/7oz/1½ cups shelled peas
Salt and pepper
1 quantity Fresh Egg Pasta (pags 47 and 51), coloured green with spinach (page 56) and cut into fettuccine (page 52)
90g/3oz/6 tbsp freshly grated Emmental cheese

Put the olive oil in a saucepan over low heat. Add the prosciutto and onions and fry, stirring frequently, for about 3 minutes. Add the asparagus and peas, cover and simmer for about 20 minutes, adding about 120 ml/4 fl oz/½ cup of water. Sprinkle with salt and pepper and keep warm.
Meanwhile, bring a large pan of water to the boil. Add salt and the fettuccine and cook until the water returns to the boil and the fettuccine float to the top. Drain well and transfer to a warmed shallow serving dish. Toss with the vegetables and half of the cheese. Sprinkle with the rest of the cheese and serve immediately.
Serves 4.

FETTUCCINE CON CARCIOFI E MOZZARELLA
Fettuccine with Artichokes and Mozzarella

The flavours of mozzarella and artichokes go well with any fresh or dry pasta but I suggest you stick with the long shapes for this recipe. This is because mozzarella melts and short pasta will stick together. A pinch of fresh thyme or mint is the perfect finishing touch.

Juice of 1 lemon
4 artichokes
4 tbsp extra virgin olive oil
1 garlic clove
Salt and pepper
1 quantity Fresh Egg Pasta (pages 47 and 51), cut into fettuccine (page 52)
210g/7oz mozzarella cheese, sliced
Pinch of fresh thyme

Stir the lemon juice into a bowl of water, large enough to hold the artichokes. Remove the outer leaves, spikes and chokes from the artichokes, then slice and drop them into the bowl of lemon water.
Heat the oil in a large frying pan. Add the garlic and the drained artichokes and sauté, stirring frequently, for about 10 minutes; discard the garlic. Add a little water and salt and pepper to taste, cover and simmer for 10 more minutes.
Meanwhile, bring a large saucepan of water to the boil. Add salt and the fettuccine and cook until the water returns to the boil and the fettuccine float to the top. Drain and add to the artichokes with the mozzarella and stir together for about 1 minute off the heat. Transfer to a warmed serving platter, add the thyme and serve immediately.
Serves 4.

TAGLIATELLE AI FUNGHI PORCINI
Tagliatelle with Porcini Mushrooms

An autumn classic in Italy when porcini are abundant in the markets, tasty and not too expensive. If porcini are not available, I suggest you try another recipe rather than substitute a different type of mushroom.
Due to the delicacy of the dish, fresh pasta is definitely a must. I also like to add a little cream to make the dish more flavourful. Herbs are not used here so they do not overwhelm the mushroom taste.

240ml/8fl oz/1 cup fresh double (heavy) cream
30g/1oz/2 tbsp unsalted butter
2 tbsp extra virgin olive oil
450g/1 lb fresh porcini mushrooms, wiped and thinly sliced
Salt and pepper
1 quantity Fresh Egg Pasta (pages 47 and 51), cut into tagliatelle (page 52)
90g/3oz/3/4 cup freshly grated Parmesan cheese

Bring a large saucepan of water to the boil. Pour the cream in a separate pan over low heat and simmer for about 5 minutes.
Meanwhile, melt the butter with the oil in a large frying pan over high heat. Add the mushrooms and sauté, stirring frequently, for about 2 minutes. Sprinkle with salt and pepper.
Add salt and the tagliatelle to the boiling water and cook until until the water returns to the boil and the tagliatelle float to the top. Drain and toss with the cream and half the cheese. Transfer to a warmed serving platter and spoon the mushrooms on top. Sprinkle with the rest of the Parmesan cheese and serve immediately.
Serves 4.

FUSILLI VERDI AI PEPERONI
Green Fusilli with Sweet (Bell) Peppers

The pepper cream sauce in this recipe perfectly coats the spirals of green fusilli or other shapes, such as pipe or eliche, and the coloured stripes make an appetizing decoration. I encourage you to buy yellow or red sweet (bell) peppers because green and other colours are not as sweet.

2 red or yellow sweet (bell) peppers, halved and seeded
120ml/4fl oz/$^{1}/_{2}$ cup extra virgin olive oil
Salt and pepper
450g/1 lb green fusilli
Handful of fresh basil leaves

Pre-heat the oven to 180°C/350°F/Gas 4. Place the sweet (bell) peppers on a baking sheet and roast them for about 40 minutes until the skins become blistered. Wrap them in foil and let them cool. Peel the peppers and cut half into strips and keep them warm. Put the rest of the peppers in a blender or food processor, add the oil and salt and pepper to taste and purée. Pour the purée into a saucepan to reheat gently.
Bring a large saucepan of water to the boil. Add salt and the fusilli and cook until *al dente*. Drain and arrange on a shallow warmed serving dish. Pour over the purée and toss together. Sprinkle with the reserved pepper strips and the basil. Serve immediately.
Serves 4.

MACCHERONI AI QUATTRO FORMAGGI
Maccheroni with Four Cheeses

Another famous recipe, with a strong flavour. I recommend using any dry pasta like maccheroni, rigatoni or ruote. But whichever shape you decide on, do not use fresh pasta because it will become very sticky.

Salt
450g/1 lb maccheroni
90g/3oz/6 tbsp unsalted butter
90g/3oz/$^{3}/_{4}$ cup Fontina cheese, cut into thin strips
90g/3oz/$^{3}/_{4}$ cup mozzarella cheese, cut into thin strips
90g/3oz/$^{3}/_{4}$ cup Emmental cheese, cut into thin strips
90g/3oz/6 tbsp freshly grated Parmesan cheese
Pepper

Bring a large saucepan of water to the boil. Add the salt and maccharoni and cook until *al dente*. Meanwhile, melt the butter without letting it brown. Drain the maccheroni and transfer it to a warmed serving bowl. Add the butter and Fontina, mozzarella and Emmental cheeses and half the Parmesan and toss together until the cheeses melt. Sprinkle with the rest of the Parmesan cheese and pepper. Serve immediately, very hot.
Serves 4.

INSALATA DI SPAGHETTI ALLE ZUCCHINE
Spaghetti Salad with Raw Courgettes (Zucchini)

In summer, spaghetti or pasta salads in general are delicious, provided they are served with very fresh ingredients and at room temperature, not straight from the refrigerator. It is always best to use dry pasta for these salads, because the taste of the eggs in cold fresh pasta is not pleasant. I think spaghetti, farfalle, radiatori and penne combine well with the many seasonal vegetables.

450g/1 lb spaghetti
120ml/4fl oz/$^{1}/_{2}$ cup extra virgin olive oil
Grated zest of 1 lemon

450g/1 lb small and fresh courgettes (zucchini), thinly sliced
Salt and pepper
Handful of fresh mint leaves

Bring a large saucepan of water to the boil. Add salt and the spaghetti and cook until *al dente*. Drain and transfer to a large bowl. Add the oil and toss together. Leave to cool to room temperature.
Stir in the lemon zest, zucchini (courgettes) and salt and pepper to taste. Toss well, sprinkle with mint and serve.
Serves 4.

MANICOTTI CON POMODORI E OLIVE
Manicotti with Tomatoes and Olives

Here's an authenic sauce from the south, a natural partner for manicotti and other dry pasta shapes, such as penne, rigatoni or zite. The small black olives from Gaeta can be replaced with Greek olives, as they have about the same flavour. I suggest you stone the olives yourself, because commercial stoned ones are usually acidic.

6 tbsp extra virgin olive oil
1 large onion, thinly sliced
450g/1 lb/3 cups ripe plum tomatoes, peeled and chopped,
or canned with the juice
1 tbsp dry oregano
1 tsp fennel seeds
Salt and pepper
180g/6oz/1 cup black olives, such as Gaeta or Greek, stoned
450g/1 lb manicotti

Heat the oil in a large frying pan over low heat. Add the onion and fry, stirring occasionally, for about 3 minutes until translucent. Add the tomatoes, oregano, fennel seeds and salt and pepper to taste. Cover and simmer for about 30 minutes. Stir in the olives and keep warm.

Meanwhile, bring a large saucepan of water to the boil. Add salt and the manicotti and cook until *al dente*. Drain and add to the frying pan with about 120 ml/4 fl oz/¹/₂ cup of the cooking water. Sauté, stirring, over medium heat for a couple of minutes. Transfer to a shallow warmed serving dish and serve immediately.
Serves 4.

MACCHERONI CON SEDANI AL FORMAGGIO
Maccheroni with Celery and Cheese

In Italy we do not often serve celery as a vegetable. But it is an important ingredient in the classic *soffritto*, so it is included in many soups, and is also served raw in Tuscan *pinzimonio*, when it is enjoyed dipped in oil. But the combination of celery with pasta is really delicious, provided that pasta is of a rustic quality. You can also use zite, bucatini or rigatoni for this dish. Always peel celery because the outer stalks are usually stringy.

450g/1 lb celery, trimmed and sliced
into pieces 2.5cm/1 inch long
3 tbsp extra virgin olive oil
120ml/4floz/¹/₂ cup meat stock (page 66)
Salt and pepper
450/1 lb maccheroni
60g/2oz/4 tbsp unsalted butter
120g/8oz/1 cup Fontina cheese, cut into thin strips

Bring a large saucepan of water to the boil. Add the celery and blanch for 3 minutes. Drain, reserving the water for cooking the pasta in.
Heat the oil in a large saucepan over medium heat. Add the celery and cook, stirring frequently, for 5 minutes. Add the stock and salt and pepper to taste. Cover, lower the heat and simmer for about 20 minutes.
Reheat the reserved water until boiling. Add the salt and maccheroni and cook until *al dente*. Melt the butter in a pan without letting it brown. Drain the pasta and transfer it to a warmed serving bowl with the butter, celery and half of the cheese and toss together. Sprinkle with the remaining cheese, and pepper. Serve immediately, very hot.
Serves 4.

ORECCHIETTE CON LE FAVE
Orecchiette with Broad (Fava) Beans

This creamy sauce, made with puréed broad (fava) beans, is delicate and very good on fresh pasta provided it has not been made with eggs. An egg-based pasta causes the sauce to become too sticky. You also can use a dry pasta such as farfalle, ruote or radiatori. If you find really fresh beans, discard just the inedible pods because the skins will be tender enough to eat. Otherwise you also have to peel them. For that reason I give the quantity of the already cleaned beans.

300g/10oz/2 cups cleaned broad (fava) beans (see above)
120ml/4fl oz/¹/₂ cup extra virgin olive oil
Salt
1 quantity Fresh Orecchiette (page 55)
90g/3oz/6 tbsp freshly grated pecorino (Romano) cheese

Bring a large saucepan of water to the boil. Add one-third of the broad (fava) beans and blanch them for 1 minute. Remove the beans with a slotted spoon and purée them with the oil and 75ml/2¹/₂fl oz/¹/₃ cup of the cooking water in a blender or food processor. Pour the sauce into a saucepan and keep warm.
Meanwhile, add the remaining beans and salt to the water and cook until the water returns to the boil. Add the orecchiette and continue cooking until the pasta is *al dente* and the beans are tender. Drain and transfer to a warmed serving platter. Add the sauce and sprinkle with the cheese and some pepper. Serve immediately, very hot.
Serves 4.

ORECCHIETTE AL TARASSACO

Orecchiette with Dandelion Greens

Dandelion greens—called *tarassaco*, *soffioni*, *erbucce*, or *dente di leone* in Italian, depending on the region— grow wild in the fields in springtime and should be picked when really small and tender, before the flowers start to form. I like to pick the dandelion greens for this myself. It is a good excuse for a walk, and I often take along my eldest grandson, Giacomo. He is starting to recognize good herbs and enjoy them.

As a substitute for the greens, you can use Belgian endive (chicory). The combination of dandelion greens with broad (fava) beans is a classic that often occurs in pasta sauces and soups.

1 small onion, chopped
2 garlic cloves, chopped
120ml/4fl oz/½ cup extra virgin olive oil
300g/10oz/2 cups ripe plum tomatoes, peeled and chopped, or canned with the juice
300g/10oz dandelion greens, well rinsed
300g/10oz/2 cups shelled broad (fava) beans
Salt and pepper
1 quantity Fresh Orecchiette (page 55)

Put the onion, garlic and oil in a large frying pan and cook gently, stirring occasionally, until translucent. Add the tomatoes, dandelion greens, broad (fava) beans and salt and pepper to taste. Cover and simmer for about 30 minutes.
Meanwhile, bring a large saucepan of water to the boil. Add salt and the orecchiette and cook until *al dente*. Drain and add to the pan with the sauce and stir together for a couple of minutes; if too dry, add a glass of the pasta cooking water. Transfer to a warmed shallow serving dish and serve immediately.
Serves 4.

PAPPARDELLE AL FINOCCHIO

Pappardelle with Fennel

Because pappardelle is such a typical Tuscan pasta, it naturally combines well with the fennel, another ingredient from the region. A large pasta like pappardelle can overwhelm the flavour of other ingredients, which is why you usually find it paired with meat sauces, especially those made with hare and duck. That is also why I've chosen it to balance the pronounced fennel flavour.

60g/2oz/4 tbsp unsalted butter
2 fennel bulbs, outer leaves removed, halved and thinly sliced lengthwise
1 tsp grated nutmeg
240ml/8fl oz/1 cup double (heavy) cream
Salt
1 quantity Fresh Egg Pasta (pages 47 and 51), shaped into pappardelle (page 52)
60g/2oz/4 tbsp freshly grated Parmesan cheese
Pepper

Melt the butter in a saucepan over medium-low heat. Add the fennel and about 120ml/4fl oz/½ cup of water and simmer, covered, for about 15 minutes until the fennel is tender. Add the nutmeg and cream and heat through; keep warm.
Bring a large saucepan of water to the boil. Add salt and the pappardelle and cook until the water returns to the boil and the pappardelle float to the top. Drain and transfer to a warmed serving bowl. Add the fennel and cream mixture and toss together. Sprinkle with the cheese and pepper. Serve immediately, very hot.
Serves 4.

PENNE ROSSE AI CARCIOFI
Red Penne with Artichokes

Artichokes are quite a tasty vegetable and their texture stands up well to the texture of penne, which is more substantial than that of the thinner shapes such as spaghetti or linguine. For the same reason, maccheroni and rigatoni are good choices for this recipe. If you would like a more delicate flavour, cook the artichokes in cream instead of tomatoes and use fresh noodles or taglierini.

4 artichokes
Juice of 1 lemon
4 tbsp extra virgin olive oil
1 onion, finely chopped
300g/10oz/2 cups plum tomatoes, peeled and chopped, or canned with the juice
Salt and pepper
450g/1 lb red penne
1 tbsp chopped flat-leaf Italian parsley

Remove the spikes, outer leaves and furry chokes from the artichokes. Slice them thinly and drop them in a bowl of water to which the lemon juice has been added to prevent them turning black.
Heat the oil in a large frying pan over low heat. Add the onion and sauté, stirring, for about 5 minutes until translucent. Add the drained artichokes and simmer, uncovered, for another 5 minutes. Add the tomatoes and salt and pepper to taste and continue simmering, covered, for about 30 minutes.
Meanwhile, bring a large saucepan of water to the boil. Add salt and the penne and cook until *al dente*. Drain and add to the pan with the artichokes. Stir in the parsley and if the sauce is too dry, add a little of the cooking water.
Sauté over medium heat for about 2 minutes. Transfer to a heated serving dish and serve immediately.
Serves 4.

PENNE ALLA NAPOLETANA
Penne with Aubergines (Eggplant) and Mozzarella

This recipe was one of my father's favourites, perhaps because of his Neopolitan heritage. He insisted that the mozzarella be only the finest quality, from the buffalos in Salerno or Battipaglia, and very fresh. At the time it was difficult to fulfill those simple requirements, unless a friend was coming to visit on the night train.

You can also use rigatoni, pennette or even ruote in this recipe. If you can't find good quality mozzarella, however, I suggest using ricotta instead. If you are afraid of deep-frying the aubergines (eggplants), you can grill (broil) them instead, but the result will not be as tasty.

1 litre/1³/₄ pints/4¹/₂ cups vegetable oil for deep-frying
450g/1 lb aubergines (eggplants), sliced
4 tbsp extra virgin olive oil
450g/1 lb/3 cups ripe plum tomatoes, peeled and chopped, or canned with the juice
Salt and pepper
450g/1 lb penne
210g/7oz mozzarella cheese sliced
Handful of fresh basil leaves

Heat the oil in a deep frying pan to 180°C/350°F/Gas 4 and deep-fry the eggplants a few at a time, until slightly golden. Drain on paper towels and sprinkle with salt.
Heat the 4 tablespoons olive oil in a saucepan over medium heat. Add the tomatoes and cook for about 30 minutes, stirring frequently, until liquid evaporates.
Add salt and pepper and keep warm.
Bring a large pan of water to the boil. Add salt and the penne and cook until *al dente*. Transfer to a warmed serving platter. Add the tomato sauce, aubergines and mozzarella and toss. Sprinkle with basil leaves and serve immediately, very hot.
Serves 4.

PENNE AL GORGONZOLA

Penne with Gorgonzola Sauce

The very tasty sauce combines wonderfully with a substantial pasta like penne, but being cream based, is also very good on almost any variety of fresh pasta. The most important requirement is that the cheese is fresh and the flavour is not too strong. Gorgonzola should be almost white and not too ripe. There are two distinct styles of this cheese, one sweet and one more pungent, almost bitter. I suggest you use the sweet type, which is readibly available around the world.

Salt
450g/1 lb penne
180g/6oz gorgonzola cheese
60g/2oz/4 tbsp unsalted butter
240ml/8fl oz/1 cup double (heavy) cream
Grated zest of 1 lemon
Pinch of grated nutmeg
Pepper

Bring a large saucepan of water to the boil. Add salt and the penne and cook until *al dente*.
Meanwhile, put the cheese, the butter, cream, lemon zest, nutmeg and a pinch of salt in another pan and simmer for about 5 minutes, stirring frequently.
Drain the pasta and transfer it to a warmed serving bowl. Add the cream sauce and toss. Sprinkle with pepper and serve immediately, very hot.
Serves 4.

PIPE ALLA LATTUGA E FAGIOLI VERDI

Pipe with Lettuce and Flageolet Beans

Green flageolet beens, fresh or even dry, can be very tender, so they make a good combination with pasta. In the United States, you can substitute white great northern beans, but do not expect the same result.

Instead of pipe, you can also use conchiglie, ruote or farfalle.

300g/10oz/just over $^3/_4$ cup fresh shelled flageolet beans, or
120g/4oz/heaped $^1/_2$ cup dried beans,
soaked in water overnight and drained
6 tbsp extra virgin olive oil
1 tbsp chopped spring (green) onion
1 head butterhead lettuce, such as Boston, thinly sliced
Salt and pepper
300g/10oz/2 cups ripe plum tomatoes, peeled,
seeded and diced
450g/2 lb pipe

Cover the beans with water and slowly bring them to the boil, then simmer for about 30 minutes for fresh beans and 1½ hours for dried. Drain and reserve.
Bring a large saucepan of water to the boil.
Meanwhile, heat the oil in a large pan. Add the onions and fry for about 3 minutes until translucent. Add the lettuce and salt and pepper and stir. When wilted, add the tomatoes and reserved beans and cook for 5 minutes more over medium heat, uncovered.
Add salt and the pipe to the boiling water and continue cooking until *al dente*. Drain and add to the pan with the sauce. Toss well and transfer to a warmed serving platter and serve immediately.
Serves 4.

FUSILLI ALLA SICILIANA

Fusilli with Olives and Cauliflower

A very hearty combination with all the Sicilian favourite flavours—olives, anchovies, cauliflowers and capers. Instead of fusilli, try bucatini or zitoni in this recipe.

Salt
450g/1 lb fusilli
450g/1 lb cauliflower, broken into florets with the stalks sliced
120ml/4fl oz/¹/₂ cup extra virgin olive oil
4 garlic cloves, chopped
90g/3oz/¹/₂ cup stoned black olives, such as Gaeta or a Greek type
4 tbsp capers in brine, rinsed
4 anchovy fillets in olive oil
2 tbsp chopped flat-leaf Italian parsley

Bring a large saucepan of water to the boil. Add the salt, fusilli and cauliflower florets and stalks and cook until the pasta is *al dente* and the cauliflower is tender.
Meanwhile, heat half the oil in a large frying pan. Add the garlic and fry, stirring often, for about 3 minutes until translucent. Add the olives, capers, anchovies, the rest of the oil and parsley and continue cooking, stirring for 2 more minutes until the anchovies break down and dissolve.
Drain the pasta and add to the pan with about 120 ml/4 fl oz/¹/₂ cup of the cooking water. Cook, stirring, for a couple of minutes until all the flavours blend. Transfer to a warmed shallow serving dish and serve immediately.
Serves 4.

RIGATONI AL CAVOLO NERO

Rigatoni with Braised Black Cabbage

This is a very hearty dish that I prepare for friends who visit me in Coltibuono in the wintertime. This is a good excuse to pour over a little of the just-pressed olive oil. Ruote or zite are a good alternative for the rigatoni.

900g/2 lb/10 cups black or savoy cabbage, thinly shredded
4 tbsp extra virgin olive oil
4 garlic cloves, chopped
4 anchovy fillets in brine or oil, drained
1 tbsp fresh thyme leaves
Salt and pepper
450g/1 lb rigatoni

Bring a large saucepan of water to the boil. Add the cabbage and blanch for about 3 minutes. Drain, reserving the water to cook pasta in.
Heat the oil in a frying pan. Add the garlic and anchovies and sauté for a couple of minutes until the garlic becomes slightly golden and the anchovies dissolve. Add the thyme and immediately the cabbage. Toss to combine the flavours, then add salt and pepper to taste. Cover and simmer over low heat for about 30 minutes, adding water a little at a time to keep the cooking juices moist.
Meanwhile, return the cabbage cooking water to the boil. Add salt and the rigatoni and cook until *al dente*. Drain and add to the pan with the cabbage and cook for a couple of minutes, stirring. Transfer to a warmed serving platter and serve immediately, very hot.
Serves 4.

Opposite page: Dried Fusilli

SPAGHETTI CACIO E PEPE

Spaghetti with Pecorino and Pepper

There's no simpler recipe than this one. This is even simpler than Garlic and Olive Oil Sauce (page 64). But, as it is a classic recipe, I wouldn't substitute any other pasta for the spaghetti. It is the most suitable pasta to be coated with this particular sauce.

Salt and pepper
450g/1 lb spaghetti
120g/4oz/1 cup freshly grated pecorino (Romano) cheese

Bring a large saucepan of water to the boil. Add salt and the spaghetti and cook until *al dente*. Drain, reserving the water, and transfer to a very hot serving bowl. Sprinkle with the cheese, abundant pepper and about 120ml/4fl oz/^{1}/$_2$ cup of the pasta cooking water. Toss and serve immediately, very hot.
Serves 4.

RUOTE CON CARDONI, PEPERONI E ACCIUGHE

Ruote with Cardoons, Sweet (Bell) Peppers and Anchovies

Cardoons are a popular winter vegetable in Italy. They have a slight artichoke flavour so artichokes are the natural substitute, but celery is also acceptable. Instead of ruote, try penne, rigatoni or manicotte.

Juice of 1 lemon.
600g/1^1/$_4$ lb cardoons
4 tbsp extra virgin olive oil
2 garlic cloves, chopped
4 anchovy fillets in brine, drained
Salt and pepper
2 yellow or red sweet (bell) peppers, halved, seeded and thinly sliced
300g/10oz/2 cups ripe plum tomatoes, peeled, or canned with the juice
450g/1 lb ruote

Pour the lemon juice in a bowl of cold water large enough to hold the sliced cardoons. Prepare the cardoons by discarding the base, the leaves and tough outer stalks. Scrape stalks with a vegetable peeler and cut them into 5cm/2 inch pieces. Drop them immediately into the bowl of lemon water.
Heat the oil in a frying pan over medium heat. Add the garlic and anchovies and cook, stirring, until translucent and the anchovies start to dissolve. Drain the cardoons and add them with salt and pepper to taste and continue cooking for 10 minutes, stirring frequently. Add the peppers and tomatoes. Cover, lower the heat and simmer for about 1 hour, adding a little water occasionally if the cooking juices dry up. Bring a large saucepan of water to the boil. Add salt and the ruote and cook until *al dente*. Drain and add to the cardoon sauce. Check the salt and transfer to a warmed serving bowl and serve immediately, very hot.
Serves 4.

TAGLIATELLE CON ASPARAGI, PISELLI E CARCIOFI
Tagliatelle with Asparagus, Peas and Artichokes

You can achieve the same nice result with tagliolini, fettuccine, *paglia e fieno* or any fresh egg pasta, or a delicate dry pasta like farfalle.

Juice of 1 lemon
2 artichokes
120ml/4fl oz/¹/₂ cup extra virgin olive oil
450g/1 lb fresh asparagus, trimmed
and tips cut into 2.5cm/1 inch pieces
Salt and pepper
210g/7oz/1¹/₄ cups shelled peas
240ml/8fl oz/1 cup double (heavy) cream
1 quantity Fresh Egg Pasta (pages 47 and 51),
cut into tagliatelle (page 52)

Pour the lemon juice into a bowl of water large enough to hold the sliced artichokes. Clean the artichokes by discarding the tough outer leaves, the furry chokes and the stalks. Slice them thinly into the bowl of lemon water. Drain and pat dry.

Heat half the oil in a saucepan over medium heat. Add the asparagus tips and artichokes and sauté for about 3 minutes, stirring occasionally. Lower the heat to minimum, add about 120ml/4fl oz/¹/₂ cup of water, cover and simmer for about 20 minutes until the artichokes become tender. Sprinkle with salt and pepper and keep warm.

Meanwhile, blanch the peas in boiling salted water for 1 minute. Drain and pour them in a blender or food processor with the rest of the oil and purée. Add the cream and blend, then pour into a saucepan over low heat and simmer for about 10 minutes to reduce; reheat when needed.

Bring a large saucepan of water to the boil. Add salt and the tagliatelle and cook until the water returns to the boil and the tagliatelle float to the top. Drain and transfer to a warmed serving bowl. Add the reheated pea and cream mixture and the asparagus and artichokes. Toss well and serve immediately, very hot.

Serves 4.

SPAGHETTI CON FAVE E POMODORO

Coloured Spaghetti with Broad (Fava) Beans and Tomatoes

Here I've chosen a simple, rustic sauce to serve with the red, green or yellow spaghetti or linguine. Fresh pasta is also suitable if you have the patience to make red, green or yellow fettuccine. I would, however, avoid using any black pasta made with squid ink for this dish. When broad (fava) beans are out of season, substitute shelled peas.

4 tbsp extra virgin olive oil
90g/3oz pancetta, chopped
1 tbsp very finely chopped onion
1 tbsp chopped celery
1 tbsp chopped flat-leaf Italian parsley
300g/10oz/2 cups plum tomatoes, peeled and chopped, or canned with the juice
300g/10oz shelled broad (fava) beans
Salt and pepper
450g/1 lb red, green or yellow spaghetti

Heat the oil in a large frying pan over medium heat. Add the pancetta, onion, celery and parsley and sauté, stirring occasionally, until the onion is translucent and the pancetta is crisp. Add the tomatoes, beans and salt and pepper to taste. Cover, lower the heat and simmer for about 30 minutes until the cooking juices are almost reduced.
Meanwhile, bring a large saucepan of water to the boil. Add salt and the spaghetti and cook until *al dente*. Drain and add to the sauce and sauté over medium heat for about 2 minutes. Transfer to a warmed serving bowl and serve immediately, very hot.
Serves 4.

TAGLIATELLE CON CIPOLLE FRITTE

Tagliatelle with Fried Onion Rings

One of my best friends is Lidia Orsi, an excellent cook. We only live three doors apart in Milan, so it's easy for us to visit each other's kitchen and experiment with new recipes. This is one of her creations, and she sometimes adds sun-dried tomatoes that have been lightly cooked in butter.

The sauce in this recipe goes really well with any kind of pasta, but I like to serve it on fresh long pasta that is not too thin. Use quite small onions so the rings are not too large.

300g/10oz small onions, thinly sliced and separated into rings
Flour for dredging
1 litre/1³/4 pints/2¹/2 cups olive oil for deep-frying
120g/4oz/8 tbsp unsalted butter
Salt
1 quantity Fresh Egg Pasta (pages 47 and 51), cut into tagliatelle (page 52)
90g/3oz/³/4 cup grated Fontina cheese
¹/2 tsp grated nutmeg

Put the onion rings in a paper bag, add the flour and shake to coat them evenly.
Bring a large saucepan of water to the boil. Pre-heat the oven to its lowest setting. Heat the oil in a large frying pan to 180°C/350°F/Gas 4. Add the onions and deep-fry them a few at a time until they are golden. Drain on paper towels and keep warm in a slightly open warm oven.
Melt the butter in a saucepan over low heat but do not let it turn brown.
Add salt and the tagliatelle to the boiling water and cook until the water returns to the boil and the tagliatelle float to the top . Drain and transfer to a warmed serving bowl. Toss with the butter and cheese. Sprinkle with the nutmeg and onion rings and serve immediately, very hot.
Serves 4.

TAGLIATELLE COI PORRI ALLA PANNA

Tagliatelle with Leeks and Cream

Leeks are a delicate vegetable which combines well with any kind of fresh egg pasta. Leeks can be time-consuming to clean, because of all the dirt between the leaves, but they must be well washed. I also recommend discarding most of the green part, which is tough. This recipe is also very tasty if you use spring (green) onions instead of leeks.

3 tbsp extra virgin olive oil
900g/2 lb leeks, halved lengthwise,
well rinsed and thinly sliced
Salt and pepper
240ml/8fl oz/1 cup double (heavy) cream
Pinch of grated nutmeg
90g/3oz/³/4 cup freshly grated Parmesan cheese
1 quantity Fresh Egg Pasta (pages 47 and 51),
cut into tagliatelle (page 52)

Heat the oil in a large frying pan over medium heat. Add the leeks and sauté for a few minutes, stirring occasionally, until they are translucent. Sprinkle with salt and pepper, add a little water, lower the heat and simmer, covered, for about 20 minutes.
Bring a large saucepan of water to the boil.
Pour the cream into another pan to heat. Add the nutmeg, and half of the Parmesan cheese and keep warm.
Add salt and the tagliatelle to the boiling water and cook until the water returns to the boil and the tagliatelle float to the top. Drain and transfer to the pan with the leeks. Add the cream and toss over low heat for 1 minute. Transfer to a warmed serving platter. Sprinkle with the rest of the Parmesan cheese and serve immediately, very hot.
Serves 4.

TAGLIERINI AI FIORI DI ZUCCA

Taglierini with Courgette (Zucchini) Flowers

When my children were small, we lived in a house with a large terrace in Milan. In the beginning the terrace was filled with just decorative plants and flowers. Slowly, however, it became more like a vegetable garden as I discovered how attractive courgettes (zucchini), green beans and peas look growing amongst other plants. This meant when unexpected guests arrived, I could pick the flowers for this recipe in a minute.

The delicacy of courgette flowers calls for a delicate pasta like taglierini, but be sure not to over-cook or they will become a mess.

300g/10oz courgette (zucchini) flowers
4 tbsp extra virgin olive oil,
plus 4 tbsp more to finish the dish
1 tbsp chopped flat-leaf Italian parsley
Salt and pepper
1 quantity Fresh Egg Pasta (pages 47 and 51),
cut into taglierini (page 52)

Bring a large saucepan of water to the boil.
Remove the courgette (zucchini) flowers' pistils by making an incision in the side of each flower.
Heat 60ml/12fl oz/4 tablespoons of the oil in a large frying pan over medium heat. Add the flowers and cook for a couple of minutes. Sprinkle with the parsley and salt and pepper to taste.
Meanwhile, add salt and the taglierini to the boiling water. Drain as soon as the taglierini come back to the surface. Add to the pan with the extra oil and toss with the courgette (zucchini) flowers for 1 minute.
Transfer to a warmed serving platter.
Serves 4.

TRENETTE AL RADICCHIO E CAPRINO

*Trenette with Radicchio and
Goat's Cheese*

Because the sauce is made with wilted vegetables, it is also nice on other long pasta shapes, such as spaghetti, linguine and bucatini. The taste is quite strong, so I suggest using dry pasta, not fresh.

90g/3oz/³/₄ cup bacon, rinded if necessary and chopped
450g/1 lb/5 cups radicchio, shredded
Salt
450g/1 lb trenette
120g/4oz fresh goat's cheese, thinly sliced
Pepper

Fry the bacon in a dry, large saucepan over low heat for about 5 minutes until the fat melts and the meat is crisp. Add the radicchio and simmer for about 20 minutes, covered, adding a little water from time to time to keep the mixture moist.
Meanwhile, bring a large pan of water to the boil. Add salt and the trenette and cook until *al dente*. Drain and add to the bacon and radicchio with a ladleful of the cooking water. Raise the heat to medium and cook for a couple of minutes, stirring. Stir in the cheese and pepper. Transfer to a warmed serving platter and serve immediately, very hot.
Serves 4.

ZITONI ALLE CIPOLLE

Zitoni with Baby (Pearl) Onions

The onions partly break up during the cooking so they weave themselves in and out of the zitoni. This is the reason why any pasta with a hole is ideal for this dish. I suggest using small flat onions, because they are more tender than baby (pearl) onions, but they are difficult to find outside Italy.

4 tbsp extra virgin olive oil
6 fresh sage leaves
450g/1 lb baby (pearl) onions
About 120ml/4fl oz/¹/₂ cup dry white wine
300g/10oz/2 cups plum tomatoes, peeled and chopped, or canned with the juice
Salt and pepper
450g/1 lb zitoni

Heat the oil in a frying pan over low heat. Add the sage leaves and fry for a couple of minutes. Add the onions and sauté for 5 more minutes, stirring occasionally. Add the wine and let it evaporate. Stir in the tomatoes and sprinkle with salt and pepper to taste. Cover and cook for about 30 minutes over low heat until almost all the liquid has been absorbed. Meanwhile, bring a saucepan of water to the boil. Add salt and the zitoni and cook until *al dente*. Drain and add to the pan with the sauce, sautéing for 2 more minutes. Transfer to a warmed serving dish.
Serves 4.

TRENETTE AL PESTO

Trenette with Pesto Sauce

Trenette al pesto is one of the best-known Genoese pasta dishes, and is usually cooked with this combination of green beans and potatoes. Pasta in Liguria is generally made without eggs, although freshly home-made, but I often use the dry, commercial variety instead. If you can't find trenette, use linguine.

Salt
300g/10oz green beans, topped and tailed
300g/10oz boiling potatoes, peeled, halved and julienned
450g/1 lb trenette
240ml/8fl oz/1 cup Pesto Sauce (page 60)

Bring a large saucepan of water to the boil. Add salt and the vegetables. When the water comes back to the boil, add the trenette and cook until *al dente*. Drain and transfer to a warmed serving bowl. Add the pesto sauce and toss well. Serve immediately, very hot.
Serves 4.

Opposite page: Trenette with Radicchio and Goat's Cheese

PASTA WITH SEAFOOD SAUCES

I CAN THINK OF NOTHING THAT MORE CLEARLY MANIFESTS THE CULINARY VERSATILITY OF PASTA THAN THE HARMONIOUS WAY WITH WHICH IT COMBINES WITH SEAFOOD OF EVERY TYPE. CERTAINLY NOTHING SHOWS A COOK'S TALENT FOR THE ART OF PREPARING PASTA MORE THAN THE ABILITY TO ACHIEVE ITS PERFECT BLEND WITH FISH. YOU NEED A DISCERNING PALATE, A GOOD EYE AND A LIGHT TOUCH. ONCE AGAIN THE SECRET OF THE ART IS SIMPLICITY.

Pasta enhanced with seafood sauce is a category of dish which is uniquely Italian, much like seafood pizza. It is difficult to duplicate it outside of Italy if you have not tasted it at its origins. The source is Mother Mediterranean and the culinary tradition that has developed along her shores from centuries of preparing the fruits fished from her seas.

Many Italian recipes for seafood sauces call for a fish or other sea creature that can only be found in the Mediterranean. Substitutes from other waters simply do not have the distinctive flavour. I would include in this category practically the whole catalogue of Mediterranean shellfish. I have never had a totally satisfying *spaghetti alle vongole veraci* (spaghetti with clam sauce), for example, away from our shores.

On the other hand, as Alan Davidson points out in *Mediterranean Seafood*, his indispensable book on the subject, the taste of many local recipes can be successfully achieved by the use of seasonings and methods of cooking that can easily be adapted. This is particularly true when it comes to seafood sauces for dressing pasta dishes.

I have chosen recipes that are easily adapted over distant seas, while still giving an idea of the range of fish it is possible to enjoy with pasta—fresh and smoked salmon, canned tuna, anchovies and sardines, dried cod, caviar, as well as a wide variety of white fish, crustaceans and moluscs. I have also paired these with a diversified selection of pasta types.

Although most of these dishes are first courses, some work well as a main course, especially the delicious skewers of fish on a bed of tagliatelle and the tasty rigatoni with squid and Swiss chard. Of course, all of the seafood pasta salads are perfect for a light summer luncheon with well-chilled white wine.

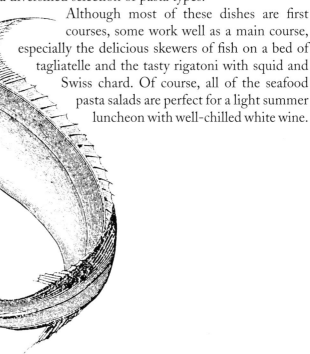

FETTUCCINE ALLE CAROTE E SCAMPI

Fettuccine with Carrots, Prawns (Shrimp) and Cheese

The unusual combination of carrots, pasta and shellfish produces a very delicate recipe, with a tendency to sweetness. Butter mixed with a little cream gives an elegant touch to this dish.

240ml/8fl oz/1 cup double (heavy) cream
30g/1oz/2 tbsp unsalted butter
2 bay leaves
Salt and pepper
210g/7oz prawns (shrimp), peeled and deveined
2 carrots, cut into very thin strips
1 quantity Fresh Egg Pasta (pages 47 and 51),
cut into fettuccine (page 52)
120g/4oz/1 cup Emmental cheese, cut into very thin strips

Bring a large saucepan of water to the boil.
Put the cream, butter, bay leaves and salt and pepper to taste in a separate pan over low heat. Add the prawn (shrimp) and simmer for 2 minutes; keep warm.
Add salt, the carrots and the fettuccine to the boiling water and cook until the pasta is *al dente* and the carrots are tender. Drain and transfer to a warmed serving dish. Stir in the cream sauce and half the cheese and toss well. Sprinkle the rest of the cheese and serve immediately, very hot.
Serves 4.

PENNE ALLA CREMA DI SARDINE

Penne with Cream of Sardines

Here's a very quick and delicious recipe that evolved some years ago when we had a small sailing boat with limited room for provisions. With four children to look after, I didn't want to spend all my time cooking, so I developed this fresh-looking dish that is easily prepared anywhere. Conchiglie or farfalle are good substitutes.

2 ripe salad tomatoes, peeled and seeded
6 tbsp extra virgin olive oil
120g/4oz sardines in oil, drained
2 anchovy fillets in brine or oil, drained
Handful of fresh basil leaves
1 tbsp capers in vinegar, drained
Salt
450g/1 lb penne

Put the tomatoes, oil, sardines, anchovies, basil and capers in a blender or food processor and blend until smooth and creamy. If the mixture is too thick, add a few tablespoons water.
Bring a large saucepan of water to the boil. Add salt and the penne and cook until *al dente*. Drain, mix with the sardine mixture and let cool to room temperature before serving.
Serves 4.

LINGUINE E SOGLIOLA AL ROSMARINO

Linguine and Sole with Rosemary

In this unusual dish, sole fillets are fried whole but they break into small pieces when combined with the linguine to become a delicious dressing. Make sure the rosemary is very finely chopped and well mixed with the flour.

Salt
300g/10oz linguine
90g/3oz/6 tbsp unsalted butter
2 tbsp finely chopped fresh rosemary
300g/10oz sole fillets, skinned
60g/2oz/¹/₂ cup plain (all-purpose) flour

Bring a large saucepan of water to the boil. Add salt and the linguine and cook until *al dente*.
Meanwhile, melt the butter in a large frying pan over low heat. Add the rosemary and fry for a couple of minutes. Dredge sole fillets in flour and shake off the excess flour. Add the fillets to the pan and sauté for about 3 minutes each side, turning them once.
Drain the linguine and transfer to warmed serving platter. Cover with sole fillets, stir together and serve immediately.
Serves 4.

INSALATA DI FARFALLE AL TONNO

Farfalle Salad with Tuna and Sweet (Bell) Peppers

This salad can be prepared ahead and kept a few hours in the refrigerator, but be sure to let it come back to room temperature before serving. Nothing is less appetizing than a cold pasta. Conchiglie or fusilli may be substituted for the farfalle.

1 yellow and 1 red sweet (bell) pepper
300g/10oz/2 cups farfalle
6 tbsp extra virgin olive oil
1 tbsp capers in brine, drained
120g/4oz/^{2}/$_3$ cup black olives,
such as Gaeta or Greek, stoned
210g/7oz tuna canned in olive oil or brine, drained
Salt and pepper
Handful of fresh basil leaves

Pre-heat oven to 180°C/350°F/Gas 4.
Arrange the peppers on a baking sheet lined with aluminium foil and bake about 40 minutes until tender. Place them in a paper bag, close and leave for about 10 minutes. Peel off the skins, halve them and remove the ribs and seeds. Cut the peppers lengthwise into strips about 1cm/^{1}/$_2$ inch wide; set aside. (If necessary, the pepper strips can be kept for a day in the refrigerator.)
Bring a large saucepan of water to the boil. Add salt and the farfalle and cook until *al dente*. Drain and transfer to a bowl. Add the olive oil and toss. Add the peppers, capers, olives and tuna and toss well. Season with salt and pepper to taste. When at room temperature, sprinkle with basil and serve.
Serves 4.

PENNE AL PESCESPADA

Penne with Swordfish

This recipe is a Sicilian speciality that is very popular in the summer, when the catch of swordfish and tuna is at its peak.

6 tbsp extra virgin olive oil
1 onion, chopped
2 garlic cloves, chopped
300g/10oz/2 cups plum tomatoes, peeled and chopped, or canned with the juice
2 tbsp capers in brine, drained
75g/2^1/$_2$oz/^{1}/$_2$ cup black olives,
such as Gaeta or Greek, stoned
Salt and pepper
300g/10oz penne
2 swordfish slices, total weight 300g/10oz, skinned and diced
1 tbsp chopped flat-leaf Italian parsley
1 tbsp chopped fresh basil

Heat the oil in a large frying pan over low heat. Add the onion and garlic and fry for about 3 minutes until translucent. Add the tomatoes, capers, olives and salt and pepper to taste. Lower the heat, cover and cook about 30 minutes until the liquid is almost absorbed.
Bring a large saucepan of water to the boil. Add salt and the penne and cook until *al dente*.
Meanwhile, add the fish to the sauce and cook for 10 minutes. Stir in the parsley and basil. Remove the fish from the sauce and keep warm. Drain the pasta and add it to the sauce. Stir together for a couple of minutes. Transfer to a warmed serving dish, arrange the fish on top and serve immediately, very hot.
Serves 4.

FETTUCCINE CON MERLUZZO E PISELLI
Fettuccine with Cod and Peas

When you are in a hurry, use dry pasta such as penne or farfalle. Or, try linguine.

4 tbsp extra virgin olive oil
2 garlic cloves, crushed
2 tbsp finely chopped flat-leaf Italian parsley
180g/6oz/1 cup shelled peas
Salt and pepper
4 cod slices, about 90g/3oz each
About 120ml/4fl oz/$\frac{1}{2}$ cup dry white wine
1 quantity Fresh Egg Pasta (pages 47 and 51),
cut into fettuccine (page 52)

Bring a large saucepan of water to the boil.
Heat the oil in a separate large pan over medium heat.
Add the garlic and parsley and fry until translucent.
Add the peas, salt and pepper and about 120ml/
4fl oz/$\frac{1}{2}$ cup of water. Lower the heat, cover and cook
for about 3 minutes. Add the fish and wine and cook,
uncovered, for 10 minutes, turning the fish only once.
Meanwhile, add salt and the fettuccine to the boiling
water and cook until the water returns to the boil and
the fettuccine float to the top. Drain and add to the
pan with the sauce and simmer, stirring, for a couple
of minutes over medium heat. Transfer to a warmed
serving platter and serve immediately, very hot.
Serves 4.

FETTUCCINE CON LE OSTRICHE
Fettuccine with Oysters

For this very delicate recipe fresh fettuccine or
taglierini are more appropriate than dry pasta.

20 large oysters
60g/2oz/$\frac{1}{2}$ cup finely grated dry breadcrumbs
4 tbsp extra virgin olive oil
Pepper
60g/2oz/4 tbsp unsalted butter
120ml/4fl oz/$\frac{1}{2}$ cup double (heavy) cream
Salt
1 quantity Fresh Egg Pasta (pages 47 and 51),
cut into fettuccine (page 52)
2 tbsp finely chopped flat-leaf Italian parsley

Bring a large saucepan of water to the boil. Pre-heat
the oven to 200°C/400°F/Gas 6.
Open the oysters and discard any empty shells.
Arrange the filled shells in an ovenproof dish and
sprinkle with the breadcrumbs, olive oil and pepper.
Bake the oysters for 10 minutes.
Meanwhile, heat the butter and cream in a pan and let
boil. Add the parsley.
Add salt and the fettuccine to the boiling water and
cook until the water returns to the boil and the
fettucine float to the top. Drain and stir into the
cream. Transfer to a warmed serving dish, cover with
the oysters and serve immediately, very hot.
Serves 4.

FETTUCCINE AL CAVIALE E RICOTTA
Fettuccine with Caviar and Ricotta

An unusual, very elegant, combination that I once
tasted in a lovely restaurant in Chicago, One
Magnificent Mile. The dish was prepared with black
and yellow fettucine, accompanied by black and red
caviar. Taglierini makes a good substitute for the fettuccine.

210g/7oz/1 scant cup fresh ricotta cheese
1 tbsp vodka
120ml/4fl oz/$\frac{1}{2}$ cup double (heavy) cream
Salt
1 quantity Fresh Egg Pasta (pages 47 and 51),
cut into fettuccine (page 52)
4 tbsp black caviar

Bring a large saucepan of water to the boil. Combine
the ricotta and vodka and keep warm in the top of a
double boiler over hot, but not boiling, water.
Heat the cream in a pan and add a little salt.
Add salt and the fettuccine to the boiling water and
cook until the water comes back to the boil and the
fettuccine float to the top. Drain and toss with the
cream in a warmed serving dish. Sprinkle with ricotta
mixture and the caviar and serve immediately,
very hot.
Serves 4.

Opposite page: Fettuccine with Caviar and Ricotta

LINGUINE AL CARPACCIO DI TONNO

Linguine with Tuna Carpaccio

I developed this recipe after I was introduced to the Japanese style of cooking on my first visit there. I learned how to prepare, eat and love raw fish. Now, to the joy of my friends, I try to "Italianize" traditional Japanese dishes.

This is a splendid pasta salad for summer that is very tasty and light. Farfalle or ruote are also suitable, and sometimes I replace the tuna with fresh anchovy fillets.

240g/8oz fresh tuna fillets, sliced paper thin
Juice of 4 lemons
300g/10oz linguine
6 tbsp extra virgin olive oil
Salt and pepper
2 tbsp finely chopped flat-leaf Italian parsley
Grated zest of 1 lemon

Arrange the tuna on a shallow dish. Cover with the lemon juice and chill for at least 2 hours but not more than 6 hours.
Meanwhile, bring a large saucepan of water to the boil. Add salt and the linguine and cook until *al dente*. Drain and transfer to a bowl. Toss with the oil and some pepper and let come to room temperature. Drain the fish, add to the pasta and toss. Sprinkle with parsley, lemon zest and more pepper. Serve.
Serves 4.

RUOTE VERDI AGLI SCAMPI E ACCIUGHE

Green Ruote with Prawns (Shrimp) and Anchovies

Spinach-flavoured green ruote, as well as any hollow, round pasta, will be well coated with this tasty anchovy sauce. The sauce takes only a few minutes to prepare, so make it while the ruote are cooking.

300g/10oz green ruote
Salt
6 tbsp extra virgin olive oil
1 garlic clove, crushed
4 anchovy fillets in oil, drained
Pinch of hot pepper flakes, crushed
300g/10oz large raw prawns (shrimp), peeled and deveined

Bring a large saucepan of water to the boil. Add salt and the ruote and cook until *al dente*.
Meanwhile, heat the oil in a pan with the garlic. Add the anchovy fillets and mash them with a fork. Add the pepper flakes and prawns (shrimp) and cook for a couple of minutes, stirring a couple of times.
Drain the pasta and add it to the pan, cooking for 2 more minutes. Toss well, transfer to a warmed serving platter and serve immediately, very hot.
Serves 4.

Opposite page: Linguine with Tuna Carpaccio

RIGATONI CON SEPPIE IN ZIMINO

Rigatoni with Squid and Swiss Chard

A very delightful and traditional Tuscan recipe. Spinach can be used instead of the Swiss chard, but—be warned—it has a stronger flavour that can overwhelm the squid.

15g/1¹/₂oz/1 tbsp dry porcini mushrooms
450g/1 lb Swiss chard, well washed and stems removed
6 tbsp extra virgin olive oil
1 small onion, chopped
300g/10oz cleaned squids, cut into strips
About 120ml/4fl oz/¹/₂ cup dry white wine
2 plum tomatoes, peeled and chopped
Salt and pepper
300g/10oz rigatoni

Soften the dry mushrooms in a bowl of water for about 30 minutes. Drain and squeeze dry, filtering and keeping the water for a risotto, a sauce or a soup. Cook the Swiss chard for 1 minute in boiling unsalted water, until just wilted. Drain and squeeze dry. Heat the oil in a large frying pan over medium heat. Add the onion and fry for about 3 minutes until translucent. Add the squid, stirring for 2 minutes, then add the wine, mushrooms, tomatoes and salt and pepper to taste. Cover, lower the heat and cook for about 30 minutes until the liquid has been absorbed. Meanwhile, bring a large saucepan of water to the boil. Add salt and the rigatoni and cook until *al dente*. Drain and add to the frying pan. Toss for a couple of minutes, then transfer to a warmed serving dish and serve immediately, very hot.
Serves 4.

RIGATONI CON LE SARDE E FINOCCHIETTO

Rigatoni with Sardines and Wild Fennel

If fresh wild fennel is difficult to obtain, fennel seeds will do. You will find them in the spice section of supermarkets or in Italian delicatessens.

450g/1 lb fresh sardines, heads and tails removed and filleted
300g/10oz rigatoni
6 tbsp extra virgin olive oil
1 tbsp chopped wild fennel or fennel seeds
1 large pinch saffron threads
2 tbsp pine nuts
Salt and pepper

Wash the sardine fillets well; set aside. Bring a large saucepan of water to the boil. Add salt and the rigatoni and cook until *al dente*. Meanwhile, heat half the oil in a large frying pan over medium heat. Add the fennel and sardine fillets and continue cooking for about 2 minutes, turning the sardines over once. Meanwhile, dissolve the saffron in 120ml/4fl oz/ ¹/₂ cup of the pasta water and add to sardines. Drain the pasta and add to the pan. Check the salt and sprinkle with pepper and pine nuts. Toss for a couple of minutes, then add the rest of the oil. Transfer to a warmed serving bowl and serve immediately, very hot.
Serves 4.

SEDANI ALLE BIETE E CAPESANTE

Sedani with Swiss Chard and Scallops

An unusual combination of flavours that is perfect for serving with sedani, because the ribbed pasta holds the green sauce. Instead of scallops, prawns (shrimp) are very suitable. Sedani can be replaced with rigatoni or penne.

450g/1 lb Swiss chard
6 tbsp extra virgin olive oil
Salt and pepper
300g/10oz sedani
300g/10oz cleaned scallops

Clean the Swiss chard, separating the green leaves and julienne the stalks vertically. Bring a large saucepan of water to the boil. Add salt and the Swiss chard leaves and boil 2 minutes. Remove the leaves with a slotted spoon and purée in a blender or food processor with 4 tablespoons of the oil and 120ml/4fl oz/$^{1}/_{2}$ cup of the cooking water to make a thin sauce. Add salt and pepper to taste.
Return the cooking water to the boil. Add the sedani and cook until *al dente*.
Heat the rest of the oil in a large pan. Add the scallops and the Swiss chard stalks. Sauté for a couple of minutes, stirring a couple of times, then add salt and pepper to taste.
Drain the pasta and toss it with the sauce. Add the scallops and stalks, mix well and serve immediately, very hot.
Serves 4.

SPAGHETTI AL MERLUZZO E ACCIUGHE

Spaghetti with Cod and Anchovies

Another very simple dish of Sicilian origin. Locally this is made with very small cod that only weigh about 210g/7oz, but slices from a larger fish are just as suitable.

4 anchovies packed in salt, heads and
tails removed and filleted
2 small cods, about 210g/7oz each, or
2 slices the same weight, skinned
Salt
300g/10oz spaghetti
6 tbsp extra virgin olive oil
4 garlic cloves, finely chopped
2 tbsp finely chopped flat-leaf Italian parsley

Wash the anchovy fillets and cod.
Bring a large saucepan of water to the boil. Add salt and the spaghetti and cook until *al dente*.
Meanwhile, heat the oil in a large saucepan over medium heat. Add the garlic and anchovies and cook, stirring frequently, until the anchovies dissolve. Add the parsley and cod and cook for a couple more minutes.
Drain the spaghetti. Transfer to a warmed serving bowl, toss with the fish and sauce and serve immediately, very hot.
Serves 4.

SPAGHETTI IN INSALATA CON PESCE E MELANZANE

Spaghetti, Fish and Aubergine (Eggplant) Salad

Any fish will do for this dish provided that it is firm enough to be boiled, such as whiting, skate, bream or grey mullet.

1 small onion, coarsely chopped
1 carrot, coarsely chopped
1 celery stalk, coarsely chopped
Handful of flat-leaf Italian parsley, chopped
450g/1 lb fish (see above)
480ml/16fl oz/2 cups vegetable oil for deep-frying
300g/10oz aubergine (eggplant), cut into 0.5cm/¼ inch slices
Salt
6 tbsp extra virgin olive oil
Juice of ½ lemon
Handful of fresh basil leaves
300g/10oz spaghetti
Pepper

Bring a large saucepan of water to the boil with the onion, carrot, celery and parsley, then lower the heat and simmer for about 1 hour; let cool.
Meanwhile, clean the fish.
Add the fish to the stock and return to the boil. Lower the heat and simmer for about 10 minutes until the fish is tender and cooked through. Drain the fish and let cool. When cool enough to handle, remove any bones and skin and break into small pieces. Transfer to a salad bowl.
Pour the vegetable oil into a large frying pan and heat to 180°C/350°F/Gas 4. Add the aubergine (eggplant) slices, a few at a time, and deep-fry until they start to become golden. Drain well on paper towels and sprinkle with salt. Dice them and add to the fish in the bowl. Gently stir in the olive oil, lemon juice and basil.
Bring a large saucepan of water to the boil. Add salt and the spaghetti and cook until *al dente*. Drain and add to the fish. Toss, sprinkle with pepper and let cool to room temperature before serving.
Serves 4.

SPAGHETTI AL BACCALÁ E PEPERONI

Spaghetti with Salt Cod and Sweet (Bell) Peppers

A very hearty southern dish typically served with spaghetti, but vermicelli or bucatini work just as well. I never peel the peppers because the skins in Italy are very thin and it isn't worth the bother. But if you want to peel them, just grill (broil) the peppers and then leave them in a closed paper bag for about 10 minutes to loosen the skins.

450g/1 lb salt cod
60g/2oz/½ cup plain (all-purpose) flour
480ml/16fl oz/2 cups vegetable oil for deep-frying
1 large onion, thinly sliced
2 yellow sweet (bell) peppers, cored, seeded and cut into 1cm/½ inch slices
4 plum tomatoes, peeled and chopped
Pinch of hot pepper flakes
Salt
300g/10oz spaghetti
1 tbsp chopped flat-leaf Italian parsley

Soak the salt cod in a bowl with enough cold water to cover for about 24 hours, change the water at least 4 times. Drain, remove any bones and skin and cut into chunks. Dredge them in flour, shaking the excess.
Heat the vegetable oil in a large saucepan to 180°C/350°F/Gas 4. Add the salt cod cubes and deep-fry until golden. Drain well on paper towels. Reserve the oil.
Heat 90ml/3fl oz/6 tbsp of the oil in a pan over medium heat. Add the onion and fry, stirring occasionally, for about 3 minutes until translucent. Add the peppers and fry for about 3 more minutes, stirring. Add tomatoes, hot pepper flakes and salt. Cover and cook for about 30 minutes over very low heat.
Meanwhile, bring a large pan of water to the boil. Add salt and the spaghetti and cook until *al dente*. Meanwhile, add the salt cod to the peppers and cook until the spaghetti is ready. Drain the spaghetti. Transfer to a warmed serving platter, add the cod and peppers with the sauce and toss well. Sprinkle with the parsley Serve immediately, very hot.
Serves 4.

SPAGHETTI ALL'ARAGOSTA

Spaghetti with Lobster

This dish is a speciality from Marettimo, a very small island near Sicily. Fortunately, there is no hotel on the island, so it remains unspoiled. We sometimes stay there in a friend's house, enjoying not only the wonderful sea and solitary swims, but also the fantastic lobster that the fishermen sell so fresh that it is still alive.

1 large or 2 small lobsters, total weight about 900g/2 lb
Salt
300g/10oz spaghetti
6 tbsp extra virgin olive oil
1 small onion, chopped
450g/1 lb/3 cups fresh ripe plum tomatoes, peeled and chopped
Pepper
1 tbsp chopped fresh chives

Remove the lobster tail meat from the shell and cube. Bring a large saucepan of water to the boil. Add salt, the lobster tail shell and the head and boil for about 1 hour.

Remove all the ingredients from the pan with a slotted spoon and return the water to the boil. Add the spaghetti and cook until *al dente*.

Meanwhile, heat the oil in a large pan over medium heat. Add the onion and cook, stirring, for about 3 minutes until translucent. Add the tomatoes and cook for 3 more minutes over high heat, stirring, so the liquid evaporates quickly. Add the cubes of lobster meat. Lower the heat and cook for 3 more minutes. Drain the spaghetti and add it to the sauce. Check the salt, sprinkle with pepper and stir for a couple of minutes. Transfer to a warmed serving bowl, garnish with chives and serve immediately, very hot.

Serves 4.

SPAGHETTI CON CALAMARI

Red Spaghetti with Squid

Another classic recipe from the southern regions and, again, spaghetti is the pasta traditionally used. The squid I cook with in Italy are usually tiny, but bigger ones work just as well. Cuttlefish is also suitable.

6 tbsp extra virgin olive oil
1 small onion, finely chopped
1 garlic clove, crushed
2 tbsp finely chopped flat-leaf Italian parsley
450g/1 lb squid, cleaned and diced
450g/1 lb/3 cups very ripe plum tomatoes,
peeled and chopped, or canned with the juice
Salt and pepper
300g/10oz red spaghetti

Heat the oil in a large frying pan over medium heat. Add the onion, garlic and parsley and cook, stirring frequently, for about 3 minutes until translucent. Add squid and sauté for about 5 minutes, stirring. Add the tomatoes and salt and pepper to taste. Lower the heat, cover and cook for about 1 hour until the liquid has been absorbed. However, if the mixture becomes too dry, just add a little water. Bring a large pan of water to the boil. Add salt and the spaghetti and cook until *al dente*. Drain and add to the frying pan. Stir over medium heat for a couple of minutes. Transfer to a warmed serving platter and serve immediately.
Serves 4.

SPAGHETTINI ALLE ACCIUGHE

Spaghettini with Anchovies and Breadcrumbs

This very simple and tasty recipe is traditionally prepared with spaghettini, but I find that spaghetti or linguine are also very nice because they get coated all round with the crumbs. Fine dry breadcrumbs may also be used instead of fresh ones.

450g/1 lb spaghettini
120ml/4fl oz/¹/₂ cup extra virgin olive oil
4 garlic cloves, very finely chopped
90g/3oz/1¹/₂ cups fresh breadcrumbs
4 anchovy fillets in oil or brine, drained
Salt and pepper
1 tbsp finely chopped flat-leaf Italian parsley

Bring a large saucepan of water to the boil. Add salt and the spaghettini and cook until *al dente*. Meanwhile, heat the oil in a large frying pan. Add the garlic, breadcrumbs and anchovies and cook, stirring until the crumbs start to change colour. Drain the spaghettini and add to the pan with a little of the cooking water. Toss over high heat for a couple of minutes. Check for salt and add pepper. Transfer to a warmed serving platter, sprinkle with parsley and serve immediately, very hot.
Serves 4.

SPAGHETTINI ALLE VONGOLE AL POMODORO

Spaghettini with Clams and Tomatoes

A very classical southern recipe. No other pasta will give the same result as spaghettini, but the clams can be replaced with mussels if you want to vary the recipe. I also suggest you make this only when tomatoes are really ripe.

900g/2 lb clams
6 tbsp extra virgin olive oil
2 garlic cloves, very finely chopped
6 ripe plum tomatoes, peeled and chopped
450g/1 lb spaghettini
Salt and pepper
1 tbsp finely chopped flat-leaf Italian parsley

Discard any clams that remain open when you tap them. Arrange the clams in a large saucepan over high heat. Cover and shake the pan for about 3 minutes until all the clams open. Discard any clams that remain closed. Filter and reserve the liquid obtained. Heat the oil in a saucepan over medium heat. Add the garlic and fry for about 3 minutes, stirring, until translucent. Add the tomatoes and continue cooking for about 10 minutes until the liquid has evaporated.
Meanwhile, bring a large pan of water to the boil. Add salt and the spaghettini and cook until *al dente*.
Add the reserved clam liquid and clams to the tomatoes and heat through. Drain the spaghettini and transfer to a warmed serving platter. Toss with the clams and tomatoes, sprinkle with pepper and parsley and serve immediately, very hot.
Serves 4.

TAGLIATELLE AL FINOCCHIO E SALMONE

Tagliatelle with Fennel and Smoked Salmon

During the winter, I always have a good provision of fresh fennel to hand. I love to eat it raw with just a little olive oil and lemon juice, and I am always experimenting with new recipes that include it. This is one result. It's particularly tasty and easy to make, and I often serve it when fish lovers are eating with us. The sweetness of the fennel is balanced by the tartness of tomatoes. The light green fennel fronds provide a natural and edible garnish.

2 fresh fennel bulbs, trimmed,
quartered and thinly sliced lengthwise
4 very ripe plum tomatoes, peeled and chopped
45g/1¹/₂oz/3 tbsp unsalted butter
Salt and pepper
1 quantity Fresh Egg Pasta (pages 47 and 51),
cut into tagliatelle (page 52)
210g/7oz thinly sliced smoked salmon,
cut into julienned strips
1 tbsp green fennel fronds, chopped

Put the fennel, tomatoes, butter and salt and pepper to taste in a saucepan over medium heat and cook, stirring occasionally, for about 10 minutes until all the liquid has evaporated.
Meanwhile, bring a large pan of water to the boil. Add salt and the tagliatelle and cook until the water returns to the boil and the tagiatelle float to the top. Transfer to a warmed serving dish. Add the smoked salmon, pour the sauce on top and mix well. Sprinkle with the fennel fronds and serve immediately, very hot.
Serves 4.

TAGLIERINI AGLI SCAMPI

Taglierini with Prawns (Shrimp)

Carlo Camerana, my very good and long-standing friend, is not only an excellent cook, but also a great opera lover. In fact, we often meet at La Scala and exchange opinions on music and various recipes. This recipe is one of his favourites. I've made this many times, and although it is best prepared at the last minute, it can also be made a few hours ahead and reheated.

350ml/12fl oz/1½ cups double (heavy) cream
30g/1oz/2 tbsp tomato purée (paste)
Salt and pepper
1 quantity Fresh Egg Pasta (pages 47 and 51),
cut into taglierini (page 52)
30g/1oz/2 tbsp unsalted butter
300g/10oz large raw prawns (shrimp), peeled and deveined
About 90ml/3fl oz/just under ⅓ cup Cognac or brandy
90g/3oz/6 tbsp freshly grated Parmesan cheese

Put the cream, tomato purée (paste) and a little salt and pepper in a saucepan over low heat and simmer for about 10 minutes to reduce.

Meanwhile, bring a large pan of water to the boil. Add the salt and taglierini and cook until the water returns to the boil and the taglierini float to the top. Melt the butter in a pan over medium heat. Add the prawns (shrimp) and sauté for about 3 minutes until the prawns turn pink and curl. Add the brandy or Cognac and let it evaporate. Add the prawns (shrimp) to the cream with the Parmesan cheese and keep warm.

Drain the taglierini and transfer to a warm serving bowl. Add the cream and prawns (shrimp) and toss. Serve immediately, very hot. Or, toss everything into an ovenproof dish, let cool and keep in refrigerator until cooking time. Cook in a preheated 180°C/350°F/Gas 4 oven for about 20 minutes until heated through.

Serves 4.

TAGLIATELLE CON SPIEDINI DI PESCE

Tagliatelle with Fish Skewers

4 thick fish slices, about 150g/5oz each
4 tbsp extra virgin olive oil
Juice of 1 lemon
Salt and pepper
12 cherry tomatoes
12 baby (pearl) onions
1 sprig fresh rosemary or a few fresh basil leaves
1 quantity Fresh Egg Pasta (pages 47 and 51),
cut into tagliatelle (page 52)
90g/3oz/6 tbsp unsalted butter, melted

Cut 4 cubes from each fish slice. Transfer to a bowl and add the oil, lemon juice, a little salt and some pepper. Let stand for about 2 hours in the refrigerator to pick up the flavours, stirring the fish a couple of times.

On to each of 4 skewers, alternate 4 pieces of fish with 3 tomatoes and 3 onions. Preheat the grill (broiler) to medium.

Grill (broil) the skewers, turning frequently and basting with the marinade, using the rosemary sprig or basil leaves like a brush, for about 10 minutes until the fish is tender and flakes easily.

Meanwhile, bring a large saucepan of water to the boil. Add salt and the tagliatelle and cook until the water returns to the boil and the tagliatelle float to the top. Drain and toss with the butter. Transfer to a warmed serving platter. Arrange the fish skewers on top and serve immediately, very hot.

Serves 4.

Opposite page: Tagliatelle with Fish Skewers

TAGLIERINI AGLI SCAMPI E FORMAGGIO FETA

Taglierini with Prawns (Shrimp) and Feta Cheese

This flavourful recipe is from an idea of Joyce Goldstein, of Square One in San Francisco, which I think one of the best Mediterranean-style restaurants in the U.S.

120ml/4fl oz/¹/₂ cup extra virgin olive oil
1 onion, chopped
2 garlic cloves, very finely chopped
4 ripe plum tomatoes, peeled and chopped
Salt and pepper
300g/10oz large raw prawns (shrimp), peeled and deveined
1 tbsp dried oregano
1 quantity Fresh Egg Pasta (pages 47 and 51),
cut into taglierini (page 52)
150g/5oz feta cheese, crumbled

Heat the oil in a saucepan over medium heat. Add the onion and garlic and cook for about 3 minutes, stirring frequently, until translucent. Add tomatoes and salt and pepper to taste and cook over high heat for about 10 minutes until all the liquid evaporates. Add the prawns (shrimp).
Meanwhile, bring a large pan of water to the boil. Add salt and the taglierini and cook until the water returns to the boil and the taglierini float to the top. Drain and add to the pan with the prawns (shrimp) and sauté for a couple of minutes over high heat, stirring, until the prawns (shrimp) turn pink and curl. Sprinkle with the oregano and feta cheese and serve immediately.
Serves 4.

TAGLIOLINI AL RAGÚ DI PESCE

Tagliolini with Fish Sauce

Fish sauce can be made with all sorts of fish, provided you bone it well before cooking. The best fish are sea bass, cod or striped bass, black fish, and I think it is best to include at least three varieties. Fresh tagliolini or chitarra are the best pastas to serve with this recipe.

4 tbsp extra virgin olive oil
4 garlic cloves, finely chopped
450g/1 lb/3 cups ripe plum tomatoes,
peeled and diced, or canned ones
450g/1 lb fish fillets, diced
1 quantity Fresh Egg Pasta (pages 47 and 51),
cut into tagliolini (page 52)
1 tbsp dried oregano
Salt and pepper

Heat the oil in a large saucepan over medium heat. Add the garlic and fry, stirring frequently, for about 3 minutes until translucent. Add the tomatoes and cook for about 10 minutes until the juices are reduced. Add the fish and cook for a few more minutes.
Meanwhile, bring a large pan of water to the boil. Add salt and the tagliolini and cook until the water almost returns to the boil. Drain and add to the pan with the fish. Sprinkle with oregano and pepper, check the salt and sauté for a couple of minutes, stirring, until warmed through and the pasta is *al dente*. Transfer to a warmed serving platter and serve immediately, very hot.
Serves 4.

TAGLIOLINI AI FUNGHI E COZZE

Tagliolini with Mushrooms and Mussels

Usually pasta with seafood should be fresh, especially when the seafood is as delicate as mussels, prawns (shrimp), salmon or clams. Here the wild mushrooms add a very special touch to an already tasty pasta.

900g/2 lb mussels
30g/1oz/2 tbsp unsalted butter
1 spring (green) onion, chopped
300g/10oz porcini mushrooms, wiped and sliced
Salt and pepper
1 quantity Fresh Egg Pasta (pages 47 and 51),
cut into tagliolini (page 52)
1 tbsp finely chopped flat-leaf Italian parsley

Bring a large saucepan of water to the boil. Discard any mussels that remain closed when you tap them. Arrange the mussels in a large pan over medium heat. Cover and shake the pan frequently for about 5 minutes until they open. Keep them warm, in the shells. Discard any mussels that remain closed. Filter the liquid obtained and boil until reduced to one glass; keep warm.

Melt the butter in a large pan over medium heat. Add the spring (green) onion and fry for about 3 minutes, stirring a couple of times, until translucent. Add the mushrooms and salt and pepper to taste and sauté for about 5 minutes, stirring a couple of times.

Add salt and the tagliolini to the boiling water and cook until the water returns to the boil and the tagliolini float to the top. Drain and add to the pan with the mushrooms with the filtered mussel cooking water. Sauté for a couple of minutes. Transfer to a warmed serving dish, cover with the mussels, sprinkle with the parsley and serve immediately, very hot.

Serves 4.

FARFALLE AL SALMONE E ZUCCHINE

Black Farfalle with Salmon and Courgettes (Zucchini)

I include this recipe in the cooking classes here at Badia a Coltibuono. It's always popular with the students, especially when they realize how easy it is to prepare such a delicious and elegant dish in less than 15 minutes–5 minutes for boiling the water, and 10 minutes for cooking the pasta and sauce.

300g/10oz/2 cups black farfalle
6 tbsp extra vigin olive oil
4 courgettes (zucchini), finely chopped
1 tbsp chopped fresh chives
Salt and pepper
4 fresh salmon slices, total weight about 300g/10oz, diced

Bring a large saucepan of water to the boil. Add the salt and the farfalle and cook until *al dente*. Meanwhile, heat the oil in a large frying pan over medium heat. Add the chives, courgettes (zucchini) and salt and pepper to taste and sauté for about 3 minutes, stirring frequently. Add the salmon and cook for another couple of minutes.

Drain the farfalle and add to the frying pan. Toss well. Transfer to a warmed serving bowl and serve immediately, very hot.

Serves 4.

INSALATA DI PASTA AL TONNO
Pasta Salad with Tuna and Mozzarella

Short, hollow pasta, such as penne or rigatoni, are excellent for pasta salads, because the ingredients fill up the holes, making the dish extra juicy and tasty. Always remember when you plan to leave pasta to cool, to dress it with olive oil as soon as you drain it so the individual pieces do not stick together. Also spread the pasta out on a large platter so it cools evenly.

Salt
300g/10oz penne
6 tbsp extra virgin olive oil
210g/7oz canned tuna, drained
210g/7oz fresh mozzarella, diced
1 hard-boiled egg, diced
20 very ripe cherry tomatoes

Handful of fresh oregano or marjoram leaves
2 tbsp chives, finely chopped
1 tbsp lemon juice
Pepper

Bring a large saucepan of water to the boil. Add salt and the penne and cook until *al dente*. Drain and toss with the oil. Spread out on a large platter and let cool. Transfer the pasta to serving dish. Add the tuna, mozzarella, egg, cherry tomatoes, oregano or marjoram, chives, lemon juice and pepper to taste and toss well. You can keep this for a couple of hours at room temperature before serving, or refrigerate for up to one day. Let the salad come back to room temperature before serving.
Serves 4.

ZITONI ALLE OLIVE E SARDINE

Zitoni with Olives, Saffron and Sardines

Zitoni are a good support for a few black olives and some sardines. Saffron not only provides a sunny colour but also a very special Mediterranean taste. Try this with rigatoni if you can't find zitoni.

Salt
450g/1 lb zitoni
4 tbsp extra virgin olive oil
1 tbsp finely chopped onion
2 garlic cloves, finely chopped
90g/3oz/³/4 cup black olives,
such as Gaeta or Greek, stoned
4 sardines in oil, drained
Generous pinch of saffron threads
4 fresh thyme sprigs
Pepper

Bring a large saucepan of water to the boil. Add salt and the zitoni and cook until *al dente*.
Meanwhile, heat the oil in a frying pan over medium heat. Add the onion and garlic and fry, stirring, for about 3 minutes until translucent. Add the olives and sardines.
Drain the pasta, reserving about 120ml/4 fl oz/¹/2 cup of the cooking water. Add the saffron to the hot water and stir. Add the pasta and saffron-flavoured water to the frying pan, sprinkle with the thyme and pepper and toss over medium heat for a couple of minutes until the zitoni are well coated with saffron and the sardines are reduced to paste-like consistency.
Transfer to a warmed serving platter and serve immediately, very hot.
Serves 4.

INSALATA DI PENNE AL PESTO E SCAMPI

Penne Salad with Pesto, Prawns (Shrimp) and Tomatoes

Nothing is more pleasant than a pasta salad in summer, but the pasta should be combined with just a few fresh flavours so you don't confuse your palate too much.

Salt
4 very ripe salad tomatoes, peeled and diced
300g/10oz penne
210g/7oz raw large prawns (shrimp) tails, peeled and deveined
4 tbsp Pesto Sauce (page 60)
4 tbsp extra virgin olive oil
Pepper

Bring a large saucepan of water to the boil. Add salt and the tomatoes and cook for 30 seconds. Remove the tomatoes and return the water to the boil. Add the penne and cook until *al dente*. Add the prawns (shrimp) and cook for 1 more minute.
Meanwhile, peel and dice the tomatoes. Place them in a deep salad bowl. Add the pesto sauce and the oil and sprinkle with pepper.
Drain the penne and prawns (shrimp) and add to the bowl. Toss well and let cool to room temperature before serving. You can refrigerate this for a few hours, but bring back to room temperature before serving.
Serves 4.

PASTA WITH MEAT SAUCES

ACCORDING TO MY PERSONAL SEASONAL CYCLE OF PASTA DISHES, I PREFER TO PREPARE MEAT SAUCES FOR A COMFORTING MID-DAY MEAL IN WINTER. ON A HOT SUMMER'S DAY I WOULD NOT USUALLY FEEL MUCH LIKE EITHER COOKING OR EATING MEAT. WHEN MY CHILDREN WERE YOUNG WE OFTEN DROVE FROM MILAN TO OUR COUNTRY ESTATE IN TUSCANY FOR WINTER WEEKENDS. I STILL REMEMBER THE DELICIOUS AROMAS THAT GREETED AND WARMED ME WHEN I ENTERED THE KITCHEN WHERE ROMOLA, THE FAMILY COOK AT COLTIBUONO, HAD BEEN SIMMERING HER *SUGO DI CARNE* (TUSCAN MEAT SAUCE) SINCE EARLY MORNING.

Meat dressings for pasta are by no means limited to the classic ragú, or stewed sauces. In this chapter you will find recipes using chicken livers, lamb, hare, ham, sweetbreads, pigeon, quail, cured pork and other kinds of meats. Some are suitable for warmer weather dining as well.

When you are serving a pasta dish with a meat sauce and a second course as well, remember not to repeat the same meat for the second course. Instead select one that is complementary or even contrasting. For example, two types of game during the hunting season, or a light pasta dressed with fowl, followed by a richer meat course.

The best type of red meat for pasta sauces are the fatty cuts, suitable for stewing, like brisket. Lean meat tends to dry out in cooking. And you should never mince (grind) the meat. Instead chop it with a knife or a mezzaluna, more or less finely depending on the recipe. Minced (ground) meat can form lumps that are unpleasant on the palate, whereas cut meat cooks to a smoother, more tender consistency.

Fowl and game birds such as chicken, turkey, pigeon and duck should be cooked whole. Take the meat off the bone with your fingers and the help of a knife, then simmer it in the sauce.

Usually recipes prescribe that you cook meat sauces in butter. You must remember that most of them originated in the north of Italy, which traditionally produced most of our meat and butter. I find that olive oil also gives excellent results, with the added advantage that the sauce is much lighter.

With the possible exception of a rustic meat sauce, grated cheese does not complement most meat sauces.

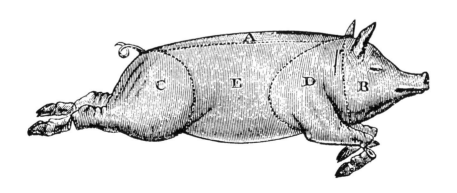

BUCATINI CON RAGÚ ALLE SPEZIE

Bucatini with Spiced Meat Sauce

Italians enjoy indulging their whims by using different herbs and spices to change the flavour of a large variety of pasta sauces. Using spices rather than herbs comes from our Renaissance heritage, and is still popular in the north of Italy.

1 tbsp extra virgin olive oil
1 tbsp unsalted butter
150g/5oz boneless stewing beef, cubed
150g/5oz boneless stewing veal, cubed
1 tbsp chopped onion
1 tbsp chopped carrot
1 tbsp chopped celery
1 tbsp chopped parsley
1 tbsp mixed ground cloves, cinnamon and nutmeg
240ml/8fl oz/1 cup dry red wine
Salt and pepper
450g/1 lb bucatini

Heat the oil and butter in a large saucepan over medium heat. Add the beef and veal and cook, stirring occasionally, until the meat starts to brown. Add the onion, carrot, celery, parsley and the mixed spices and continue cooking, stirring for a couple of minutes. Add the wine, lower the heat to minimum, add salt and pepper to taste and cook for about 1 hour, checking the liquid, and adding more wine if necessary to keep the sauce moist.
Let any excess liquid evaporate and pour the contents of the saucepan on to a chopping board. Chop the meat very finely and return to the saucepan. Continue cooking for one more hour, adding more wine or water if the sauce starts to dry out. Let the excess liquid evaporate and keep warm.
Bring a large pan of water to the boil. Add salt and the bucatini and cook until *al dente*. Drain and transfer to a warmed serving bowl. Pour on the sauce, toss well and serve immediately.
Serves 4.

CONCHIGLIE AI BROCCOLI E PANCETTA

Conchiglie with Broccoli and Pancetta

This is one of my favourite winter recipes, capturing all the flavours from the south. It can easily be enjoyed as a main course, maybe followed by a salad. Smoked mozzarella or provola are easy to find in Italian speciality shops, but in desperation you can substitute Emmental cheese. You can also achieve the smoky taste by using smoked bacon instead of pancetta, but remember bacon is fattier.

1kg/2¼ lb broccoli, broken into florets
with the stalks chopped
120ml/4fl oz/½ cup extra virgin olive oil
90g/3oz pancetta, chopped
Salt and pepper
450g/1 lb conchiglie
120g/4oz smoked mozzarella or provola, shredded

Keep the broccoli florets in a bowl of cold water. Cook the stalks in boiling salted water for about 15 minutes until tender.
Heat 1 tablespoon of the oil in a large frying pan. Add the pancetta and fry, stirring, for about 2 minutes until crisp; set aside.
Drain the broccoli stalks and cool in a bowl of iced water. Drain and purée them with the rest of the oil in a blender or food processor, adding salt and pepper to taste; keep warm in a pan over very low heat.
Bring a large pan of water to the boil. Add salt and the conchiglie and broccoli florets and cook until the pasta is *al dente* and the florets are tender. Drain and transfer to a warmed serving bowl. Add the broccoli sauce and the cheese and mix well. Sprinkle with the pancetta and serve immediately.
Serves 4.

Opposite page: Conchiglie with Broccoli and Pancetta

PICI AI FEGATINI DI POLLO E RADICCHIO
Pici with Chicken Livers and Radicchio

Pici is a thick spaghetti that is a speciality of the town of Montepulciano in Tuscany, but is now popular all over the region. Pici should really be home-made, but if you don't have the time, you can substitute 360g/12oz tagliatelle.

60g/2oz/4 tbsp unsalted butter, softened
1 tbsp wholegrain Dijon mustard
1 quantity Fresh Pici (page 54)
240g/8oz chicken livers, trimmed and sliced
1 small head red radicchio, thinly sliced crosswise
Salt and pepper

Use a fork to mash together 45g/1½oz/3 tbsp of the butter and the mustard.
Bring a large saucepan of water to the boil. Add salt and the pici and cook until the water returns to the boil and the pici float to the top.
Melt the rest of the butter in a large frying pan over medium heat. Add the chicken livers and sauté for about 3 minutes, stirring a couple of times. Stir in the radicchio and add salt and pepper. Cover and cook for 1 minute until wilted.
Drain the pici and transfer to a warmed serving platter. Add the mustard butter and toss until it melts. Arrange the livers and radicchio on top and serve immediately, very hot.
Serves 4.

LINGUINE AL MAIALE E MELANZANE
Linguine with Pork and Aubergines (Eggplants)

This dish is also quite tasty if you grill (broil) the aubergine (eggplants) instead of deep-frying them as specified in this recipe. Do not salt the aubergines before you cook them or they will become tasteless and mushy. If they are fresh, they should be quite firm. If you can only find large aubergines for this, quarter the slices. This is one of the few recipes in this book when I use minced (ground) meat.

1 litre/1¾ pints/4½ cups vegetable oil for deep-frying
4 small aubergines (eggplants) or 2 large ones, sliced about 0.5cm/¼ inch thick
15g/12oz/1 tbsp unsalted butter
2 tbsp extra virgin olive oil
300g/10oz minced (ground) pork
4 garlic cloves, chopped
4 spring (green) onions, chopped
450g/1 lb tomatoes, peeled, or canned with the juice
½ tsp hot pepper flakes
Salt
450g/1 lb linguine
1 tbsp capers in brine, drained
Handful of black olives, such as Gaeta or Greek, stoned

Heat the oil in a large, deep frying pan. Deep-fry the aubergines (eggplants) in the oil until slightly golden, working in batches. Drain on paper towels; set aside.
Melt the butter with the oil in a large saucepan over medium heat. Add the pork and cook, stirring, for about 5 minutes until brown. Add the garlic and onions and cook for 2 more minutes. Add the tomatoes, hot pepper flakes and salt. Cover, lower the heat and simmer for about 1 hour until the liquid is reduced.
Meanwhile, bring a large pan of water to the boil. Add salt and the linguine and cook until *al dente*.
While the pasta is cooking, add the capers, olives and aubergines to the sauce. Check the salt. Drain the pasta and transfer to a warmed serving bowl. Mix with the sauce and serve immediately, very hot.
Serves 4.

Opposite page: Linguine with Pork and Aubergines (Eggplants)

LINGUINE AL SUGO D'AGNELLO

Linguine with Lamb Sauce

Here's a sauce that isn't harmed at all by being prepared in advance and chilled until you are ready to serve. It is also delicious on bread slices with a glass of wine as an appetizer. Instead of linguine, you can also use spaghetti.

This recipe comes from Nanni Guiso, a great cook, a great host, a great writer and the most famous collector of theatre puppets. Although now living in Siena, he was born on Sardinia and cherishes the island's food, which he prepares for friends. This dish often features as the first course for New Year's Eve dinner in his beautiful home. Following dinner, just after midnight, his guests are treated to a puppet show of famous operas with his puppets and the voices of Callas, Domingo and Carreras.

15g/^{1}/$_2$oz/1 tbsp dry porcini mushrooms (optional)
30g/1oz/2 tbsp unsalted butter
1 tbsp extra virgin olive oil
450g/1 lb any cut of lamb, chopped into large pieces
1 carrot, diced
1 celery stalk, diced
About 120ml/4fl oz/^{1}/$_2$ cup dry white wine
300g/10oz/2 cups plum tomatoes peeled and diced,
or canned with the juice
Salt and pepper
About 450ml/16fl oz/2 cups light meat stock (page 66)
450g/1 lb linguine

Soak the mushrooms in 240m/8fl oz/1 cup water for about 30 minutes.
Melt the butter with the oil in a large, flameproof heavy-based casserole over medium heat. Add the lamb and cook for about 10 minutes, stirring a couple of times, until golden.
Drain the mushrooms, filtering and reserving the soaking water. Add them with the carrot and celery to the lamb. Add the wine and simmer until it evaporates. Add the tomatoes and salt and pepper to taste. Lower the heat, cover and continue simmering for about 5 hours, adding a little stock each time the cooking juices dry up.
Remove the pan from the heat. When the meat is cool enough to handle, remove the meat from the

bones. Pass the meat and cooking juices through a food mill with small holes. If it is too dry, add the mushroom soaking liquid. Reheat and boil until it reaches the consistency of a tomato sauce.
Meanwhile, bring a large saucepan of water to the boil. Add salt and the linguine and cook until *al dente*. Drain and mix with the lamb sauce. Transfer to a warmed serving platter and serve immediately.
Serves 4.

FUSILLI ALLA SALSICCIA E BROCCOLI

Fusilli with Sausage and Broccoli

Serving a bowl of crisp, fried breadcrumbs for sprinkling over the top of each portion adds extra flavour and texture. The crumbs make a good alternative to grated Parmesan cheese on many dishes.

1 tbsp extra virgin olive oil
240g/8oz sweet Italian sausages, casings
removed and crumbled
Salt
450g/1 lb broccoli, broken into florets with stalks diced
450g/1 lb fusilli
60g/2oz/^{1}/$_2$ cup Fried Breadcrumbs (page 67)

Heat the oil in a large frying pan over medium heat. Add the sausage meat and stir gently with a wooden spoon until the sausage becomes slightly brown; set aside.
Bring a large saucepan of water to the boil. Add salt and the broccoli stalks and the fusilli and cook until the pasta is almost *al dente*. Add the broccoli florets and when the water comes to the boil again, drain.
Reheat the sausage mixture. Add the pasta and broccoli and sauté for a couple of minutes. Transfer to a warmed serving platter and serve immediately, accompanied by the breadcrumbs for everyone to sprinkle over the top.
Serves 4.

MANICHE AL BAGÚ D'AGNELLO ALLA MENTA

Maniche with Minted-Lamb Sauce

Italian lamb is very small and one leg will weigh approximately 600g/1¼ lb. If you have a larger piece, make extra sauce for another time and freeze it. The fresh taste of the mint can be replaced with 1 tablespoon of thyme leaves.

2 tbsp extra virgin olive oil
15g/12oz/1 tbsp unsalted butter, diced
600g/1¼ lb piece of leg of lamb
4 garlic cloves, thinly sliced
Handful of fresh mint leaves
Salt and pepper
About 120ml/4fl oz/½ cup white wine
Grated zest of ½ lemon
450g/1 lb maniche

Put oil and butter into a roasting pan. Slit the meat lengthwise with small incisions and fill the incisions with the garlic and mint. Rub the meat with salt and pepper. Place the lamb in the pan and put in a cold oven. Set the oven to 180°C/350°F/Gas 4 and roast the lamb for about 1½ hours. Add the wine and lemon zest and continue roasting for 30 more minutes. When the meat is cool enough to handle, remove the bone. Chop the meat with the lemon zest and return it to the roasting pan with the cooking juices. Keep in refrigerator until required.
Bring a large pan of water to a boil. Add salt and the maniche and cook until *al dente*. Drain, reserving some water and place in the roasting pan. Sauté for a couple of minutes on top of the hob (stove) over high heat with about 120ml/4fl oz/½ cup of the pasta water, stirring throughly. Transfer to a warmed serving platter and serve immediately, very hot.
Serves 4.

PAPPARDELLE CON OSSOBUCHI AL FINOCCHIO

Pappardelle with Ossobuchi and Fennel

The refreshing flavour of fennel helps reduce the rich taste of the meat. The marrow can be easily scooped out from the bones with a small spoon.

2 ossobuchi, about 450g/1 lb total weight
Flour for dredging
15g/12oz/1 tbsp unsalted butter
1 tbsp extra virgin olive oil
About 120ml/4fl oz/½ cup dry white wine
Salt and pepper
1 fennel bulb, halved and thinly sliced
1 tbsp grated orange zest
1 quantity Fresh Egg Pasta (pages 47 and 51),
cut into pappardelle (page 52)

Dredge the ossobuchi in flour, shaking off any excess. Melt the butter with the oil in a heavy-based frying pan over low heat. Add the ossobuchi and raise the heat to medium. Brown the meat on all sides for about 10 minutes. Add the wine, lower the heat to minimum and sprinkle with salt and pepper to taste. Cover and cook for about 1 hour, adding a little water from time to time to keep the cooking juices moist. Add the fennel to the ossobuchi and continue cooking for 1 more hour. Remove the pan from the heat and when cool enough to handle, remove the meat from the bones, scooping out the marrow. Chop the meat roughly and put it back with the marrow in the pan; add the orange zest and keep it warm. The meat can also be cooked one day ahead and refrigerated. Reheat the sauce. Bring a large saucepan of water to the boil. Add salt and the pappardelle and cook until the water returns to the boil and the pappardelle float to the top. Drain, reserving 120ml/4fl oz/½ cup of the water, and add the sauce. Add the water to the pan and cook, stirring for a couple of minutes. Transfer to a heated serving platter and serve immediately, very hot.
Serves 4.

PAPPARDELLE AL SUGO DI CONIGLIO

Pappardelle with Rabbit Sauce

When we eat meat sauces in Italy, we tend to pair them with fresh or dry egg pasta, and this is especially true with rabbit or game sauces. This recipe is also delicious made with hare during the season. This sauce keeps for a few days in the refrigerator, or can be frozen.

3 tbsp extra virgin olive oil
½ small onion, chopped
1 carrot, chopped
1 celery stalk, chopped
½ rabbit, about 600g/1¼ lb, cut into large pieces
About 120ml/4fl oz/½ cup dry white wine
1 tbsp fresh thyme leaves
Salt and pepper
1 quantity Fresh Egg Pasta (pages 47 and 51),
cut into pappardelle (page 52)

Heat the olive oil in a large saucepan over high heat. Add the onion, carrot, celery and the rabbit. Sauté, stirring occasionally, until slightly brown. Add the wine, thyme and salt and pepper and lower the heat to minimum. Cover and cook for about 1 hour, adding a little water if necessary to keep the sauce moist. Remove the pan from the heat and when the rabbit is cool enough to handle, remove the bones, discarding them. Put everything back into the pan and reheat.
Meanwhile, bring a large pan of water to the boil. Add the salt and the pappardelle and cook until the water returns to the boil and the pappardelle float to the top. Drain, reserving 120ml/4fl oz/½ cup of the cooking water. Add the pappardelle and the water to the rabbit sauce and cook over medium heat for a couple of minutes. Transfer to a warmed serving platter and serve immediately, very hot.
Serves 4.

PENNE AI FEGATINI DI POLLO E PEPERONI

Penne with Chicken Livers and Sweet (Bell) Peppers

When I make this recipe, I often prepare a larger quantity of the yellow peppers to keep for a couple of days covered with a little oil. That way when I feel like eating them, I just add a little chopped garlic and fresh basil or dry oregano, depending on the season.

1 yellow sweet (bell) pepper, halved lengthwise
Salt
450g/1 lb penne
45g/1½oz/3 tbsp unsalted butter
2 tbsp extra virgin olive oil
210g/7oz chicken livers, trimmed and thinly sliced
1 anchovy fillet in brine, drained
1 tbsp capers in brine, drained

Preheat the oven to 180°C/350°F/Gas 4. Place the peppers in the oven for about 40 minutes, sprinkled with salt, until they are charred and softened. Place them in a closed paper bag for about 10 minutes. Peel them, then slice them lengthwise about 0.5cm/¼ inch thick.
Bring a large saucepan of water to the boil. Add salt and the penne and cook until *al dente*.
Meanwhile, melt 15g/½oz/1 tbsp of the butter with the oil in a heavy-based frying pan over medium heat. Add the chicken livers, anchovy fillet and capers and sauté for about 3 minutes, stirring occasionally. Add the peppers and keep warm.
Melt the rest of butter in a pan. Drain the pasta and transfer to a warmed serving platter. Pour over the melted butter and toss. Arrange the livers and peppers on top and serve immediately, very hot.
Serves 4.

Opposite page: Penne with Chicken Livers and Sweet (Bell) Peppers

BUCATINI AL MAIALE AFFINOCCHIATO
Bucatini with Fennel and Pork

In summer most parts of central and southern Italy are blooming with wild fennel and it is very easy to pick up enough seeds to last the whole winter. Fennel seeds are also sold in the spice section of supermarkets. You can use them whole or ground.

Salt
450g/1 lb bucatini
2 tbsp extra virgin olive oil
225g/8oz sweet Italian sausages, casings removed
225g/8oz very finely chopped pork
1 tbsp fennel seeds
About 120ml/4fl oz/½ cup of dry white wine

Bring a large saucepan of water to the boil. Add salt and the bucatini and cook until *al dente*.
Meanwhile, heat the oil in a large frying pan over medium heat. Add the sausage meat and pork and sauté for about 5 minutes until golden. Add the fennel seeds and the wine and continue cooking for a few more minutes.
Drain the pasta and add it to the pan with a glass of the cooking water. Cook for a couple of minutes to blend the flavours. Transfer to a warmed serving platter and serve immediately, very hot.
Serves 4.

RUOTE VERDI CON PETTO DI POLLO
Green Ruote with Chicken Breast

A delicate pasta salad that can be served on a bed of crispy lettuce leaves. You can prepare this a few hours in advance and keep it in the refrigerator, but be sure to serve it at room temperature, refreshed by adding a little more oil at the last minute.

480ml/16fl oz/2 cups vegetable stock (page 66)
1 whole chicken breast (2 halves)
450g/1 lb green ruote
2 tbsp raisins
1 fennel bulb, outer leaves removed, halved and cut into very fine slices
8 walnuts, shelled and chopped
4 tbsp extra virgin olive oil
Salt and pepper

Bring the stock to the boil in a saucepan. Add the chicken and simmer for about 20 minutes until it is tender and the juices run clear if you pierce it with the tip of a knife.
Bring a large pan of water to the boil. Add salt and the ruote and cook until *al dente*. Drain and transfer to a serving bowl. Add the raisins, fennel, walnuts, oil and salt and pepper to taste. Mix well and let cook completely before serving.
Serves 4.

PENNE AL PROSCIUTTO E CARCIOFI
Penne with Prosciutto and Artichokes

Here's another very quick recipe. If the artichokes are cleaned ahead of time and kept in a bowl of water with a few drops of lemon juice, you can make the sauce while the penne are boiling.

4 artichokes
1 tbsp lemon juice
Salt
450g/1 lb penne
120ml/4fl oz/½ cup extra virgin olive oil
90g/3oz prosciutto, roughy chopped
1 tbsp fresh thyme leaves
Salt and pepper

Clean the artichokes, discarding the stalks, tough leaves and chokes. Slice them thinly into a bowl with water and the lemon juice.
Bring a large saucepan to the boil. Add salt and the penne and cook until *al dente*.
Meanwhile, drain the artichokes. Heat the oil in a large heavy-based frying pan over medium heat. Add the prosciutto and artichokes and sauté for about 5 minutes, stirring occasionally. Add the thyme, salt and pepper to taste and 120ml/4fl oz/½ cup of the cooking pasta water. Drain the pasta and add it to the pan. Cook for 2 more minutes, stirring continuously.
Transfer to a warmed serving bowl and serve immediately, very hot.
Serves 4.

FUSILLI VERDI CON PROSCIUTTO E CIPOLLINE

Green Fusilli with Ham and Onions

The spinach-flavoured green pasta makes a pleasant contrast with the pink of the ham and the white of the onions in this recipe that combines the northern flavour of spices and ham with the southern shape of fusilli. The slight sweetness of the raisins gives the dish a Renaissance touch.

450g/1 lb small baby (pearl) onions
30g/1oz/2 tbsp unsalted butter
1 clove
3cm/1¼ inch cinnamon stick
Salt and pepper
Handful of raisins
240ml/8fl oz/1 cup double (heavy) cream
180g/6oz/1 heaped cup cooked ham, chopped
450g/1 lb green fusilli

Bring a large saucepan of salted water to the boil. Blanch the onions for about 1 minute. Drain and peel.

Melt the butter in a saucepan over low heat. Add the onions, clove, cinnamon and salt and pepper to taste. Cover and simmer for about 20 minutes, shaking the pan frequently, until tender. Stir in the raisins, cream and ham and continue simmering, stirring occasionally.

Meanwhile, bring another large pan of water to the boil. Add salt and the fusilli and cook until *al dente*. Drain and pour the pasta into the ham and onion mixture. Simmer, stirring, 2 more minutes to blend the flavours. Check the salt and transfer to a warmed serving platter. Serve immediately, very hot.

Serves 4.

PIZZOCCHERI CON PICCIONE E CREMA D'AGLIO

Pizzoccheri with Pigeon and Roasted Garlic

Pizzoccheri, a speciality from the region of Valtellina in northern Italy, are like tagliatelle, but made with buckwheat. I first had pizzoccheri at the home of Ugo Mulas, a photographer. His wife, Nini, an extremely good cook who is originally from Valtellini, made them for dinner for a group of friends. The conversation switched easily from sculpture and children's books to good food, with the help of a few glasses of our Chianti.

The noodles can be home-made following the recipe on page 54, or bought. They have a pleasant strong taste that goes well with the pigeon.

30g/1oz/2 tbsp unsalted butter
1 tbsp extra virgin olive oil
4 garlic heads, cloves separated but skins left on
2 pigeons, cleaned
About 120ml/4fl oz/½ cup dry white wine
1 quantity Fresh Pizzoccheri (page 54),
or 360g/12oz bought pizzoccheri
Salt

Preheat the oven to 180°C/375°F/Gas 4.

Melt the butter with the oil in a heavy-based flameproof casserole over low heat. Raise to medium, add the garlic cloves and pigeons and sauté for about 10 minutes until the pigeons are brown, turning them over several times. Put the casserole in the oven and roast for about 1 hour, uncovered, turning the pigeons a couple of times.

Remove the casserole from the oven. Take out the garlic cloves and pass them through a food mill. When the pigeons are cool enough to handle, remove the bones and chop the meat roughly. Return the garlic cream to the casserole. Add the wine and cook over low heat to reduce the sauce by half. Add the meat and keep warm. You can prepare the sauce to this stage a few hours ahead and keep in the refrigerator until needed.

Bring a large saucepan of water to the boil. Add salt and the pizzoccheri and cook until the water returns to the boil and the pizzoccheri float to the top. Drain, mix with the sauce and serve immediately, very hot.

Serves 4.

ORECCHIETTE ALL'AGNELLO

Orecchiette with Stewed Lamb

This recipe comes from Puglia, in southern Italy, where lamb and greens are very popular.

2 tbsp extra virgin olive oil
2 garlic cloves, chopped
450g/1 lb lamb, chopped
About 120ml/4fl oz/$^{1}/_{2}$ cup dry white wine
450g/1 lb/3 cups ripe plum tomatoes, peeled and chopped, or canned with the juice
Salt and pepper
450g/1 lb broccoli, separated into florets with the stalks thinly sliced
1 quantity Fresh Orecchiette (page 55), or 360g/12oz bought orecchiette

Heat the oil in a heavy flameproof casserole over medium heat. Add the garlic and lamb and cook, stirring a couple of times, until the lamb is brown. Add the wine, the tomatoes and salt and pepper to taste. Cover and cook over low heat for about 30 minutes. Add the broccoli stalks and keep cooking, uncovered, until the stalks are tender and the liquid from the tomatoes has evaporated. Remove the casserole from the heat and when the lamb is cool enough to handle, remove any bones. (The sauce can be kept a few hours in the refrigerator.)
Bring a large saucepan of water to the boil. Add salt and the orecchiette and cook until *al dente*; it can take almost 20 minutes, depending on the brand. Meanwhile, reheat the lamb sauce. Drain the orecchiette and transfer to a warmed serving platter. Pour the sauce on top, mix well and serve immediately, very hot.
Serves 4.

RIGATONI AL BRASATO

Rigatoni with Braised Beef

Braised beef sauces are popular and every region has its own version. I really should say that every chef has his or her own recipe. Yet, the one part of the recipe that never changes is that the meat should cook very slowly so all the flavours blend and it is meltingly tender.

15g/$^{1}/_{2}$oz/1 tbsp unsalted butter
60g/2oz pancetta, chopped
300g/10oz braising beef, cut into bite-size pieces
About 120ml/4fl oz/$^{1}/_{2}$ cup good-quality red wine, possibly aged
1 carrot, chopped
1 onion, chopped
1 celery stalk, chopped
1 bay leaf
1 tbsp chopped flat-leaf Italian parsley
2 cloves
1 anchovy fillet in brine or oil, drained (optional)
60ml/2fl oz/$^{1}/_{4}$ cup double (heavy) cream
Salt
450g/1 lb rigatoni

Melt the butter in a heavy flameproof casserole over high heat. Add the pancetta and beef and cook, stirring frequently, until brown on all sides, the pancetta fat melts and the meat is crisp. Add the wine, carrot, onion, celery, bay leaf, parsley, cloves and anchovy fillet. Cover, lower the heat to minimum and cook for about 2 hours, adding a little water when necessary to keep the cooking juices moist.
Remove from the heat and let cool a bit. Finely chop the meat. Return to the casserole, add the cream and continue cooking while preparing the pasta. (The sauce can also be kept in refrigerator for a few hours and reheated when needed.)
Bring a large saucepan of water to the boil. Add salt and the rigatoni and cook until *al dente*. Drain and transfer to a warmed serving platter. Add the hot meat sauce, mix well and serve immediately, very hot.
Serves 4.

RIGATONI CON LA PEVERADA

Rigatoni with Peppery Mint Sauce

This sauce is a speciality from the Veneto region, and usually used to accompany birds or hare. I've made a few changes to serve it with pasta and I think the result is really delicious.

120g/4oz Italian salami, casing removed
and very finely chopped
120g/4oz chicken livers, trimmed and very finely chopped
2 anchovy fillets in brine or oil, drained
and very finely chopped
1 garlic clove, very finely chopped
1 tbsp grated lemon zest
60g/1oz/2 cups fine dry breadcrumbs
Salt
450g/1 lb rigatoni
6 tbsp extra virgin olive oil
Pepper

Mix the salami, chicken livers, anchovies, garlic, lemon zest and breadcrumbs together.
Bring a large saucepan of water to the boil. Add salt and the rigatoni and cook until *al dente*. Meanwhile, heat the oil in a heavy-based frying pan over medium heat. Add the breadcrumbs mixture and fry for about 3 minutes, stirring with a wooden spoon, until slightly golden.
Drain the rigatoni, reserving some of the water. Add the pasta to the mixture with one ladleful of the pasta cooking water and cook for a couple of minutes. Add abundant freshly ground black pepper and serve immediately.
Serves 4.

SPAGHETTI ALLA CARBONARA

Spaghetti with Eggs and Pancetta

A very traditional Roman dish that my son, Guido, particularly likes. I fondly remember making immense portions of this during parents' weekend at his boarding school, where hundreds of boys from different countries shared his love of *spaghetti alla carbonara*.

This is sometimes also made with bucatini, a pasta similar to spaghetti but with a hole in the centre. It can be quite difficult to eat for anyone not used to it. If you can't find pancetta, use smoked bacon as the smoky taste works very well with this dish.

3 tbsp extra virgin olive oil
1 garlic clove, peeled but left whole
120g/4oz pancetta, chopped
450g/1 lb spaghetti
2 eggs
60g/2oz/1/2 cup freshly grated Parmesan cheese
60g/2oz/1/2 cup freshly grated pecorino (Romano) cheese
Salt and pepper

Bring a large saucepan of water to the boil.
Heat the oil in a large frying pan over medium heat. Add the garlic and fry until it is just golden. Discard the garlic, add the pancetta to the pan and continue frying until golden; set aside.
Add salt to the boiling water, then add the spaghetti and cook until *al dente*. Beat the eggs in a large bowl, then add the cheeses and salt and pepper. Reheat the oil and pancetta.
Drain the spaghetti, reserving 120ml/4fl oz/1/2 cup of the water, and immediately add the pasta and water to the pancetta. Cook for a couple of minutes, stirring, then take the pan off the heat and stir in the eggs and cheese. Transfer to a warmed serving platter and serve immediately, very hot.
Serves 4.

FARFALLE AL PROSCIUTTO E LATTUGA

Farfalle with Ham and Lettuce

This is one of my favourite recipes when I have unexpected guests. It is very easy and quick, but tasty. The presentation is nice and delicate, but to make it even more elegant, I sometimes sprinkle the farfalle with pine nuts just before serving. Chopped almonds or hazelnuts are just as effective.

1 head lettuce, separated into leaves
30g/1oz/2 tbsp unsalted butter
210g/7oz/1½ cups cooked ham, well trimmed
and cut into matchsticks
Salt and pepper
240ml/8oz/1 cup double (heavy) cream
450g/1 lb farfalle

Bring a large saucepan of water to the boil. Blanch the lettuce leaves for 30 seconds. Use a slotted spoon to remove and place them in a bowl of iced water. Squeeze out all the moisture and slice.
Melt the butter in a frying pan over low heat. Add the lettuce, ham and salt and pepper to taste and cook for a couple of minutes, stirring. Add the cream and cook for about 10 minutes to reduce.
Meanwhile, return the lettuce cooking water to the boil. Add salt and the farfalle and cook until *al dente*. Transfer to a warmed serving dish, pour the ham and lettuce sauce on top and mix well. Serve immediately.
Serves 4.

PICI ALLA SALSICCIA E FUNGHI

Pici with Sausages and Wild Mushrooms

This very tasty recipe calls for marjoram, a herb not easy to find everywhere, but it can be replaced with thyme. Also, the wild mushrooms can be replaced with cultivated or shittaki mushrooms, or even better, a mixture of the two.

4 tbsp extra virgin olive oil
1 small onion, chopped
2 garlic cloves, chopped
300g/10oz sweet Italian sausages,
casings removed and crumbled
300g/10oz wild mushrooms, such as porcini,
wiped and thinly sliced
450g/1 lb/3 cups plum tomatoes, peeled and chopped, or
canned with the juice
Handful of marjoram leaves, or 1 tbsp fresh thyme leaves
Salt and pepper
1 quantity Fresh Pici (page 54)

Heat the oil in a large frying pan over medium heat. Add the onion and garlic and fry for about 3 minutes until transparent. Add the sausages and sauté until slightly golden. Add the mushrooms and continue cooking for 3 more minutes, stirring a couple of times. Add the tomatoes, marjoram and salt and pepper to taste. Lower the heat and cook, covered, for about 30 minutes.
Meanwhile, bring a large saucepan of water to the boil. Add salt and the pici and cook until the water returns to the boil and the pici float to the top. Drain and add to the sauce in the pan. Stir for a couple of minutes, then transfer to a warmed serving platter and serve immediately, very hot.
Serves 4.

Opposite page: Pici with Sausages and Wild Mushrooms

SPAGHETTI AL SUGO DI CARNE

Spaghetti with Meat Juices

One of the best-known Italian chefs, Nino Bergese, who recently died, used to make a risotto with the cooking juices of beef fillet at his restaurant, La Santa in Genoa. It was one of the best risottos I ever had, and I've used the same technique to make a pasta sauce with a cheaper cut of meat. Save the meat for making into croquettes.

450g/1 lb topside (beef bottom round)
120g/4oz pancetta, diced
30g/1oz/2 tbsp unsalted butter
2 tbsp extra virgin olive oil
1 sprig fresh rosemary
Handful of fresh sage leaves
Salt and pepper
About 120ml/4fl oz/$\frac{1}{2}$ cup dry white wine
450g/1 lb spaghetti

Make small incisions all round the beef and fill them with the pieces of pancetta. Put the butter and olive oil into a heavy-based flameproof casserole and arrange the meat on top. Add the rosemary and sage and salt and pepper to taste. Cook over medium heat for about 10 minutes, turning the meat a couple of times until it is golden brown on each side. Stir in the wine, lower the heat, cover and continue cooking for a couple of hours, adding about 120ml/4fl oz/$\frac{1}{2}$ cup of water at a time, whenever the cooking juices become dry. In the end you will obtain a good quantity of a dark sauce. Strain the sauce, removing the sage and rosemary. The sauce, with the fat, can be kept in the refrigerator for a couple of weeks.
When ready to serve, bring a large saucepan of water to the boil. Add salt and the spaghetti and cook until *al dente.*
Meanwhile, reheat the sauce with the fat. Drain the spaghetti and transfer it to a warmed serving platter. Mix well with the sauce and serve immediately, very hot.
Serves 4.

SPAGHETTI ALLA SALSICCIA E OLIVE

Spaghetti with Sausages and Olives

This dish features the very unusual and tasty combination of sausage, fennel seeds, olives and orange zest. During the summer I garnish this with the fresh fennel that grows wild and abundantly in every field in Tuscany.

Salt
450g/1 lb spaghetti
4 tbsp extra virgin olive oil
210g/7oz sweet Italian sausages,
casings removed and crumbled
4 garlic cloves, chopped
Grated zest of 1 orange
1 tbsp fennel seeds
120g/4oz/1 cup black olives, such as Gaeta or Greek, stoned

Bring a large saucepan of water to the boil. Add salt and the spaghetti and cook until *al dente.*
Meanwhile, heat the oil in a pan over medium heat. Add the sausage and fry for a couple of minutes, stirring occasionally. Add the garlic, orange zest, fennel seeds and olives and fry for 2 more minutes until the sausage becomes slightly brown.
Drain the spaghetti and transfer to a warmed serving bowl. Add the sausage sauce, toss well and serve immediately, very hot.
Serves 4.

TAGLIATELLE CON STRACCI AL ROSMARINO
Tagliatelle with Meat Sautéed in Rosemary

I am very fortunate to have seven grandchildren, and even more fortunate that they are all here in Coltibuono around me. We often eat together. This is their favourite dish – it combines their beloved pasta with the meat they love even more, probably because it has all the perfume of our herb garden.

If you put the meat in the freezer for one hour, you'll be able to slice it paper thin. Or, ask your butcher to slice it with a machine.

120ml/4fl oz/^{1}/$_2$ cup extra virgin olive oil
4 sprigs fresh rosemary
4 garlic cloves, thinly sliced
1 quantity Fresh Egg Pasta (pages 47 and 51), cut into tagliatelle (page 52)
300g/10oz top rump (top round of beef), sliced paper thin
Juice of ^{1}/$_2$ lemon
Salt and pepper

Bring a large saucepan of water to the boil.
Heat the oil in a large frying pan over medium heat.
Add the rosemary and garlic.
Add salt and the tagliatelle to the boiling water and cook until the water returns to the boil and the tagliatelle float to the top.
Meanwhile, add the meat to the pan and sauté for a couple of minutes, turning the slices only once. Stir in the lemon juice and salt and pepper to taste. Drain the tagliatelle, add to the pan and sauté, stirring, for 1 more minute. Transfer to a warmed serving platter and serve immediately, very hot.
Serves 4.

TAGLIATELLE CON CONIGLIO ALLA PASTA D'OLIVE
Tagliatelle with Rabbit and Olive Paste

Prepared olive paste is readily available, but I like to make my own. Just mash a few black olives (preferably Gaeta) with a little olive oil and add a flavouring such as garlic, grated orange zest or dry oregano. It will keep, covered, in the refrigerator for at least one week.

45g/1^1/$_2$oz/3 tbsp unsalted butter
1 tbsp extra virgin olive oil
450g/1 lb rabbit, cut into bite-size pieces
About 120ml/4fl oz/^{1}/$_2$ cup dry white wine
Salt and pepper
About 120ml/4fl oz/^{1}/$_2$ cup light meat stock (page 66)
60g/2oz/4 tbsp olive paste
1 quantity Fresh Egg Pasta (pages 47 and 51), cut into tagliatelle (page 52)

Melt 15g/^{1}/$_2$oz/1 tbsp of the butter with the olive oil in a heavy-based, flameproof casserole over medium heat. Add the rabbit and brown evenly, stirring a couple of times, for about 10 minutes. Add the wine, lower the heat to minimum and sprinkle with salt and pepper. Cover and cook for about 1^1/$_2$ hours, adding the stock when needed to keep the cooking juices moist. Stir in the olive paste and keep warm. You can also keep the rabbit in the refrigerator for a few hours and reheat when it is time to serve.
Bring a large saucepan of water to the boil. Add salt and the tagliatelle and cook until the water returns to the boil and the tagliatelle float to the top.
Meanwhile, melt the rest of the butter without letting it brown.
When the tagliatelle are done, drain and transfer to a warmed serving platter. Pour over the melted butter and toss. Arrange the rabbit and sauce on top and serve immediately.
Serves 4.

TAGLIATELLE COL SUGO DI QUAGLIA
Tagliatelle with Quail Sauce

Quails are easy to find because they are raised commercially. Of course in the hunting season, they are more tasty. Partridge is also a wonderful substitute. One is enough for the recipe.

4 quail cleaned
4 pancetta slices, chopped
120g/4oz/8 tbsp unsalted butter
Handful of fresh sage leaves
Salt
1 quantity Fresh Egg Pasta (pages 47 and 51),
cut into tagliatelle (page 52)

Stuff the quails with the pancetta.
Melt 15g/½oz/1 tbsp of the butter in a large frying pan or flameproof casserole over medium heat. Add the sage and quails and fry for about 30 minutes, turning them gently a few times, until brown. Add a little water after about 20 minutes of cooking.
Remove the pan from the heat. When the quails are cool enough to handle, remove the bones and chop them roughly; keep warm.
Melt the rest of the butter in a saucepan. Bring a large pan of water to the boil. Add salt and the tagliatelle and cook until the water returns to the boil and the tagliatelle float to the top. Drain and transfer to a warmed serving bowl. Add the melted butter and the quail sauce and mix well. Serve immediately, very hot.
Serves 4.

TAGLIERINI AL FOIE GRAS
Taglierini with Foie Gras

My father was a connoisseur of fine food, and at one time we were fortunate enough to have the best home cook in Milan. This is her rich and elegant recipe, that she often presented in a case of home-made puff pastry (page 67) and garnished with shaved white truffles. In the autumn, I also garnish this with shaved white truffles, and I suggest you do the same at least once because it is a real treat.

30g/1oz/2 tbsp unsalted butter
240ml/8fl oz/1 cup double (heavy) cream
60g/2oz/½ cup freshly grated Parmesan cheese
2 tbsp brandy
Salt and pepper
210g/7oz canned foie gras
1 quantity Fresh Egg Pasta (pages 47 and 51),
cut into taglierini (page 52)

Bring a large saucepan of water to the boil.
Melt the butter in a pan over low heat. Add the cream and simmer for about 10 minutes to reduce. Stir in the cheese, brandy and salt and pepper to taste; keep warm.
Slice thinly the foie gras. Add salt and the taglierini to the boiling water and cook about 1 minute until barely *al dente*. Drain and transfer to a warmed serving platter. Add the cream mixture and mix well. Top with the foie gras and serve immediately, very hot.
Serves 4.

ELICHE ALLO SPECK
Eliche with Speck

Speck is a smoked ham speciality from a northern region of Alto Adige, and it is becoming very popular throughout Italy. If you can't find any, use bacon, but remember to pour off all the fat that melts in the pan. Provola is a cheese from the South, also with a smoky taste. Look for it in Italian speciality shops.

Salt
450g/1 lb eliche
30g/1oz/2 tbsp unsalted butter
150g/5oz speck, diced
240ml/8fl oz/1 cup double (heavy) cream
150g/5oz smoked provola, grated

Bring a large saucepan of water to the boil. Add salt and the eliche and cook until *al dente*. Meanwhile, melt the butter in a large frying pan over medium heat. Add the speck and fry until the fat becomes golden. Stir in the cream.
Drain the pasta, add to the pan and simmer, stirring, for a couple of minutes to blend the flavours. Transfer to a warmed serving platter. Sprinkle with the grated provola and toss. Serve immediately, very hot.
Serves 4.

TAGLIERINI ALLE ANIMELLE E TARTUFI NERI

Taglierini with Sweetbreads and Black Truffles

Black truffles are a speciality from the little town of Norcia in Umbria. They last longer and cost much less than white truffles, and although they do not have much perfume, they have a very distinctive taste. They also survive the canning process without losing too much flavour.

300g/10oz sweetbreads
15g/12oz/1 tbsp unsalted butter
30g/1oz fresh or canned black truffles, julienned
240ml/8fl oz/1 cup double (heavy) cream
Salt
1 quantity Fresh Egg Pasta (pages 47 and 51),
cut into taglierini (page 52)

Soak the sweatbreads in cold water for about 2 hours. Put them in a saucepan, cover with cold water and bring to the boil. Lower the heat and cook over low heat for about 20 minutes. Drain and when cool enough to handle, discard the membranes and veins. Slice them thinly. At this point they can be kept, covered, a few hours in the refrigerator.
Bring a large pan of water to the boil.
Melt the butter in a flameproof casserole over low heat. Add the truffles and cream and bring to the boil. Add the sweetbreads.
Add salt and the taglierini to the boiling water and cook until the water returns to the boil and the taglierini float to the top. Drain and transfer to a warmed serving platter. Mix with the cream and sweetbreads and serve immediately, very hot.
Serves 4.

TAGLIATELLE CON SCALOPPINE ALLA RUCOLA

Tagliatelle with Veal and Rocket (Arugula)

Italians tend to over-cook their vegetables, but eating in American restaurants I have learned how vegetables can be sautéed very briefly and kept crispy. That certainly is the case with rocket (arugula)—the less cooking the better.

240ml/8fl oz/1 cup double (heavy) cream
450g/1 lb veal escalopes (scaloppini), thinly sliced and pounded until very thin
Flour for dredging the meat
60g/2oz/4 tbsp unsalted butter
Salt and pepper
1 quantity Fresh Egg Pasta (pages 47 and 51),
cut into tagliatelle (page 52)
About 120ml/4fl oz/$^1\!/_2$ cup dry white wine
210g/7oz rocket (arugula)

Bring a large saucepan of water to the boil. Place the cream in a separate pan over high heat and slowly boil for about 5 minutes to reduce; keep warm.
Dredge the veal in the flour, shaking off any excess. Melt the butter in a frying pan large enough so the pieces of veal do not overlap over high heat. Add the veal and salt and pepper and cook for a couple of minutes each side.
Meanwhile, add salt and the tagliatelle to the boiling water and cook until the water returns to the boil and the tagliatelle float to the top. Add the wine to the veal, scrape the base of the pan and stir in the rocket (arugula). Drain the tagliatelle and add to the cream, mixing well. Transfer to a warmed serving platter, arrange the veal on top and serve immediately, very hot.
Serves 4.

STUFFED PASTA DISHES

THIS CATEGORY OF PASTA DISH IS MADE ONLY WITH FRESH EGG PASTA, THE BEST OF WHICH, OF COURSE, IS HOME-MADE. ALTHOUGH TODAY MOST ITALIANS USE THE GOOD-QUALITY PACKAGED FRESH PASTA SO READILY AVAILABLE, THOSE WHO HAVE MASTERED THE CRAFT WILL TAKE THE TIME TO MAKE RAVIOLI AND OTHER SHAPES AND KINDS OF STUFFED PASTA FOR SPECIAL OCCASIONS.

One advantage of making your own, besides the superior taste and texture of the pasta, is you can fill them with many different and delicious stuffings that cannot be found in the store variety, which usually consist of basic meat and cheese fillings. In these recipes I have used anchovies, caviar and other kinds of seafood, herbs, greens and all sorts of vegetables, game, oxtail and cured meats, as well as a variety of cheeses.

Be especially careful not to over-cook stuffed pasta as the little packet containing the filling will become unsealed and the stuffing will empty into the water. The best way to test when it is ready is to cut off a bit of the edge of a piece. When it is still quite firm to the bite, or *al dente*, remove them from the water.

When you cook filled pasta, carefully slide it into the boiling water. When it is done, gently transfer it from the pan of water to the colander or with a slotted spoon directly to the serving dish.

Filled pasta should be brought to the table spread out on a warmed serving platter, rather than served in a bowl as you would noodles. You want to taste all the flavours in the filling, so use a light touch when the recipe calls for dressing stuffed pasta with other ingredients, such as cream, cheese or butter.

AGNOLOTTI AI TARTUFI NERI
Agnolotti with Black Truffles

The black truffle is less expensive than the white and has less aroma but a stronger taste. Black truffles are easily available between October and March in Tuscany, and especially in Umbria.

4 potatoes
60g/2oz fresh black truffles, cleaned with a brush and very finely chopped
2 egg yolks, size 3 (U.S. large), lightly beaten
Salt and pepper
1 quantity Fresh Egg Pasta (pages 47 and 51)
6 tbsp extra virgin olive oil
4 anchovy fillets in oil or brine, drained
1 garlic clove, mashed

Boil the potatoes in their skins until tender. Drain, peel and mash with a fork. Add half the truffles to the potatoes with the egg yolks and mix together. Add salt and pepper to taste.
Prepare the agnolotti following the instructions on page 54, filling them with the truffle and potato mixture.
Bring a large saucepan of water to the boil. Heat the oil in the top of a double boiler so it does not fry. Add the anchovies, the rest of the truffles and the garlic and mash with a fork until the anchovies dissolve.
Add salt and the agnolotti to the boiling water and cook for 2 minutes after the water returns to the boil. Drain and transfer to a warmed serving platter. Pour the oil and truffle mixture on top, mix delicately and serve immediately, very hot.
Serves 4.

AGNOLOTTI RIPIENI AL CERVO
Agnolotti with Deer Meat

During hunting season filling pasta with game meat is very popular, especially in Tuscany where lots of people go hunting. Deer is a slightly sweet meat, and it can be replaced in this recipe with wild boar.

30g/1oz/2 tbsp unsalted butter
1 small carrot, finely chopped
1 small onion, finely chopped
1 celery stalk, finely chopped
450g/1 lb boneless deer meat, diced
2 ripe plum tomatoes, peeled and chopped
120ml/4fl oz/^{1}/$_2$ cup aged red wine
1 clove
240ml/8fl oz/1 cup meat stock (page 66)
Salt and pepper
1 quantity Fresh Egg Pasta (pages 47 and 51)

Melt the butter in a large saucepan over medium heat. Add the carrot, onion and celery and sauté, stirring occasionally, for about 3 minutes until translucent. Add the deer meat and sauté for about 10 more minutes until slightly coloured. Stir in the tomatoes, wine and clove. Lower the heat, cover and continue simmering for about 2 hours, adding the stock a little at a time, to keep the cooking juices moist.
Sprinkle with salt and pepper and let cool. Pick up the meat and chop it finely. Pass the cooking vegetables through a food mill and add to the meat. Prepare agnolotti following the instructions on page 54, filling them with half the prepared meat. Reheat the remaining meat mixture, adding a little water to make a sauce; it shouldn't be too liquid. Bring a large pan of water to the boil. Add salt and the agnolotti and cook for 2 minutes after the water returns to the boil. Drain and transfer to a warmed serving platter. Cover with the sauce and serve immediately, very hot.
Serves 4.

Opposite page: Agnolotti with Black Truffles

AGNOLOTTI AL PROSCIUTTO

Agnolotti with Ham

This is one of the simplest ways of making the filling. For a variation, you can substitute sweet Italian sausage or mortadella for the ham. The agnolotti can be shaped as squares or rounds.

210g/7oz cooked ham, finely chopped
1 egg, lightly beaten
90g/3oz/³/4 cup freshly grated Parmesan cheese
Handful of boiled spinach, squeezed dry and finely chopped
Pinch of grated nutmeg
Salt and pepper
1 quantity Fresh Egg Pasta (pages 47 and 51)
90g/3oz/6 tbsp unsalted butter
Handful fresh sage leaves

Combine the ham, egg, half the cheese, the spinach and nutmeg and add salt and pepper to taste.
Prepare the agnolotti following the instructions on page 54, filling them with the ham mixture.
Bring a large saucepan of water to the boil. Melt the butter with the sage in a pan over medium heat, and cook for a couple of minutes.
Add salt and the agnolotti to the boiling water and cook for about 2 minutes after the water returns to the boil. Drain. Transfer to a warmed serving platter. Sprinkle with the rest of Parmesan and the sage-flavoured butter and serve immediately, very hot.
Serves 4.

AGNOLOTTI DI POLLO E SPINACI

Agnolotti with Chicken and Spinach

This is a variation of a classic Tuscan recipe, which uses a spinach and ricotta filling. To make this dish lighter, just dress the agnolotti with melted butter and fresh sage leaves.

15g/¹/2oz/1 tbsp unsalted butter
1 tbsp extra virgin olive oil
210g/7oz boneless chicken breast, diced
About 60ml/2fl oz/¹/4 cup dry white wine
Salt and pepper
210g/7oz fresh spinach, washed and tough stalks removed
1 quantity Fresh Egg Pasta (pages 47 and 51)
40g/1 lb/2 cups Meat Sauce (page 58)

Melt the butter with the oil in a frying pan over medium heat. Add the chicken and sauté for about 10 minutes, stirring occasionally, until slightly golden.
Add the wine and salt and pepper to taste. Cover, lower the heat and simmer for 10 more minutes until tender.
Meanwhile, cook the spinach in boiling salted water for about 5 minutes. Drain well, squeeze dry and stir into the chicken. Let cool, then chop very finely; set aside.
Prepare the agnolotti following the instructions on page 54, filling them with the chicken and spinach mixture. Bring a large pan of water to the boil. Add salt and the agnolotti and cook for 2 minutes after the water returns to the boil.
Meanwhile, reheat the meat sauce.
Drain the agnolotti. Transfer to a warmed deep serving platter and stir gently with half the sauce. Top with the rest of the sauce and serve immediately, very hot.
Serves 4.

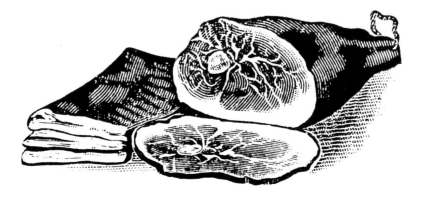

CANNELLONI VERDI AI FUNGHI

Green Cannelloni with Mushrooms

Cannelloni should always be prepared ahead and covered with cream or a white sauce before baking. They can be kept in the refrigerator up to 24 hours before cooking. For this recipe I usually use wild porcini mushrooms, but shittake or cultivated mushrooms will do just as well.

90g/3oz/6 tbsp unsalted butter
210g/7oz wild porcini mushrooms, wiped and thinly sliced
Salt and pepper
60g/2oz/4 tbsp plain (all-purpose) flour
600ml/20fl oz/2$\frac{1}{2}$ cups milk
90g/3oz/$\frac{3}{4}$ cup freshly grated Parmesan cheese
1 egg, size 3 (U.S. large)
1 quantity Fresh Egg Pasta (pages 47 and 51), coloured green with spinach (page 56)
60g/2oz/4 tbsp finely chopped cooked ham

Melt 30g/1oz/2 tbsp of the butter in a large saucepan over medium heat. Add the mushrooms and sauté for about 5 minutes, stirring occasionally. Add salt and pepper to taste and set aside to cool, then finely chop. Melt the rest of the butter in a pan over medium heat. Stir in the flour and cook, stirring, for about 2 minutes. Add half of the milk, a little at a time, stirring constantly with a wooden spoon, until a fairly thick white sauce forms.
Put half of the sauce in another pan and thin with the rest of the milk. Add half the cheese and salt and pepper to taste. Stir the thick sauce into the chopped mushrooms. Let cool, then add the egg and the rest of the Parmesan. Add salt and pepper to taste.
Prepare the cannelloni following the instructions on page 54.
Bring a large pan of water to the boil. Add salt and the cannelloni and cook for 2 minutes after the water returns to the boil.
Meanwhile, preheat the oven to 180°C/350°F/Gas 4. Drain the cannelloni and put on a cloth to dry. Fill with the mushroom mixture. Roll up and arrange in a buttered ovenproof dish. Sprinkle with the ham and the remaining white sauce. Bake for about 20 minutes until bubbling hot. Serve very hot.
Serves 4.

CANNELLONI ALLA SALSICCIA E POMODORO

Cannelloni with Sausages and Tomato Sauce

Fresh sweet sausages are popular all over Italy—sometimes they are oval and fat; sometimes long and thin like the *Milanese luganeghe.*

6 tbsp extra virgin olive oil
210g/7oz Italian sweet sausages, casings removed, crumbled
2 garlic cloves, chopped
$\frac{1}{2}$ small onion, chopped
600g/20oz/4 cups plum tomatoes, peeled and chopped, or canned with the juice
Salt and pepper
120g/4oz/$\frac{1}{2}$ cup ricotta cheese
60g/2oz/$\frac{1}{2}$ cup freshly grated Parmesan cheese
1 quantity Fresh Egg Pasta (pages 47 and 51)

Heat 1 tablespoon of the oil in a saucepan over medium heat. Add the sausage and fry for about 5 minutes, stirring occasionally. Put the garlic, onion and the rest of the oil in a separate pan for about 3 minutes, stirring, until the onion is translucent. Add the tomatoes and salt and pepper to taste. Cover, lower the heat and simmer about 30 minutes until all the liquid is absorbed.
Stir the ricotta into the sausages with the Parmesan cheese and mix well.
Prepare the cannelloni following the instructions on page 54. Bring a large pan of water to the boil. Add salt and the cannelloni and cook for 2 minutes after the water returns to the boil. Drain and put on a cloth to dry.
Meanwhile, preheat the oven to 180°C/350°F/Gas 4. Fill the cannelloni with the sausage and ricotta cheese mixture. Arrange them in a buttered ovenproof dish and cover them with the tomato sauce. Bake for about 20 minutes until bubbling hot. Serve immediately, very hot.
Serves 4.

TORTELLONI ALLE ZUCCHINE E DRAGONCELLO

Tortelloni with Courgettes (Zucchini) and Tarragon

This is one of the favourite recipes at the Badia a Coltibuono restaurant, because it is so tasty and light. No cheese is added so the flavour remains very fresh.

120ml/4fl oz/¹/₂ cup extra virgin olive oil
4 courgettes (zucchini), finely chopped in a food processor
2 tbsp fresh chopped tarragon leaves
Salt and pepper
1 quantity Fresh Egg Pasta (pages 47 and 51)
1 tbsp chopped fresh flat-leaf Italian parsley

Heat 4 tablespoons of the oil in a large frying pan over medium heat. Add the courgettes (zucchini) and sauté, stirring occasionally, for about 3 minutes. Add the tarragon and sauté for 1 more minute. Remove from the heat and let cool. Sir in the salt and pepper to taste; set aside.
Prepare the tortelloni following the instructions on page 54, filling with the courgette (zucchini) mixture. Bring a large saucepan of water to the boil. Add salt and the tortelloni and cook for 2 minutes after the water returns to the boil. Drain and arrange on a warmed platter. Sprinkle with the parsley, the remaining oil and serve immediately, very hot.
Serves 4.

RAVIOLI DI RADICCHIO

Ravioli with Radicchio

The best radicchio for these ravioli is from Treviso, because it is less bitter than other varieties. If you can't find that, substitute escarole, which also has a slightly bitter taste.

60g/2oz smoked bacon, chopped
210g/7oz/2 heaped cups radicchio, finely shredded
60g/2oz/¹/₂ cup smoked mozzarella cheese, grated
1 large egg, size 3 (U.S. large)
Salt and pepper
1 quantity Fresh Egg Pasta (pages 47 and 51)
90g/3oz/6 tbsp unsalted butter

Place the bacon in a frying pan over low heat and fry for about 5 minutes, stirring, until the fat melts and the meat becomes crisp. Add the radicchio and cook, covered, for about 10 minutes. If necessary, add a little water. Let cool and stir in the mozzarella and the egg. Sprinkle with salt and pepper to taste. Blend well and reserve.
Prepare the ravioli following the instructions on page 54, filling with the radicchio mixture. Bring a large pan of water to the boil. Add salt and the ravioli and cook for 2 minutes after the water returns to the boil. Meanwhile, melt the butter in a pan over medium heat. Drain the ravioli and transfer to a warmed serving platter. Cover with the butter and serve immediately.
Serves 4.

CAPPELLACCI AL CAPRINO E MELANZANE
Cappellacci with Aubergine (Eggplant) and Goat's Cheese

Cappellacci are larger than cappelletti. To make them, use rounds of pasta about 9cm/3½ inches in diameter, using the same technique that I give you for making cappelletti (page 54).

1 large aubergine (eggplant)
4 tbsp extra virgin oil
1 tbsp tomato purée (paste)
Handful of fresh basil leaves, chopped
Salt and pepper
90g/3oz/6 tbsp ricotta cheese
90g/3oz/6 tbsp fresh goat's cheese
2 egg yolks, size 3 (U.S. large)
1 quantity Fresh Egg Pasta (pages 47 and 51)

Preheat the oven to 180°C/350°F/Gas 4. Bake the aubergine (eggplant) whole for about 20 minutes until soft. When cool enough to handle, peel and mash with the oil and the tomato purée (paste). Stir in the basil and salt and pepper to taste; set aside.

Mix both cheeses with the egg yolks and salt and pepper.

Prepare the cappellacci following the instructions for cappelletti on page 54, filling them with the cheese mixture. Re-heat the sauce and, if necessary, thin with a little water.

Bring a large saucepan of water to the boil. Add salt and the cappellacci and cook for 2 minutes after the water returns to the boil. Drain and transfer to a warmed serving platter. Cover with the aubergine sauce and serve immediately, very hot.

Serves 4.

TORTELLI ALLA RICOTTA AL LIMONE

Tortelli with Lemon Ricotta

These tortelli are very quick to prepare but absolutely delicious. If lemon thyme is difficult to find, use ordinary thyme.

210g/7oz/scant 1 cup fresh ricotta
2 egg yolks
Finely grated zest of 2 lemons
1 tbsp fresh lemon thyme leaves
Salt and pepper
1 quantity Fresh Egg Pasta (pages 47 and 51)
60g/2oz/4 tbsp unsalted butter

Put the ricotta in a bowl and mash with a fork to break up any lumps. Add the egg yolks, lemon zest, thyme leaves and salt and pepper to taste; set aside. Prepare the tortelli following the instructions on page 54, filling with the tortelli mixture. Bring a large saucepan of water to the boil. Add salt and the tortelli and cook for 2 minutes after the water returns to the boil.

Meanwhile, melt the butter. Drain the tortelli and transfer to a warmed serving platter. Pour the butter over and serve immediately, very hot.

Serves 4.

RAVIOLI ALLA PANCETTA E PATATE

Ravioli with Bacon and Potatoes

The fat produced by melting the bacon is very tasty on the ravioli, making this perfect for a winter evening, when not so many fresh ingredients are available.

120g/4oz/1 cup smoked bacon,
rinded if necessary and chopped
4 potatoes, peeled and thinly sliced
1 large onion, thinly sliced
1 clove, ground
Salt and pepper
1 quantity Fresh Egg Pasta (pages 47 and 51)
90g/3oz/6 tbsp freshly grated Fontina cheese

Put the bacon in a frying pan over low heat and fry, stirring frequently, until the fat melts and the meat is crisp. Remove the bacon with a slotted spoon and set aside. Drain off most of the fat from the frying pan and reserve.

Add the potatotes and onion to the fat remaining in the pan and increase the heat to medium. Cook, covered, for about 10 minutes, stirring frequently, until soft. If necessary, add a little water. Add the clove and salt and pepper to taste and set aside to cool completely. Mash with a fork and stir in the bacon. Prepare the ravioli following the instructions on page 54, filling with the potato and bacon mixture. Bring a large pan of water to the boil. Add salt and the ravioli to the water and cook for 2 minutes after the water returns to the boil.

Meanwhile, reheat the reserved bacon fat. Drain the pasta and transfer to a warmed serving platter. Sprinkle with the Fontina and spoon over the bacon fat. Serve immediately, very hot.

Serves 4.

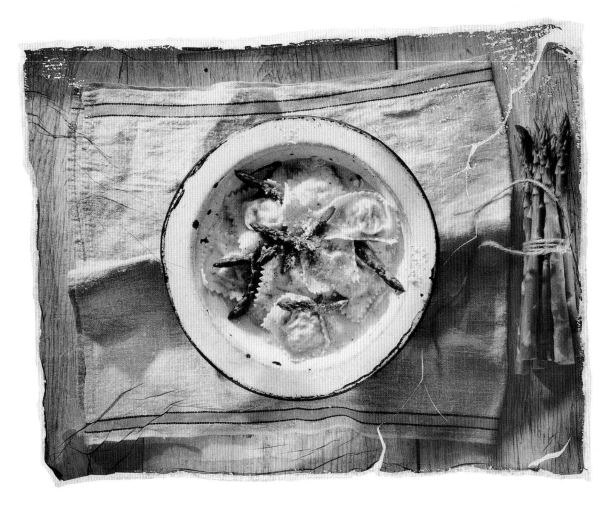

RAVIOLI CON ASPARAGI ALLA PARMIGIANA
Ravioli with Asparagus Parmigiana

Parmigiana is the Italian word that lets you know a recipe contains Parmesan cheese and melted butter. The asparagus can be replaced with artichokes, cleaned, sliced and sautéed with the same method.

90g/3oz/6 tbsp unsalted butter
900g/2 lb fresh asparagus, tough ends discarded
Salt
120g/4oz/¹/₂ cup fresh ricotta cheese
120g/4oz/1 cup freshly grated Parmesan cheese
1 egg yolk, size 3 (U.S. large)
Pepper
1 quantity Fresh Egg Pasta (pages 47 and 51)

Melt 30g/1oz/2 tbsp of the butter in a large frying pan over low heat. Add the asparagus tips and cook, covered, for 3 minutes. Add salt and a little water, cover again and continue cooking for about 10 more minutes until tender. Let cool and finely chop half of the tips; set aside the rest.

Mix the chopped tips with ricotta, half the Parmesan cheese and the yolk. Sprinkle with pepper and let cool.

Prepare the ravioli following the instructions on page 54, filling with the asparagus mixture. Bring a large saucepan of water to the boil. Add salt and the ravioli and cook for 2 minutes after the water returns to the boil. Meanwhile, heat the rest of the butter until it is sizzling. Add the remaining asparagus tips. Drain the ravioli and transfer to a warmed deep serving platter. Sprinkle with the rest of the Parmesan and spoon over the butter with asparagus tips. Serve immediately, very hot.
Serves 4.

RAVIOLI ALLE ACCIUGHE
Ravioli with Fresh Anchovies

If you find the taste of anchovies too strong, substitute sole fillets and cook them the same way. Dry breadcrumbs can be bought in Italian speciality shops if you don't have time to make your own. They will keep for a long time, provided they are in an airtight container.

300g/10oz fresh anchovies
90g/3oz/³/₄ cup fine dry breadcrumbs
2 tbsp finely chopped flat-leaf Italian parsley
1 tbsp dry oregano
120ml/4fl oz/¹/₂ cup extra virgin olive oil
Salt and pepper
1 quantity Fresh Egg Pasta (pages 47 and 51)

Preheat the oven to 180°C/350°F/Gas 4.
Clean the anchovies, opening them in half and removing all the bones and cutting off the heads and tails. Wash them carefully.
Place the anchovies in an ovenproof dish, greased with a little olive oil. Sprinkle the crumbs, parsley, oregano, half the oil and salt and pepper to taste over the top. Bake for about 20 minutes until the flesh flakes easily. Let cool completely, then mash the anchovies and topping with a fork.
Prepare the ravioli following the instructions on page 54, filling them with the anchovy mixture. Bring a large pan of water to the boil. Add salt and the ravioli and cook for 2 minutes after the water returns to the boil.
Meanwhile, heat the oil without letting it fry. Drain the ravioli. Transfer it to a warmed serving platter, pour over the oil and mix together carefully. Serve immediately, very hot.
Serves 4.

RAVIOLI ALLA CODA DI BUE
Ravioli with Oxtail

Sometimes the cheapest cuts of meat are the best, provided they are cooked correctly. Oxtail, for example, needs slow cooking to transform it into a tender, succulent piece of meat. I will always remember a wonderful oxtail prepared for me years ago by Andreas Hellrig, of Palio, in New York City. It had been completely de-boned and reconstructed.

15g/¹/₂oz/1 tbsp unsalted butter
2 tbsp extra virgin olive oil
900g/2 lb oxtail, each piece halved
1 onion, chopped
1 celery stalk, finely chopped
2 sweet (bell) peppers, grilled (broiled), peeled and chopped
4 plum tomatoes, peeled and chopped
1 quantity Fresh Egg Pasta (pages 47 and 51)
Salt

Melt the butter with the oil in a large frying pan over medium heat. Add the oxtail and onion and cook until slightly browned. Add the celery, peppers and tomatoes. Lower the heat, cover and cook for about 4 hours, adding some water, a little at a time, to keep the cooking juices moist. Drain the oxtail, reserving the vegetables. De-bone and chop the meat; reserve half. Add the rest to the vegetables and re-heat to make the sauce.
Prepare the ravioli following the instructions on page 54, filling with the reserved meat. Bring a large saucepan of water to the boil. Add salt and the ravioli and cook for 2 minutes after the water returns to the boil. Drain and transfer to a warmed serving platter. Cover with the sauce and serve immediately, very hot.
Serves 4.

RAVIOLI ALLE PATATE E CAVOLFIORE
Ravioli with Potatoes and Cauliflower

The mixture of potatoes and cauliflower is enhanced by a few capers and anchovies. Dry oregano gives a typically southern flavour.

210g/7oz cauliflower
210g/7oz potatoes, peeled and diced
4 anchovy fillets in oil or brine, drained
1 tbsp capers in salt or brine, drained
1 tbsp dry oregano
Salt and pepper
1 quantity Fresh Egg Pasta (pages 47 and 51)
6 tbsp extra virgin olive oil
1 tbsp chopped flat-leaf Italian parsley

Bring a large saucepan of water to the boil. Add the cauliflower and cook about 10 minutes until tender. Remove with a slotted spoon and set aside. Add the potatoes to the water and boil for a few minutes until tender. Drain and let cool. Put the potatoes, cauliflower, anchovies and capers in a food processor and process. Add the oregano and salt and pepper to taste and mix well.
Prepare the ravioli following the instructions on page 54, filling with the vegetable mixture. Bring a large pan of water to the boil. Add salt and the ravioli and cook for 2 minutes after the water returns to the boil. Meanwhile, heat the oil without letting it turn brown. Drain the ravioli. Sprinkle with oil and parsley, mix carefully and transfer to a warmed serving platter.
Serve immediately, very hot.
Serves 4.

RAVIOLI AL CAVIALE NERO E ROSSO
Ravioli with Black and Red Caviar

My best friend, Maria Louisa de'Banfield, is a specialist in the cuisine of northern Italy, having been born in Trieste. (Her father is the pilot Goffredo de'Banfield, a hero from World War I.) But she is also curious about other cuisines, and has access to recipes from the many famous home cooks who work for all her friends. This is one of her recipes that I especially love.

Black and red caviar are not too expensive and make a lovely presentation with the ravioli. Using squid ink in the pasta dough, instead of one of the eggs, makes black ravioli for an even more dramatic look.

120g/4oz/$\frac{1}{2}$ cup ricotta cheese
60g/2oz/4 tbsp black caviar
60ml/2fl oz/$\frac{1}{4}$ cup sour cream
Salt and pepper
1 quantity Fresh Egg Pasta (pages 47 and 51)
(blackened with squid ink for black pasta, see page 56)
90g/3oz/6 tbsp unsalted butter
60g/2oz/4 tbsp red caviar

Combine the ricotta, black caviar and sour cream. Add very little salt to taste and pepper.
Prepare the ravioli following the instructions on page 54, filling with the ricotta mixture. Bring a large pan of water to the boil. Add salt and the ravioli and cook for 2 minutes after the water returns to the boil. Meanwhile, melt the butter. Drain the ravioli. Transfer to a warmed serving platter, pour the butter on top, sprinkle with red caviar and serve immediately, very hot.
Serves 4.

RAVIOLI CON CAPESANTE

Ravioli with Scallops

Fish ravioli is one of my favourites, although fish is not easily found in Chianti. Scallops are a speciality in Venice, like spider crab (*granceola*) that, in fact, can be substituted for the scallops in this recipe.

120ml/4fl oz/¹/₂ cup extra virgin olive oil
2 garlic cloves, very finely chopped
12 scallops, removed from the shells and sliced
About 60ml/2fl oz/¹/₄ cup dry white wine
2 tbsp finely chopped flat-leaf Italian parsley
1 quantity for Fresh Egg Pasta (pages 47 and 51)
Salt

Heat half the oil in a frying pan over medium heat. Add the garlic and sauté for about 3 minutes, stirring occasionally, until translucent. Add the scallops and sauté 2 more minutes. Add the wine and let it evaporate. Sprinkle with half the parsley and set aside. Prepare the ravioli following the instructions on page 54, filling with the scallop mixture. Bring a large pan of water to the boil. Add salt and the ravioli and cook for 2 minutes after the water returns to the boil. Drain and transfer to a warmed serving platter. Sprinkle with the rest of parsley, the rest of oil and serve immediately, very hot.
Serves 4.

RAVIOLI DI RICOTTA

Ravioli with Ricotta

These are especially delicious when you use sheep's milk ricotta, like cooks do in Tuscany or Umbria. But cow's milk ricotta is a good substitute, provided it is very fresh.

210g/7oz/scant 1 cup fresh ricotta cheese
2 egg yolks
90g/3oz/³/₄ cup freshly grated Parmesan cheese
Handful of chopped fresh basil leaves
Pinch of grated nutmeg
Salt and pepper
1 quantity Fresh Egg Pasta (pages 47 and 51)
Handful of whole basil leaves
4 tbsp extra virgin olive oil

Mix together the ricotta, egg yolks, Parmesan cheese, chopped basil, nutmeg and salt and pepper to taste. Prepare the ravioli following the instructions on page 54, filling them with the ricotta mixture. Bring a large saucepan of water to the boil. Add salt and the ravioli and cook for 2 minutes after the water returns to the boil. Drain and transfer to a warmed serving platter. Sprinkle with the whole basil leaves and the oil. Serve immediately, very hot.
Serves 4.

RAVIOLI AL SALMONE

Ravioli with Smoked Salmon

A simple variation in this recipe is to replace the smoked salmon with smoked trout. If you can't find fennel seeds, sprinkle grated lemon zest on the cream.

210g/7oz smoked salmon, chopped
90g/3oz/6 tbsp fresh ricotta cheese
Salt and pepper
2 egg yolks
1 quantity Fresh Egg Pasta (pages 47 and 51)
240ml/8fl oz/1 cup double (heavy) cream
1 tbsp fennel seeds

Mix together the salmon and ricotta with a little salt and pepper to taste. Stir in the egg yolks and set aside. Prepare the ravioli following the instructions on page 54, filling with the salmon mixture. Bring a large saucepan of water to the boil. Add the ravioli and salt and cook for 2 minutes after the water returns to the boil.
Meanwhile, heat the cream in a pan over low heat. Add a little salt and pepper to taste. Drain the ravioli and transfer to a warmed serving platter. Sprinkle with the fennel seeds and serve immediately, very hot.
Serves 4.

Opposite page: Fresh Ravioli and Tortelli

TORTELLONI CON BRESAOLA E FORMAGGIO DI CAPRA
Tortelloni with Bresaola and Goat's Cheese

Bresaola is a delicious cold meat speciality from a northern valley called Valtellina. It is very tasty dried beef that Italians eat with just a bit of lemon juice and extra virgin olive oil.

210g/7oz fresh goat's cheese, mashed with a fork
120ml/4fl oz/¹/₂ cup extra virgin olive oil
Salt and pepper
120g/4oz bresaola, sliced paper thin
1 quantity Fresh Egg Pasta (pages 47 and 51)

Mix together the goat's cheese, 2 tablespoons of the oil and salt and pepper to taste. Lay the bresaola slices flat and spoon the goat's cheese mixture down the centre of each. Fold up the slices, to make little parcels.
Prepare the tortelloni following the instructions on page 54, filling with the bresaola parcels. Bring a large saucepan of water to the boil. Add salt and the tortelloni and cook for 2 minutes after the water returns to the boil.
Meanwhile, heat the rest of the oil. Drain the tortelloni and transfer to a warmed serving platter. Pour the heated oil on top and sprinkle with more pepper. Serve immediately, very hot.
Serves 4.

RAVIOLI ALLE ERBE
Ravioli with Herbs

The simple ricotta filling is enhanced by the flavour of various herbs added just before serving. I use fresh rosemary, sage, thyme and chives, which produce quite a strong flavour.

210g/7oz/scant 1 cup fresh ricotta cheese
60g/2oz/4 tbsp freshly grated Parmesan cheese
2 egg yolks, size 3 (U.S. large)
Salt and pepper
1 quantity Fresh Egg Pasta (pages 47 and 51)
6 tbsp extra virgin olive oil
1 tbsp finely chopped fresh rosemary
1 tbsp finely chopped fresh sage
1 tbsp finely chopped fresh thyme
1 tbsp finely chopped fresh chives
2 garlic cloves, finely chopped

Mix together the ricotta, Parmesan cheese, egg yolks; add salt and pepper to taste; set aside.
Prepare the ravioli following the instructions on page 54, filling them with the ricotta mixture. Bring a large saucepan of water to the boil. Add salt and the ravioli and cook for 2 minutes after the water returns to the boil.
Meanwhile, heat the oil in a large pan. Add the herbs and garlic and cook for about 3 minutes. Drain the ravioli and transfer to a warmed serving platter. Pour the oil and herbs on top and serve immediately, very hot.
Serves 4.

Opposite page: Ravioli with Herbs

TORTELLI NERI CON SEPPIOLINE E PATATE
Black Tortelli with Cuttlefish and Potatoes

When I was newly married and first had a house of my own, I had to teach our cook how to prepare the recipes I particularly liked. For my first dinner party, I wanted to serve this dish with black pasta for fun. In those days it was not easy to find squid ink, so first the cook and I had to kill a couple of cuttlefish instead. The result was that more ink seemed to go all around the kitchen, rather than into the pasta dough. Since then I have become expert in the art of black pasta.

In Italy, we are lucky enough to get baby cuttlefish, but one larger one will do.

6 tbsp extra virgin olive oil
1 small onion, chopped
210g/7oz cuttlefish, cleaned and sliced
210g/7oz/1½ cups potatoes, peeled and diced
Salt and pepper
1 quantity Fresh Egg Pasta (pages 47 and 51)
blackened with squid ink (page 56)
240ml/8fl oz/1 cup Alfredo Sauce (page 64)

Heat the oil in a large frying pan over medium heat. Add the onion and fry, stirring, for about 3 minutes until translucent. Add the fish, potatoes and salt and pepper to taste and mix well. Lower the heat, cover and cook for about 30 minutes, stirring occasionally and, if necessary, adding a little water at a time to keep the cooking juices moist.
Raise the heat, uncover and finish cooking until all the liquid evaporates. Pass everything through a food mill or chop in a food processor; set aside to cool completely.
Prepare the tortelli following the instructions on page 54, filling them with the cuttlefish mixture. Bring a large saucepan of water to the boil. Add salt and the tortelli and cook for 2 minutes after the water returns to the boil.
Meanwhile, heat the Alfredo sauce. Drain the tortelli and transfer to a deep warmed serving platter. Add the sauce, mix carefully and serve immediately, very hot.
Serves 4.

TORTELLONI CON CAPESANTE AL CURRY
Tortelloni with Scallops in a Curry Sauce

I developed this recipe after my first trip to India about 30 years ago. Since then, I return almost every year, because I think India is one of the most beautiful places in the world with gracious people and astonishing art. This is a recipe I particularly like when I want to get away from strictly Italian food.

30g/1oz/2 tbsp unsalted butter
1 onion, chopped
8 savoy cabbage leaves, shredded
240ml/8fl oz/1 cup milk
2 tbsp curry powder
Salt and pepper
12 scallops, cleaned and washed
1 quantity Fresh Egg Pasta (pages 47 and 51)

Melt the butter in a large frying pan over medium heat. Add the onion and cabbage and sauté for about 3 minutes, stirring occasionally. Add the milk and curry powder and continue cooking about 30 minutes until the vegetables are soft. Add salt and pepper to taste and purée in a blender or food processor. Reheat and add the scallops, cooking them for just a few minutes until they turn opaque. Remove the scallops with a slotted spoon and reserve.
Prepare the tortelloni following the instructions on page 54, filling with the scallops. Bring a large saucepan of water to the boil. Add salt and the tortelloni and cook for 2 minutes after the water returns to the boil.
Meanwhile, reheat the sauce. Drain the tortelloni and transfer to a warmed serving platter. Cover with the sauce and serve immediately, very hot.
Serves 4.

TORTELLONI ALLO SPADA E OLIVE

Tortelloni with Swordfish and Olives

Tuna is a good substitute for the swordfish, because its flavour also stands up well against the strong taste of the olives and capers.

120ml/4fl oz/½ cup extra virgin olive oil
2 garlic cloves, chopped
360g/12oz swordfish, sliced
Juice of ½ lemon
Salt and pepper
90g/3oz/¾ cup black olives,
such as Gaeta or Greek, stoned and chopped
1 tbsp capers in brine or salt, drained
1 quantity Fresh Egg Pasta (pages 47 and 51)
1 tbsp grated orange zest
1 tbsp chopped flat-leaf Italian parsley

Heat half of the oil in a large frying pan over low heat. Add the garlic and cook until translucent. Raise the heat to medium, add the fish and sauté for about 3 minutes each side until golden brown. Sprinkle with lemon juice and salt and pepper to taste; set aside to cool.
Remove any skin and bones from the fish and finely chop. Add half of the olives to the fish and mix well. Prepare the tortelloni following the instructions on page 54, filling with the fish mixture. Bring a large saucepan of water to the boil. Add salt and the tortelloni and cook for 2 minutes after the water returns to the boil.
Meanwhile, heat the rest of the oil in a pan over medium heat. Add the remaining chopped olives, the capers and orange zest. Drain the tortelloni and transfer to warmed serving platter. Sprinkle with the olive oil mixture and parsley and serve immediately, very hot.
Serves 4.

TORTELLONI CON TONNO E PISELLI

Tortelloni with Tuna and Peas

I do not like, nor rarely use, frozen produce, but in the case of peas I sometimes break my rule. This is because peas are often better and sweeter when they have been commercially frozen than some of the fresh ones you buy. To defrost them, just put them in cold water for a few minutes.

210g/7oz tuna in oil or brine, drained
210g/7oz/1½ cups shelled fresh peas, blanched in boiling water for a couple of minutes, or defrosted
Salt and pepper
1 quantity Fresh Egg Pasta (pages 47 and 51)
6 tbsp extra virgin olive oil
240ml/8fl oz/1 cup Cooked Tomato Sauce (page 64)
1 tbsp flat-leaf Italian parsley

Pass the tuna and peas through a food mill or chop in a food processor. If necessary, add a little salt to taste and sprinkle with pepper; set aside.
Prepare the tortelloni following the instructions on page 54, filling with the tuna and pea mixture. Bring a large saucepan of water to the boil. Add salt and the tortelloni and cook for 2 minutes after the water returns to the boil.
Meanwhile, reheat the tomato sauce and add the parsley. Drain the tortelloni and transfer to a warmed serving platter. Mix with the sauce and serve immediately.
Serves 4.

TORTELLI AI FIORI DI ZUCCA

Tortelli with Courgette (Zucchini) Flowers

Courgette (zucchini) flowers have a brief life in June when the plants produce more flowers than fruits. Only the male flowers are good to eat, and the flowers from the top of the plants should not be used.

120g/4oz/8 tbsp unsalted butter
210g/7oz courgette (zucchini) flowers, pistils removed and chopped
Salt and pepper
90g/3oz/6 tbsp fresh ricotta cheese
1 quantity Fresh Egg Pasta (pages 47 and 51)
60g/2oz/4 tbsp Emmental cheese, grated

Melt 30g/1oz/2 tbsp of the butter in a frying pan over medium heat. Add the courgette (zucchini) flowers and sauté for 3 minutes, stirring occasionally. Sprinkle with salt and pepper and let cool. Stir in the ricotta and reserve.
Prepare the tortelli following the instructions on page 54, filling them with the flower and cheese mixture.
Bring a large saucepan of water to the boil. Add salt and the tortelli and cook for 2 minutes after the water returns to the boil.
Meanwhile, melt the rest of butter. Drain the tortelli and transfer to a warmed serving platter. Sprinkle with the Emmental cheese and the butter. Serve immediately, very hot.
Serves 4.

CAPPELLETTI GRATINATI ALLA PANNA

Cappelletti au Gratin with Cream

This dish can be assembled ahead of time so you just add the cream at the last minute. I particularly like to serve this when white truffles are in season so I can sprinkle shavings of them over the top.

30g/1oz/2 tbsp unsalted butter
210g/7oz boneless veal meat, diced
1 boneless leg of chicken, diced
1 egg yolk
Pinch of grated nutmeg
60g/2oz/4 tbsp freshly grated Parmesan cheese
60g/2oz/4 tbsp finely grated Fontina cheese
Salt and pepper
1 quantity Fresh Egg Pasta (pages 47 and 51)
480ml/16fl oz/2 cups double (heavy) cream
60g/2oz/1/2 cup finely chopped cooked ham

Melt the butter in a large frying pan over medium heat. Add the veal and chicken and sauté, stirring occasionally, until well browned. Place in a food processor and finely chop. When cool, add the egg yolk, nutmeg, half the Parmesan, half the Fontina cheese and salt and pepper to taste and blend again.
Prepare the cappelletti following the instructions on page 54, filling with the prepared meat mixture.
Bring the cream to the boil in a saucepan and reduce by one-third over low heat.
Bring a large pan of water to the boil. Add salt and the cappelletti and cook for 2 minutes after the water returns to the boil. Meanwhile, preheat the grill (broiler) to medium-high.
Drain and arrange the pasta in a buttered flameproof dish. Sprinkle with the ham and remaining Fontina cheese. Cover with cream. Sprinkle with the remaining Parmesan. Put under the grill (broiler) for about 10 minutes until bubbling and golden brown. Serve immediately, very hot.
Serves 4.

Opposite page: Fresh Cappelletti and Cappellacci

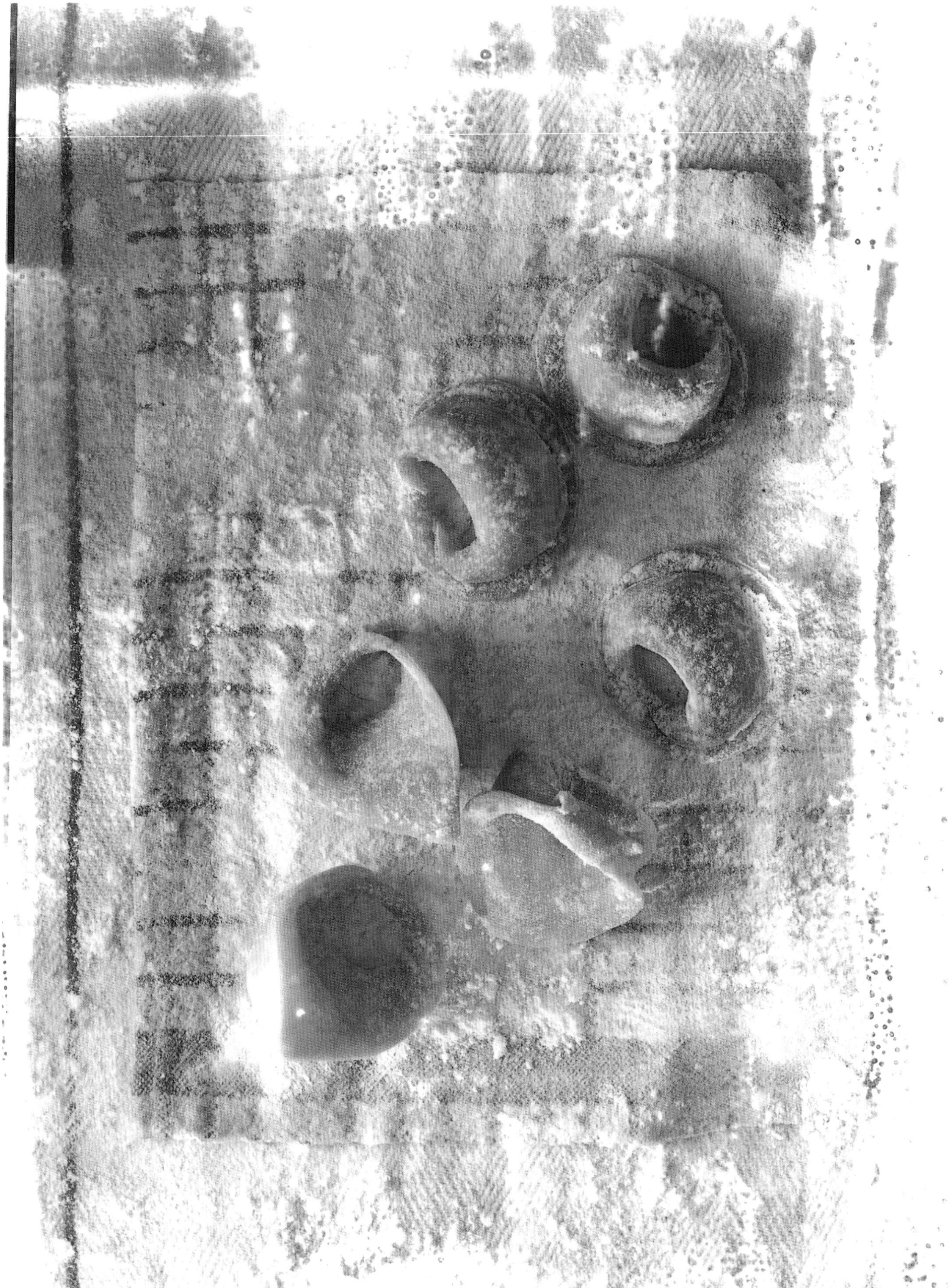

MOULDED AND BAKED PASTA DISHES

IN THIS CHAPTER I HAVE INCLUDED RECIPES FOR A CATEGORY OF PASTA DISH THAT, APART FROM LASAGNE, IS NOT WIDELY KNOWN OUTSIDE OF ITALY. THIS IS A PITY, SINCE THESE DISHES ARE SO DELICIOUS AND SO ESPECIALLY SUITABLE FOR ENTERTAINING. MOST OF THEM CAN BE PREPARED WELL AHEAD OF TIME AND PUT IN THE OVEN TO BAKE WHILE YOU ARE ENJOYING A DRINK WITH YOUR GUESTS. MANY ARE SUBSTANTIAL ENOUGH THAT THEY DO PERFECTLY FOR A ONE-COURSE MEAL, FOLLOWED, PERHAPS, BY SALAD AND FRUIT. SOME ARE IDEAL FOR BRUNCH AND BUFFET LUNCHEONS AND SUPPERS.

Besides lasagne and casserole-type dishes, this category includes moulds, rings, pies, shells and tarts, filled with pasta and sometimes encased in a pastry crust. There are several different types of moulded pasta dishes, variously named, and not all cookery writers use the same word to refer to the same kind of dish. Older recipe books made a basic distinction between a *pasticcio* and a *timballo*. A *pasticcio* was a baked dish, filled with pasta and various other ingredients and enclosed within a pastry case–*en croûte*, as the French would say. Whereas a *timballo* was a high-sided moulded dish with pasta and other ingredients, but not enclosed within pastry. Now the term *pasticcio* is not normally used in recipes, maybe because it more commonly means a "mess", something to be avoided both in the kitchen and at the table. Today *timballo*, from the French *timbale*, is applied to pasta pies, as well as dishes prepared in a mould. A *timballo* is often made in a ring mould and when it is unmoulded, the hole is filled with a rich sauce.

In Italy at an elegant, more formal meal at which you want your food to taste and look special, we would not serve a plate of pasta, a dish most families eat every day. This does not mean my guests have to forego the pleasure of pasta for the sake of etiquette. Instead, I present them with a tasty pasta tart or a sumptuous pasta timbal, dishes guaranteed to increase the enjoyment of pasta at the table.

This social convention has a long and venerable history. Moulded pasta dishes were known to the ancient Romans, and the great chefs of the Renaissance brought them to the zenith of their richness for the grandiose banquets of that era. Fifteenth- and sixteenth-century recipes list endless ingredients that filled these sweet and savoury creations: every kind of meat, game, fish and vegetable mixed with delicacies such as truffles and ostrich eggs, seasoned with exotic spices.

Some historians think these elaborate pasta pies may have been used as a way round the papal sumptuary laws, enacted in the Italian papal states to restrain the excesses of the wealthy classes, whose feasting had gotten out of hand. Among other regulations, these laws prohibited more than three courses at a banquet. For those accustomed to sitting down to an average of thirty or so different dishes, this was a painful austerity measure. As a solution to this problem a pasta pie was served as the second course. Within an ample crust of ravioli and maccheroni almost all the ingredients of the banished courses could be distributed between alternating layers of pastry within the same pie.

A mouth-watering description of a traditional moulded pasta dish is given by Giuseppe Tommaso di Lampedusa in his novel, *Il Gattopardo* (*The Leopard*). The setting is a meal served in an aristocratic country home in nineteenth-century Sicily. The description, however, could only have come from personal experience of similar pasta *timballi* savoured by Lampedusa himself in his own home during the first half of this century. I hope the text will serve as a source of inspiration when you go about preparing these dishes:

The burnished gold of the crusts, the fragrance of the sugar and cinnamon they exuded, were but preludes to the delights released from the interior when the knife broke the crust; first came a spice-laden haze, then chicken livers, hard-boiled eggs, sliced ham, chicken and truffles in masses of piping hot, glistening macaroni, to which the meat juice gave an exquisite hue of suede.

PASTICCIO DI BUCATINI CON ANIMELLE

Bucatini Mould with Sweetbreads

There was a time when we regularly ate much more for dinner. After the soup and before the main course, for example, there would be a middle course, such as a vegetable mould or an omelette. Vegetable moulds were always accompanied by a "little something", such as sautéed cock comb, chicken livers or sweetbreads. This dish is a remembrance of those times of abundance.

If you are in the mood, you can completely cover the mould with the bucatini, one strand next to another one and not overlapping, to make a very neat presentation, and fill the mould with the sweetbreads. Otherwise, just mix together the bucatini and sweetbreads and fill the mould with the combination.

300g/10oz sweetbreads
60g/2oz prosciutto, chopped
1 small onion, chopped
Salt and pepper
210g/7oz/1½ cups shelled peas
120g/4oz/8 tbsp unsalted butter
300g/10oz bucatini
90g/3oz/¾ cup freshly grated Parmesan cheese

Soak the sweetbreads in cold water for about 2 hours, changing the water once. Bring a saucepan of water to the boil. Add the sweetbreads and cook for 5 minutes. Drain, and place them under cold water to stop the cooking. Pat them dry and remove the membranes and veins. Slice them about 0.5cm/¼ inch thick. Sauté the prosciutto and onion in a large frying pan over medium heat for a couple of minutes. Add the sweetbreads and salt and pepper to taste and cook for 5 minutes. Lower the heat, cover and continue cooking for about 10 more minutes, adding a little water to keep the cooking juices moist; set aside to cool.
Meanwhile, blanch the peas in boiling water for about 2 minutes, then drain; set aside.
Butter a deep 23cm/9 inch ring mould. Sprinkle with the Parmesan and put in the refrigerator.
Preheat the oven to 180°C/350°F/Gas 4.
Bring a large pan of water to the boil. Add salt and the bucatini and cook until *al dente*. Drain and mix with the rest of the butter, the peas and the Parmesan. Fill the mould and bake for about 20 minutes. Meanwhile, gently reheat the sweetbreads. Unmould the bucatini on to a warmed serving platter. Fill the centre with the sweetbreads and serve immediately, very hot.
Serves 4.

PASTICCIO DI BUCATINI E SCAMPI

Bucatini and Prawn (Shrimp) Mould

The flavour of the prawns (shrimp) makes this into a nice party dish that can be prepared ahead of time. You can also use other shellfish, such as clams or mussels, instead of the prawns (shrimp).

3 tbsp extra virgin olive oil
4 leeks, halved lengthwise, well rinsed and sliced
300g/10oz large raw prawns (shrimp), peeled and deveined
1 tbsp grated lemon zest
Salt and pepper
180g/6oz/1 cup Emmental cheese, grated
240ml/8fl oz/1 cup White Sauce (page 62)
15g/12oz/1 tbsp unsalted butter
60g/2oz/½ cup dry fine breadcrumbs
300g/10oz bucatini

Heat the oil in a saucepan over medium heat. Add the leeks and sauté about 3 minutes, stirring, until translucent. Add the prawns (shrimp), lemon zest and salt and pepper to taste and sauté for 3 more minutes, stirring occasionally. Remove from heat and stir in the cheese and white sauce; set aside.
Preheat the oven to 180°C/350°F/Gas 4.
Grease a 20cm/8inch springform pan with the butter and coat with the breadcrumbs. Bring a large pan of water to the boil. Add salt and the bucatini and cook until *al dente*. Drain the pasta and stir with the prawn mixture. Press into the prepared mould. Bake in the oven for about 50 minutes. Loosen the edges with a knife and invert on to a warmed serving platter. Serve at once.
Serves 4.

TIMBALLO DI BUCATINI E PICCIONE

Bucatini and Pigeon Timbal

This is an elegant dish for an elegant dinner. It can be prepared a day in advance and kept in the refrigerator until it is time for it to be baked.

120g/4oz/8 tbsp unsalted butter
2 pigeons, cleaned, rinsed inside and out, and quartered
1 carrot, chopped
1 celery stalk, chopped
1 bay leaf
1 small onion, chopped
60g/2oz prosciutto, chopped
1 fresh sprig rosemary
30g/1oz/2 tbsp plain (all-purpose) flour
About 120ml/4fl oz/½ cup dry white wine
Salt and pepper
300g/10oz bucatini
450g/1 lb Shortcrust (Piecrust) Pastry (page 67)
About 120ml/4fl oz/½ cup double (heavy) cream

Melt 15g/½oz/1 tbsp of the butter in a large frying pan over medium heat. Add the pigeon pieces and sauté until slightly brown. Add the carrot, celery, bay leaf, onion, prosciutto and rosemary. Sprinkle with the flour and cook for a couple of minutes. Add the wine and salt and pepper to taste. Lower the heat, cover and cook for about 1 hour, adding some water a little at a time to keep the cooking juices moist.
Meanwhile, preheat the oven to 180°C/350°F/Gas 4. Bring a large pan of water to the boil. Add salt and the bucatini and cook until *al dente*. Drain and toss with the rest of butter, except 15g/½oz/1 tbsp.
With the rest of the butter grease a 20cm/8 inch springform pan and dust with the flour. Roll out three-quarters of the pastry (dough) and cover the bottom and sides of the pan. Add the cream to the pigeons and scrape the bottom of the pan. Pick up the pieces of meat and reserve. Mix the juices with the bucatini. Layer the bucatini and pigeon pieces in the springform pan to fill the crust.
Roll out the remaining pastry (dough) and use to cover the top. Cut off the excess and prick the top with a fork. Bake for about 1 hour, covering the top if the crust is browning too much. Let cool slightly before unmoulding. Transfer to a warmed serving platter.
Serves 4.

BUCATINI CON PROVOLA AFFUMICATA

Bucatini Pie with Smoked Provola Cheese

A pasta like bucatini, penne or rigatoni is best for a baked pasta dish because it does not easily over-cook. This is important because the pasta is cooked twice, once in boiling water and once in the oven.

300g/10oz bucatini
90g/3oz/6 tbsp unsalted butter
150g/5oz pancetta or bacon, chopped
240ml/8fl oz/1 cup double (heavy) cream
150g/5oz/1¼ cups smoked provola cheese, chopped
90g/3oz/¾ cup freshly grated Parmesan cheese
Salt and pepper
90g/3oz Shortcrust (Piecrust) Pastry (page 67)
1 egg yolk, lightly beaten

Bring a large saucepan of water to the boil. Add salt and the bucatini and cook until *al dente*. Drain and mix with 30g/1oz/2 tbsp of the butter; set aside.
Melt another 30g/1oz/2 tbsp butter in a large frying pan over medium heat. Add the pancetta and fry until the fat melts and the meat is slightly golden. Add to the pasta.
In a separate pan, heat the cream almost to the boil. Add the provola and Parmesan cheeses and a little salt and pepper. Add to the pasta and toss well.
Spread the rest of the butter in an ovenproof serving dish. Transfer the pasta into it.
Roll out the pastry (dough) in the shape of the dish until it is about 0.5cm/¼ inch thick, sealing the edges to the dish with a little water. Add 2 drops of water to the egg yolk and brush the surface of the pastry (dough). Bake for about 20 minutes until the surface is golden. Serve immediately, very hot.
Serves 4.

TIMBALLO DI BUCATINI ALLE MELANZANE
Bucatini Timbal with Grilled Aubergines (Broiled Eggplant)

One of my favourite hotels is the Sirenuse, in Postiano, famous for its beautiful architecture and position. It was once the Sersale family palace, and is now run as a hotel by Antonio Sersale of the younger generation. Its restaurant is famous for its pasta, and the chef occasionally prepares the buffet with thirty pasta dishes. He taught me the expression "pasta all'impiedi", which means pasta should be underdone, or still standing. In fact, the less pasta is cooked, the easier it is to digest.

This recipe is a speciality from the hotel. Like all other timbals, moulds and tarts, this is perfect for parties, because it can be prepared in advance and kept for a few hours in the refrigerator before baking.

6 tbsp extra virgin olive oil
2 garlic cloves, chopped
450g/1 lb/3 cups ripe plum tomatoes, peeled and chopped, or canned with the juice
Pinch of hot pepper flakes
Salt and pepper
2 oval aubergines (eggplants), about 300g/10oz, trimmed and cut lengthwise into 0.3cm/1/8 inch thick slices
15g/1/2oz/1 tbsp unsalted butter
60g/2oz/1/2 cup fine dry breadcrumbs
300g/10oz bucatini
Handful of fresh basil leaves

Heat the oil in a saucepan over low heat. Add the garlic and sauté for about 3 minutes until translucent. Add the tomatoes, pepper flakes and salt and pepper to taste and cook, covered, for about 30 minutes until all the liquid is absorbed.
Preheat the grill (broiler) and the oven to 180°C/350°F/ Gas 4.
Grill (broil) the aubergines (eggplants) for about 1 minute on each side. Grease a 20cm/8 inch springform pan with the butter and coat the bottom and sides evenly with the breadcrumbs. Line the bottom and sides with the aubergines, overlapping them slightly; reserve any leftover slices.
Bring a large pan of water to the boil. Add salt and the bucatini and cook until *al dente*. Drain and transfer to a bowl. Add the sauce, leftover aubergines and basil, and toss. Transfer to the prepared springform pan and press down lightly to pack. Bake for about 50 minutes. Invert on to a warmed serving platter and serve immediately, very hot.
Serves 4.

PASTICCIO DI VERMICELLI E RICOTTA
Vermicelli and Ricotta Mould

A little bit of cinnamon and sugar will give this elegant dish the right touch.

15g/1/2oz/1 tbsp unsalted butter
4 tbsp finely grated dry breadcrumbs
150g/5oz/2/3 cup fresh ricotta cheese
4 eggs, size 3 (U.S. large)
240ml/8fl oz/1 cup milk
30g/1oz/2 tbsp sugar
1/2 tbsp ground cinnamon
450g/1 lb vermicelli
Salt and pepper

Preheat the oven to 180°C/350°F/Gas 4.
Butter a 23cm/9 inch springform mould and sprinkle with the breadcrumbs. Shake off any excess; set aside. Mix the ricotta in a bowl with the eggs, one at a time. Stir in the milk, sugar and cinnamon, and blend well. Bring a large saucepan of water to the boil. Add salt and the vermicelli and cook until *al dente*. Drain the vermicelli and toss with the ricotta mixture. Check the salt and add pepper. Arrange in the prepared mould and cook for about 1 hour, or until a wooden stick inserted in the centre comes out clean. Invert on to a warmed serving platter, giving a firm shake half way over. Remove the mould and serve immediately, very hot.
Serves 4.

Opposite page: Bucatini Timbal with Grilled Aubergines (Broiled Eggplant)

TORTA DI FETTUCCINE AL PECORINO E MENTA

Fettuccine Tart with Pecorino and Mint

The fresh fettuccine in this recipe can be replaced with linguine or even a short pasta like penne, if you like a more rustic feeling. The freshness of the mint balances the tartness of the cheese.

240ml/8fl oz/1 cup double (heavy) cream
Handful of fresh mint leaves
180g/6oz/1¹/₂ cups pecorino (Romano) cheese, grated
Salt and pepper
15g/¹/₂oz/1 tbsp unsalted butter
300g/10oz Shortcrust (Piecrust) Pastry (page 67)
300g/10oz Fresh Egg Pasta (pages 47 and 51), cut into fettuccine (page 52)

Preheat the oven to 180°C/350°F/Gas 4.
Put the cream into a saucepan over medium heat, with the mint, cheese and salt and pepper and stir for a couple of minutes; set aside.
Butter a 20cm/8 inch tart pan with a removable base. Roll out the pastry (dough) thinly until it is large enough to cover the base and the side of the pan.
Trim the edges and prick the base. Bake for about 30 minutes, or until it is a golden colour. If the pastry puffs up, just press it down with the palm of your hand.
Meanwhile, bring a large saucepan of water to the boil. Add salt and the fettuccine and cook until the water returns to the boil and the fettucine float to the top. Drain and mix with the sauce.
Fill the tart shell with the fettuccine and bake for 20 more minutes. Unmould the tart on to a warmed serving platter and serve immediately.
Serves 4.

TORTA DI CONCHIGLIE AL PATE D'OLIVE

Conchiglie Tart with Olive Paste

Olive paste is a traditional Ligurian appetizer that is also excellent to use as a pasta sauce. It is very easy to prepare at home in a blender or food processor, and this version, with a bit of lemon zest, is particularly delicate.

180g/6oz/1¹/₂ cups black olives, such as Gaeta or Greek, stoned
Grated zest of 1 lemon
2 garlic cloves, peeled
6 tbsp extra virgin olive oil
Salt and pepper
15g/¹/₂oz/1 tbsp unsalted butter
300g/10oz Shortcrust (Piecrust) Pastry (page 67)
300g/10oz conchiglie

Preheat the oven to 180°C/350°F/Gas 4.
Put the olives in a blender or food processor with the lemon zest, garlic, olive oil and salt and pepper to taste. Blend until creamy. Butter a 20cm/8 inch tart pan with removable base. Roll out the pastry (dough) thinly until it is large enough to cover the base and sides of the pan. Trim the edges and prick the base.
Bake for about 40 minutes, or until golden. If the pastry puffs up, just press it down with the palm of your hand.
Meanwhile, bring a large pan of water to the boil. Add salt and the conchiglie and cook until *al dente*. Add one glass of the pasta cooking water to the olive paste mixture in the blender or food processor and blend for a couple of seconds.
Drain the pasta and toss with the olive paste. Unmould the tart on to a warmed serving plate. Fill with pasta mixture and serve immediately, very hot.
Serves 4.

CONCHIGLIE E SCAMPI AL GRATIN
Conchiglie with Prawns (Shrimp) au Gratin

You can assemble this dish up to three months in advance and freeze it. Just be sure to bring it back to room temperature before baking. Penne or rigatoni are also suitable.

60g/2oz/4 tbsp unsalted butter
450g/1 lb large raw prawns (shrimp), peeled and deveined
About 90ml/3fl oz/just under ¹/₃ cup brandy or Cognac
Salt and pepper
300g/10oz conchiglie
240ml/8fl oz/1 cup double (heavy) cream
90g/3oz/³/₄ cup freshly grated Parmesan cheese

Melt half the butter in a large frying pan over medium heat. Add the prawns (shrimp) and sauté, stirring a couple of times, for about 3 minutes until the prawns turn pink and curl. Add brandy or Cognac and let it evaporate. Sprinkle with salt and pepper; set aside

Preheat the oven to 180°C/350°F/Gas 4. Use 15g/¹/₂oz/1 tbsp of the butter to grease an ovenproof serving dish.

Bring a large pan of water to the boil. Add salt and the conchiglie and cook until *al dente*.

Meanwhile, whip the cream until soft peaks form. Drain the pasta and mix with half the cream and half the prawns. Transfer to the prepared dish. Cover with half the cheese, the rest of the pasta, prawns and cream. Sprinkle with rest of Parmesan. Bake for about 20 minutes until slightly golden on top. Serve immediately, very hot.
Serves 4.

LASAGNE ALL'ARANCIA
Lasagne with Orange Zest

Try this light and pleasant dish, with its delicate flavour, for dinner. I tasted this for the first time at the home of my good friend, Maria Luisa de'Banfield. It has since become one of my favourite dishes. For variety, I sometimes use lemon zest instead of orange, in which case I sprinkle the lasagne with a little black caviar as it comes out of the oven.

1 quantity Fresh Egg Pasta (pages 47 and 51), cut into lasagne (page 52)
60g/2oz/4 tbsp unsalted butter, diced
Finely grated zest and juice of 1 orange
About 90ml/3fl oz/just under ⅓ cup of brandy
240ml/8fl oz/1 cup double (heavy) cream
Salt and pepper

Bring a large saucepan of water to the boil. Add salt and the lasagne, a few sheets at a time, and cook until the water returns to the boil and the lasagne float to the top. Drain and put in a bowl of cold water. Drain again and put on a cloth to dry.
Preheat the oven to 180°C/350°F/Gas 4 and grease an ovenproof serving dish with 15g/½oz/1 tbsp of the butter.
Heat the orange zest and juice, brandy and cream until just warm. Add salt and pepper to taste.
Layer the lasagne with the orange-cream sauce in the ovenproof dish. Dot with the remaining butter. Cook for about 20 minutes until bubbling. Serve immediately, very hot.
Serves 4.

LASAGNE ALL'UMIDO
Lasagne with Braised Meat

This is a typical Roman dish that is usually served with the lasagne as a first course, followed by the beef surrounded by all the vegetables.

900g/2 lb braising beef
150g/5oz lard, cut into matchsticks
10 cloves
Salt and pepper
1 onion, chopped
1 carrot, chopped
1 celery stalk, chopped
240ml/8fl oz/1 cup dry white wine
300g/10oz/2 cups ripe plum tomatoes, peeled and chopped, or canned with the juice
15g/½oz/1 tbsp unsalted butter
1 quantity Fresh Egg Pasta (pages 47 and 51), cut into lasagne (page 52)

Preheat the oven to 180°C/350°F/Gas 4.
Make incisions in the meat with a small knife and fill them with half the lard pieces and all the cloves. Rub the meat with salt and pepper and tie with a string.
Melt the rest of the lard in a roasting pan or flameproof casserole on top of the stove over low heat.
Add the meat, turn the heat up to high and cook, turning the meat a couple of times, until it takes a brown colour. Lower the heat, add onion, carrot and celery and sauté for a couple more minutes. Add the wine, tomatoes and salt and pepper. Cover and cook in the oven for about 4 hours until the meat becomes very tender, adding water a little at a time if necessary to keep the juices moist.
Untie the meat. Slice it and keep warm for serving later. Do not turn off the oven.
Pass the cooking juices and vegetables through a food mill.
Meanwhile, grease an ovenproof serving dish with the butter. Bring a large saucepan of water to the boil. Add salt and the lasagne, a few sheets at a time, and cook until the water returns to the boil and the lasagne float to the top. Drain and put in a bowl of cold water. Drain again and put on a cloth to dry.
Layer the lasagne with the meat juices and vegetable mixture in the serving dish. Cook for about 20 minutes. Serve immediately accompanied by the meat.
Serves 4.

LASAGNE ALLO STINCO
Lasagne with Veal Shank

If you are in a real hurry you can substitute rigatoni for the lasagne, but the dish will lose its delicacy. You can get a special long, slim spoon to extract the marrow from the cooked shank, but a slim knife will do.

90g/3oz pancetta, choppped
1 small onion, chopped
1 carrot, chopped
1 celery stalk, chopped
1 bay leaf
1 veal shank
About 375ml/12¹/2fl oz/just over 1¹/2 cups dry white wine
1 tbsp tomato purée (paste)
1 tbsp fresh thyme leaves
Salt and pepper
1 quantity Fresh Egg Pasta (pages 47 and 51), cut into lasagne (page 52)
15g/12oz/1 tbsp unsalted butter
240ml/8fl oz/1 cup White Sauce (page 62)

Preheat the oven to 180°C/350°F/Gas 4. Fry the pancetta in a flameproof casserole over low heat until the fat melts. Add the onion, carrot, celery and bay leaf and cook, stirring frequently, for about 3 minutes until translucent. Add the veal shank and cook over medium heat until golden on all sides, turning the meat to colour it evenly. Add 120ml/4fl oz/¹/2 cup of the wine, the tomato purée (paste), thyme and salt and pepper to taste. Cover and cook in the oven for about 4 hours, until very tender, adding the rest of the wine a little at a time. If the cooking juices get too dry, add a little water.
When cool enough to handle, remove all the meat from the shank bone.
Bring a large pan of water to the boil. Add salt and the lasagne, a few sheets at a time, and cook until the water returns to the boil and the lasagne float to the top. Drain and put in a bowl of cold water. Drain again and put on a cloth to dry.
Reheat the oven to 180°C/350°F/Gas 4 and grease an ovenproof serving dish with the butter.
Layer the lasagne in the serving dish with the veal and the white sauce ending with a layer of white sauce. Cook for about 20 minutes until bubbling hot.
Serve immediately.
Serves 4.

LASAGNE VERDI CON AGNELLO E PEPERONI
Green Lasagne with Lamb and Sweet (Bell) Peppers

Salt
1 quantity Fresh Egg Pasta (pages 47 and 51), flavoured and coloured with spinach (page 56), cut into lasagne (page 52)
4 tbsp extra virgin olive oil
1 onion, chopped
300g/10oz lamb, cut into bite-size pieces
450g/1oz ripe plum tomatoes or canned with the juice
1 tbsp fresh thyme leaves
1 bay leaf
Small pinch of hot pepper flakes
2 red sweet (bell) peppers, cored, seeded and thinly sliced
15g/¹/2oz/1 tbsp unsalted butter
240ml/8fl oz/1 cup White Sauce (page 62)

Bring a large saucepan of water to the boil. Add salt and lasagne, a few sheets at a time, and cook until the water returns to the boil and the lasagne float to the top. Drain and put in a bowl of cold water. Drain again and arrange on a cloth towel to dry.
Heat the oil in a large saucepan over medium heat. Add the onion and fry for about 3 minutes, stirring occasionally, until translucent. Add the lamb and cook for 5 more minutes, stirring occasionally. Add the tomatoes, thyme, bay leaf, pepper flakes and salt to taste. Cover, lower the heat and cook for about 1¹/2 hours until almost all the liquid is absorbed.
Stir in the peppers and cook for 10 more minutes. Meanwhile, preheat the oven to 180°C/350°F/Gas 4 and grease an ovenproof serving dish with the butter. Layer the lasagne, meat sauce and white sauce in the serving dish, ending with the white sauce. Cook for about 20 minutes. Serve immediately, very hot.
Serves 4.

LASAGNE CON LENTICCHIE
Lasagne with Lentils

The lentils I like best are those from Castelluccio, a small village in central Italy. They are tasty and very small. But any lentils will do, provided you soak them in cold water for 12 hours.

180g/6oz/1 cup lentils
60g/2oz pancetta in one slice, diced
1 onion, chopped
1 bay leaf
450g/1 lb/3 cups plum tomatoes, peeled and chopped, or canned with the juice
Salt and pepper
4 tbsp extra virgin olive oil
1 quantity Fresh Egg Pasta (pages 47 and 51), cut into lasagne (page 52)
15g/½oz/1 tbsp unsalted butter

Soak the lentils in cold water for about 12 hours. Discard any that are still floating on surface and drain. Put the pancetta and onion in a frying pan over medium heat and fry, stirring, for about 5 minutes. Add the bay leaf, tomatoes and lentils and sprinkle with salt and pepper to taste. Lower the heat and cook for about 1 hour, adding water a little at a time to keep the lentils moist. Take off the heat and pour in the oil.
Meanwhile, bring large pan of water to the boil. Add salt and the lasagne, a few sheets at a time, and cook until the water returns to the boil and the lasagne float to the top. Drain and put in a bowl of cold water. Drain again and put on a cloth to dry.
Preheat the oven to 180°C/350°F/Gas 4 and grease an ovenproof serving dish with the butter.
Layer the lasagne with the lentil mixture in the serving dish, ending with the lentil mixture. Cook for about 20 minutes until piping hot. Serve immediately.
Serves 4.

LASAGNE ALLA MOZZARELLA E SALSICCE
Lasagne with Mozzarella and Sausages

Here's quite a filling dish that can be served as a one-dish meal. Substitute diced cooked ham for the sausages if you want a milder flavour.

Salt
1 quantity Fresh Egg Pasta (pages 47 and 51), cut into lasagne (page 52)
240ml/8fl oz/1 cup double (heavy) cream
60g/2oz/4 tbsp freshly grated Parmesan cheese
15g/½oz/1 tbsp unsalted butter
180g/6oz mozzarella cheese, thinly sliced
180g/6oz sweet Italian sausages, casings removed and crumbled
Pepper

Bring a large saucepan of water to the boil. Add salt and the lasagne, a few sheets at a time, and cook until the water returns to the boil and the lasagne float to the top. Drain and put in a bowl of cold water. Drain again and put on a cloth to dry.
Mix the cream with the Parmesan. Preheat the oven to 180°C/350°F/Gas 4 and grease an ovenproof serving dish with the butter. Add one layer of lasagne. Cover with half the mozzarella and half the sausages. Pour in half of the cream and cover with the rest of the lasagne. Add the rest of the mozzarella and sausages and end with the remaining cream. Sprinkle with pepper. Cook for about 20 minutes until bubbling and slightly golden on top. Serve immediately.
Serves 4.

LASAGNE AI SEMI DI PAPAVERO
Lasagne with Poppy Seeds

A typical dish from Alto Adige, combining the salted taste of lasagne with a little sugar. Poppy seeds have a distinctive flavour that I like to sometimes add to bread, like they do in Germany. This unusual dish is especially good for a brunch.

Salt
1 quantity Fresh Egg Pasta (pages 47 and 51), cut into lasagne (page 52)
105g/3¹/₂oz/7 tbsp unsalted butter
60g/2oz/4 tbsp poppy seeds
60g/2oz/4 tbsp sugar
240ml/8fl oz/1 cup double (heavy) cream

Bring a large saucepan of water to the boil. Add salt and the lasagne, a few sheets at a time, and cook until the water returns to the boil and the lasagne float to the top. Drain and put in a bowl of cold water. Drain again and put on a cloth to dry.
Preheat the oven to 180°C/350F/Gas 4 and grease an ovenproof serving dish with 15g/¹/₂oz/1 tbsp of the butter.
Melt the remaining butter in a pan over low heat. Add the poppy seeds and sugar and cook, stirring occasionally, for about 5 minutes. Stir in the cream; set aside.
Layer the lasagne and the cream sauce in the ovenproof dish, ending with the cream sauce.
Cook for about 20 minutes until piping hot.
Serve immediately.
Serves 4.

LASAGNE AL BACCALÀ IN UMIDO
Lasagne with Salt Cod

In Italy it is possible to buy salt cod already soaked, otherwise you must soak it yourself for about 24 hours, changing the water at least 4 times.

Salt
1 quantity Fresh Egg Pasta (pages 47 and 51), cut into lasagne (page 52)
3 tbsp extra virgin olive oil
300g/10oz salt cod, already soaked in water and patted dry
1 shallot, chopped
About 60ml/2fl oz/¹/₄ cup dry white wine
240ml/8fl oz/1 cup double (heavy) cream
Pepper
15g/¹/₂oz/1 tbsp unsalted butter

Bring a large saucepan of water to the boil. Add salt and lasagne, a few sheets at a time, and cook until the water returns to the boil and the lasagne float to the top. Drain and put in a bowl of cold water. Drain again and put on a cloth to dry.
Heat the oil in a pan over medium heat. Add the salt cod and shallot and cook, stirring occasionally, for a few minutes each side until just beginning to become golden. Add the wine and let it evaporate. Add the cream and pepper to taste and bring to the boil. At that point the cod will break up into small, irregular pieces.
Meanwhile, preheat the oven to 180°C/350°F/Gas 4 and grease an ovenproof serving dish with the butter.
Layer the lasagne and salt cod mixture in an ovenproof serving dish, ending with salt cod mixture.
Cook for about 20 minutes until bubbling. Serve immediately, very hot.
Serves 4.

TORTA DI LINGUINE AL PESTO DI FAVE

*Linguine Tart with
Broad (Fava) Bean Pesto*

When I cannot use broad (fava) beans freshly picked from my garden, I blanch the beans very quickly. This removes the slightly bitter taste they develop when they are not very fresh.

15g/^{1}/₂oz/1 tbsp unsalted butter
450g/1 lb Shortcrust (Piecrust) Pastry (page 67)
1kg/2^1/₄ lb/5 cups fresh broad (fava) beans, shelled and peeled (about 100g/3^1/₂oz/^{1}/₂ cup shelled)
6 tbsp extra virgin olive oil
60g/2oz/^{1}/₂ cup pecorino (Romano) cheese, freshly grated
6 fresh mint leaves
Salt and pepper
300g/10oz linguine

Preheat the oven to 180°C/350°F/Gas 4. Butter a 20cm/8 inch tart pan with a removable base. Roll out the pastry (dough) very thinly on a lightly floured surface and transfer to the pan. Trim the edges. Prick the bottom with a fork. Bake for about 30 minutes, or until the bottom is golden. If it puffs up, just press down once with the palm of your hand. Meanwhile, put the beans, olive oil, cheese, mint leaves and salt and pepper in a blender or food processor and blend until creamy.
Bring a large pan of water to the boil. Add salt and the linguine and cook until *al dente*. Before you drain the pasta, add 120ml/4fl oz/^{1}/₂ cup of the cooking water to the food processor and process again. Drain the linguine and toss with the sauce. Unmould the tart shell and fill with the linguine mixture. Serve immediately, very hot.
Serves 4.

TORTA DI LINGUINE IN SALSA DI NOCI

Linguine Tart with Walnut Sauce

The linguine can be replaced with fettuccine or taglierini if you feel like preparing a fresh pasta, but do not use spaghetti or any of the short pastas, which are better suited to less delicate sauces.

15g/^{1}/₂oz/1 tbsp unsalted butter
120g/4oz/^{2}/₃ cup shelled hazelnuts
30g/1oz/2 tbsp pine nuts
1 garlic clove
Handful of flat-leaf Italian parsley
4 tbsp extra virgin olive oil
60ml/2fl oz/4 tbsp milk
Salt and pepper
120g/4oz/^{1}/₂ cup ricotta cheese
120ml/4fl oz/^{1}/₂ cup double (heavy) cream
450g/1 lb Shortcrust (Piecrust) Pastry (page 67)
300g/10oz linguine

Preheat the oven to 180°C/350°F/Gas 4. Butter a 20cm/8 inch tart pan with a removable bottom. Put the hazelnuts, pine nuts, clove, parsley, oil, milk and salt and pepper to taste in a blender or food processor. Purée until almost creamy. Add the ricotta cheese and the cream and blend a few more seconds.
Roll out the pastry (dough) on a lightly floured work surface until 25cm/10 inches round and transfer to the tart pan. Trim the edges. Prick the bottom with a fork. Bake for about 30 minutes, or until the bottom is golden. If the pastry puffs up just press down with the palm of your hand. Do not turn off the oven.
Bring a large saucepan of water to the boil. Add salt and the linguine and cook until *al dente*. Drain and return to the pan. Add the sauce and stir together. Transfer to the tart shell and bake for 20 more minutes. Unmould and serve immediately.
Serves 4.

Opposite page: Linguine Tart with Broad (Fava) Bean Pesto

TORTA DI TAGLIATELLE ALLA FONTINA
Truffle Tagliatelle Tart with Fontina Cheese

Truffle-flavoured tagliatelle, although expensive, are now available in the shops, and I sometimes use them. Still, I prefer to mix truffle butter with the pasta or in a sauce because I think it has a better taste. The trouble with truffle pasta is that much of the flavour gets diluted in the cooking water. This tart can be prepared in advance and kept in the refrigerator for about 8 hours before cooking. For a simpler version, use dry linguine.

300g/10oz Shortcrust (Piecrust) Pastry (page 67)
120g/4oz/8 tbsp unsalted butter
Salt
360g/¹/₂oz truffle-flavoured tagliatelle
120g/4oz/1 cup Fontina cheese, finely shredded
Pepper
60g/2oz/¹/₂ cup freshly grated Parmesan cheese

Roll out the pastry (dough) on a lightly floured surface until 25cm/10 inches round. Use 15g/¹/₂oz/ 1 tbsp of the butter to butter a 20cm/8 inch tart pan with a removable bottom. Transfer the pastry to the tart pan and trim the edges. Keep in the refrigerator. Bring a large saucepan of water to the boil. Add salt and the tagliatelle and cook until *al dente*. Meanwhile, preheat the oven to 180°C/350°F/Gas 4. Melt the rest of the butter. Drain the pasta and toss with the melted butter. Add the Fontina cheese and some pepper. Fill the tart shell with the pasta mixture and sprinkle with the Parmesan cheese. Cook for about 40 minutes, or until the crust becomes golden. Unmould on to a warmed serving platter and serve immediately, very hot.
Serves 4.

TORTA DI FETTUCCINE
Fettuccine Tart with Veal Sauce

This kind of tart is popular all over Italy—sometimes they are savoury and served as a first dish, sometimes they are sweet and served for dessert. This particular one is made with a veal sauce and you can serve the meat cold afterwards as a second course, accompanied by a green salad.

60g/2oz/4 tbsp unsalted butter
2 tbsp extra virgin olive oil
2 onions, finely chopped
900g/2 lb veal suitable for roasting
Flour for dusting the meat
About 120ml/4fl oz/¹/₂ cup dry white wine
Salt and pepper
300g/10oz Shortcrust (Piecrust) Pastry, (page 67)
300g/10oz fettuccine
240ml/8fl oz/1 cup double (heavy) cream

Preheat the oven to 180°C/350°F/Gas 4.
Melt half the butter with the oil in a roasting pan or large flameproof dish over medium heat. Add the onions and fry for about 3 minutes, stirring, until translucent.
Roll the veal in flour and add to the baking dish. Cook for about 10 minutes until the meat starts to colour on all sides. Pour in the wine.
Put the pan or casserole in the oven for about 1¹/₂ hours, turning the meat over a couple of times and adding about 240ml/8fl oz/1 cup of water, a little at a time, to keep the cooking juices moist. Add salt and pepper to taste.
Grease a 20cm/8 inch tart pan with a removable base with the remaining butter. Roll out the pastry (dough) until it is about 3mm/¹/₈ inch thick and large enough to cover the base and sides of the pan. Trim the edges and prick the base.
Bring a large pan of water to the boil. Add salt and the fettuccine and cook until *al dente*. Drain and mix with half the cream. Reserve the meat for the main course and add the rest of the cream to the roasting pan or casserole, scraping the base over medium heat on top of the oven. If the sauce is too thick, add a little bit of water.
Add the sauce to the fettuccine, toss well and put in the tart shell. Bake for about 30 minutes or until the pastry becomes golden. Let cool slightly on a wire rack and unmould on to a warmed serving platter.
Serve very hot.
Serves 4.

PASTICCIO DI PENNE AL RADICCHIO
Penne Mould with Radicchio

A colourful dish for wintertime, when bright-red radicchio is less expensive and tastier. There are many qualities of red radicchio available, and the best is the one with long leaves, not curly, called radicchio di Treviso. Maccheroni also works well in this.

300g/10oz penne
6 tbsp extra virgin olive oil
1 red onion, chopped
300g/10oz red radicchio, sliced
240ml/8fl oz/1 cup White Sauce (page 62)
2 eggs, size 3 (U.S. large)
Salt and pepper
15g/¹/₂oz/1 tbsp unsalted butter
60g/2oz/4 tbsp freshly grated Parmesan cheese

Bring a large saucepan of water to the boil. Add salt and the penne and cook until *al dente*. Drain and toss with half the oil; set aside.
Heat the rest of the oil in a pan over medium heat. Add the onion and cook for about 3 minutes until translucent. Add the radicchio, lower the heat and cook for about 10 more minutes until tender. Stir in the white sauce and let cool. Add the eggs and salt and pepper to taste.
Preheat the oven to 180°C/350°F/Gas 4. Butter a deep 900g/2 lb/4 cup mould and dust with the Parmesan cheese.
Add the rest of the Parmesan to the pasta and stir in the radicchio mixture. Fill the mould. Cook for about 50 minutes until bubbling hot. Let rest a couple of minutes. Release from the mould with the point of a knife and invert on to a warmed serving platter, giving a firm shake. Remove the mould and serve immediately, very hot.
Serves 4.

TAGLIERINI IN TORTIERA AL ROGNONE
Taglierini and Kidney Pie

Veal kidneys are the most delicate, but beef ones also work well in this tasty dish. Instead of taglierini, you can also use dry linguine.

60g/2oz/4 tbsp unsalted butter
Handful of fresh sage leaves
1 onion, finely chopped
1 fresh rosemary sprig
300g/10oz veal kidneys, cleaned, trimmed and thinly sliced
About 120ml/4fl oz/¹/₂ cup dry white wine
Salt and pepper
300g/10oz taglierini
360g/12oz Shortcrust (Piecrust) Pastry (page 67)

Melt 45g/1¹/₂oz/3 tbsp butter in a large frying pan over high heat. Add the sage, onion, rosemary and the kidneys and cook, stirring occasionally, for about 5 minutes. Add the wine and salt and pepper to taste. Lower the heat to minimum and simmer for 3 more minutes. Discard the sage and rosemary and pass everything through a food mill, or purée in a blender.
If too thick, add a little bit of water; set aside.
Pre-heat the oven to 180°C/350°F/Gas 4. With the rest of the butter grease a 20cm/8 inch round ovenproof dish. Bring a large pan of water to the boil. Add salt and the taglierini and cook until *al dente*. Drain and toss with the kidney sauce and transfer to the prepared dish.
Roll out the pastry on a lightly floured surface into a 20cm/8 inch round. Cover the dish with it, sealing all around. Prick the surface with a fork to allow the steam to come out. Bake for about 20 minutes or until the surface becomes golden. Serve immediately, very hot.
Serves 4.

ANELLO DI TAGLIERINI CON RICOTTA E POMODORO

Taglierini Ring with Ricotta and Tomatoes

Here's a rustic recipe that is equally suitable for brunch or an elegant lunch. For quicker preparation, use linguine.

6 tbsp extra virgin olive oil
2 garlic cloves, chopped
900g/2 lb/6 cups ripe plum tomatoes, peeled and chopped, or canned with the juice
Salt and pepper
Handful of fresh basil leaves
15g/1oz/1 tbsp unsalted butter
60g/2oz/¹/₂ cup fine dry breadcrumbs
1 quantity Fresh Egg Pasta (pages 47 and 51), cut into taglierini (page 52)
240g/8oz/1 cup ricotta cheese

Heat the oil in a saucepan over medium heat. Add the garlic and sauté, stirring, for about 3 minutes until translucent. Add the tomatoes and salt and pepper to taste. Lower the heat and simmer, stirring occasionally, for about 1 hour until all the excess liquid has evaporated. Add the basil leaves; set aside.
Preheat the oven to 180°C/350°F/Gas 4. Grease a 23cm/9 inch ring mould with the butter and coat evenly with the breadcrumbs.
Bring a large pan of water to the boil. Add salt and taglierini and cook until the water returns to the boil and the taglierini float to the top. Drain and toss in a bowl with half the tomato sauce and all the ricotta cheese.
Press the dressed pasta into the mould. Cook for about 20 minutes, until bubbling hot. Loosen the mould with the point of a knife and invert on to a warmed serving platter, giving a firm shake. Remove the mould and fill the centre with the rest of the sauce. Serve immediately, very hot.
Serves 4.

SFOGLIATA DI TAGLIERINI AL TARTUFO

Taglierini with Puff Pastry and White Truffles

A very elegant dish for a first course, that can be followed by meat or fish. The amount of truffle used is up to everyone's generosity, but I suggest at least 30g/1oz.

360g/12oz Puff Pastry (page 67)
Salt
1 quantity Fresh Egg Pasta (pages 47 and 51), cut into taglierini (page 52)
90g/3oz/6 tbsp unsalted butter
90g/3oz/³/₄ cup freshly grated Parmesan cheese
1 tsp grated nutmeg
Pepper
1 white truffle (optional; see above)

Preheat the oven to 180°C/350°F/Gas 4.
Roll out two-thirds of the puff pastry (dough) on a lightly floured surface until about 25cm/10 inches round. Transfer to a 23cm/9 inch springform pan. Trim the edge. Roll out the rest of the pastry in a 23cm/9 inch round. Bake both for about 30 minutes until golden brown and puffed up.
Meanwhile, bring a large saucepan of water to the boil. Add salt and the taglierini and cook until the water returns to the boil and the taglierini float to the top. Melt the butter in a pan. Drain the taglierini and place in a bowl. Add the butter, cheese, nutmeg and pepper and mix well.
Remove the side of the pan from the puff pastry case. Fill with the taglierini mixture and shave truffle on top. Cover with the pastry lid and serve immediately.
Serves 4.

CROSTATA DI LINGUINE ALLA CREMA DI FORMAGGIO

Linguine Tart with Cheese Sauce

When white truffles are in season, I sprinkle them over the top of this tart. And, when porcine are readily available, I do the same with them.

360g/12 oz Shortcrust (Piecrust) Pastry (page 67)
240ml/8fl oz/1 cup double (heavy) cream
180g/6oz/1¹/2 cups freshly grated Parmesan cheese
Salt and pepper
3 egg yolks, size 3 (U.S. large)
300g/10oz linguine

Preheat the oven to 180°C/350°F/Gas 4. Roll out the pastry (dough) on a lightly floured work surface until 25cm/10 inches round. Transfer to a 23cm/9 inch tart pan with a removable bottom that is 2.5cm/1 inch deep. Trim the edges well. Prick the bottom with a fork and bake for about 30 minutes, or until barely golden. If the bottom puffs up during baking, press down with the palm of your hand. Do not turn off the oven.
Meanwhile, bring the cream to the boil, then simmer for about 10 minutes. Stir in the cheese and add salt and pepper to taste. Let cool and stir in the egg yolks.
Bring a large pan of water to the boil. Add salt and the linguine and cook until *al dente*. Drain, add to the cream mixture and toss well. Transfer the linguine to the tart shell and bake for about 20 minutes until bubbling hot. Unmould and serve immediately.
Serves 4.

CROSTATA DI BUCATINI CON LA ZUCCA

Bucatini Tart with Pumpkin

A perfect dish for the autumn when pumpkins are tasty and very big. Bucatini is the best shaped pasta to use for timbals because when you cut a slice it will hold together, unlike penne which will fall apart.

600g/20oz pumpkin with peel and seeds
4 amaretto biscuits (cookies), crumbled
1 egg
60g/2oz/4 tbsp finely grated Parmesan cheese
Pinch of grated nutmeg
Salt and pepper
240ml/8fl oz/1 cup double (heavy) cream
300g/10oz Shortcrust (Piecrust) Pastry (page 67)
15g/¹/2oz/1 tbsp unsalted butter
300g/10oz bucatini

Preheat the oven to 180°C/350°F/Gas 4. Cook the pumpkin for about 30 minutes until tender; do not turn off the oven. Peel and seed the pumpkin. Purée through a food mill or in a blender or food processor. Stir in the amaretto biscuits (cookies), egg, Parmesan cheese, nutmeg and little salt and pepper. Add the cream.
Butter a 20cm/8 inch tart pan with a removable base. Roll out the pastry until it is large enough to cover the base and sides of the pan. Prick the base with a fork. Bake for about 30 minutes, or until barely golden. If the pastry puffs up, just press it down with the palm of your hand.
Meanwhile, bring a large pan of water to the boil. Add salt and the bucatini and cook until *al dente*. Drain and toss with the pumpkin sauce. Fill the tart shell and bake for about 20 minutes until bubbling hot. Unmould the tart on to a warmed serving plate. Serve immediately, very hot.
Serves 4.

Diuersi uasi

stufaroro

nauicella cō piastrelle et quattro piedi

nauicella cō piastrelle et 4 piedi

Conserua

nauicella senza piedi

nauicella senza piedi

stufator ouato

Conserua bassa

Conserua grande

padella p fare oui frittolate

stufaroro largo

tortera con il coperto

nauicella bassa

conca

nauicella alta

9

VERMICELLI AI PETTI DI POLLO

Vermicelli with Chicken Breasts

Optional in this dish, and I would use them, are black truffles, a speciality from Umbria, where they are widely served on pasta and meat dishes.

Salt
300g/10oz vermicelli
90ml/3fl oz/6 tbsp double (heavy) cream
60g/2oz/4 tbsp unsalted butter
2 chicken breasts (or 1 whole breast), about 300g/10oz total weight, cut into matchstick strips
60g/2oz prosciutto, chopped
300g/10oz Meat Sauce (page 58)
1 black truffle, about 30g/1oz, thinly sliced (optional; see above)

Bring a large saucepan of water to the boil. Add salt and the vermicelli and cook until *al dente*. Drain and dress with the cream.
Preheat the oven to 180°C/350°F/Gas 4.
Melt half the butter in a pan over medium heat. Add the chicken and prosciutto and sauté for about 3 minutes, stirring a couple of times. Add to the meat sauce. Toss in the vermicelli.
With the rest of the butter, grease an ovenproof serving dish. Fill with the pasta. Cook for about 20 minutes until bubbling hot. Cover with truffle slices, if you are using them, and serve immediately, very hot.
Serves 4.

RIGATONI AL SUGO DI CONIGLIO

Rigatoni Baked with Rabbit Sauce

Dried rigatoni are perfect for this dish, but can easily be replaced with lasagne if you want to make fresh pasta. Never buy dry lasagne, because it is difficult to cook, it sticks and is not very tasty.

2 tbsp extra virgin olive oil
90g/3oz pancetta, chopped
1/2 rabbit, about 600g/1¼ lb, cut into large pieces
1 onion, chopped
2 garlic cloves, chopped
1 carrot, chopped
1 celery stalk, chopped
1 clove
Pinch of ground cinnamon
About 375ml/12½fl oz/just over 1½ cups good red wine
450g/1 lb/3 cups ripe plum tomatoes, peeled and chopped, or canned with the juice
Salt and pepper
300g/10oz rigatoni
15g/12oz/1 tbsp unsalted butter
240ml/8fl oz/1 cup White Sauce (page 62)

Heat the oil and pancetta in a large saucepan over medium heat. Add the rabbit, onion, garlic, carrot and celery, and fry, stirring, for about 5 minutes. Add the clove, cinnamon and red wine and continue cooking until almost all the liquid evaporates. Add the tomatoes and sprinkle with salt and pepper to taste. Lower the heat to a minimum, cover and cook for about 1½ hours.
Let the mixture cool and bone the rabbit, discarding the bones. Return the meat pieces to the pan.
Meanwhile, bring a large pan of water to the boil.
Add salt and the rigatoni and cook until *al dente*.
Preheat the oven to 180°C/350°F/Gas 4 and grease an ovenproof serving dish with the butter.
Drain the rigatoni and mix with the rabbit sauce.
Transfer to the prepared dish, cover with the white sauce and bake for about 20 minutes until bubbling hot. Serve immediately, very hot.
Serves 4.

TIMBALLO DI MACCHERONI AI FUNGHI

Maccheroni Timbal with Mushrooms

Fresh mushrooms, such as shittake, porcini or morels, make a delicious mixture for this lovely timbal. Long maccheroni or bucatini should be used because they are the most suitable for the impressive presentation.

4 tbsp extra virgin olive oil
1 onion, chopped
2 garlic cloves, chopped
450g/1 lb mixed mushrooms, wiped and sliced
300g/10oz/2 cups plum tomatoes, peeled and chopped, or canned with the juice
Salt and pepper
15g/¹/₂oz/1 tbsp unsalted butter
300g/10oz long maccheroni
240ml/8fl oz/1 cup White Sauce (page 62)

Heat the oil in a saucepan over low heat. Add the onion and garlic and cook, stirring, for about 3 minutes until translucent. Add the mushrooms, raise the heat to medium and sauté for about 5 minutes, stirring. Add the tomatoes and cook for 20 more minutes, or until the excess liquid has evaporated. Add salt and pepper to taste.
Bring a large pan of water to the boil. Add salt and the maccheroni and cook until *al dente*. Drain and leave on a cloth to dry, separating the strands.
Preheat the oven to 180°C/350°F/Gas 4. Grease a 1 litre/1³/₄ pint/4¹/₂ cup ovenproof mould with the butter. Start covering the inside with the maccheroni. Make a spiral, starting on the bottom and continue adding the pasta, strand by strand, until you arrive at the top. Press each strand firmly into the butter so they stick to the inside of the mould.
Cut the leftover maccheroni into small pieces and mix with the mushrooms and white sauce. Spoon into the mould. Cook for about 30 minutes until bubbling hot. Release the timbal from the mould with the point of a knife and invert on to a warmed serving platter, giving a firm shake. Remove the mould and serve immediately, very hot.
Serves 4.

TIMBALLO DI RIGATONI E MELANZANE

Rigatoni and Aubergine (Eggplant) Timbal

Penne or bucatini can also be used instead of rigatoni.

1 litre/1³/₄ pints/4¹/₂ cups olive oil for deep-frying
2 aubergines (eggplants), thinly sliced
4 tbsp extra virgin olive oil
180g/6oz minced (ground) beef
4 ripe plum tomatoes, peeled and chopped
Salt and pepper
300g/10oz rigatoni
3 eggs, size 3 (U.S. large), lightly beaten
Pinch of grated nutmeg
60g/2¹/₂oz/¹/₂ cup freshly grated Parmesan cheese

Heat the oil in a large saucepan to 180°C/350°F. Add the aubergine (eggplant) slices, a few at a time, and fry until tender. Drain on paper towels; set aside.
Heat 3 tbsp of the extra virgin oil in a saucepan over medium heat. Add the meat and fry, stirring occasionally, for about 10 minutes. Add the tomatoes and salt and pepper and cook for 20 more minutes until all the excess liquid has evaporated. Let cool completely.
Bring a large pan of water to the boil. Add salt and the rigatoni and cook until *al dente*.
Meanwhile, add the eggs, nutmeg and cheese to the meat. Drain the rigatoni and toss with the prepared sauce and the aubergines.
Preheat the oven to 180°C/350°F/Gas 4. Grease a 1 litre/1³/₄ pint/4¹/₂ cup deep ovenproof mould with the rest of the oil.
Fill the mould with the rigatoni mixture. Cook for about 50 minutes until bubbling hot and the eggs are completely set. Release from the mould with the point of a knife and invert on to a warmed serving platter, giving a firm shake. Remove the mould and serve immediately, very hot.
Serves 4.

Opposite page: Dried Rigatoni

INDEX

ACKNOWLEDGEMENTS

The publishers wish to thank the following copyright holders
for their permission to reproduce illustrations supplied:

Vintage Magazine Picture Library: *pages 13, 16, 26–27 and 39.*
Robert Opie Collection: *pages 39 and 145.*
Mansell Collection Limited: *pages 12, 14-15 and 21.*
Fotomas Index Picture Library: *pages 8-9, 11, 23, 31, 46, 52, 70, 112 and 184.*
John Heseltine Archive: *page 56.*
Mary Evans Picture Library: *pages 6, 29, 33, 37 and 38.*
Advertising Archive Limited: *page 16.*
Museo della Pasta, Rome: *pages 20, 21, 25 and 55.*
Dover Publications

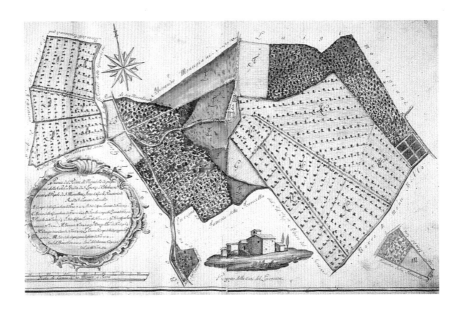